Language, Meaning and the Law

For my mother, Patricia Barnacle Hutton

Language, Meaning and the Law

CHRISTOPHER HUTTON

EDINBURGH UNIVERSITY PRESS

© Christopher Hutton, 2009

Edinburgh University Press Ltd
22 George Square, Edinburgh

Typeset in 10/12 Times New Roman
by Servis Filmsetting Ltd, Stockport, Cheshire, and
Printed by the MPG Books Group in the UK

A CIP record for this book is available from the British Library

ISBN 978 0 7486 3350 0 (hardback)
ISBN 978 0 7486 3351 7 (paperback)

The right of Christopher Hutton
to be identified as author of this work
has been asserted in accordance with
the Copyright, Designs and Patents Act 1988.

Contents

Acknowledgements

For moral support and many fascinating discussions on a wide range of topics I would like to thank my colleagues and friends in the School of English, the Faculty of Arts and the Registry of the University of Hong Kong. Working with Roy Harris on our joint publication *Definition in Theory and Practice* (2007) was important preparation for writing this book. Grant Evans and Gary Wickham provided many suggestions for readings; Katherine Baxter directed me towards Dada for the motto for Chapter 7. Mick Fisher of Hong Kong University's SPACE has been most supportive of my somewhat erratic attempts to obtain a legal education. The University of Hong Kong provided study leave for the academic year 2007–8. My gratitude goes to Sarah Edwards and the staff of Edinburgh University Press for their advice and patience.

Preface: The Scope of the Book

This book is concerned with approaches to language, meaning and interpretation that have been discussed within the legal context. Though many of these approaches are frequently formulated in a manner unique to law, they have been shaped by constant dialogue with philosophy, political theory, sociology, literary studies and linguistics. The aim of this book is *not* to improve how lawyers deal with words and their meanings (which is not to say that no improvement is possible), but to use law to reflect on the nature of language, its role within social life, and the theories with which legal theorists and practising lawyers, linguists and philosophers attempt to make sense of it. The underlying presumption is that in looking from the outside at this complex of problems, opinions and ideologies, we gain insights of wider significance for the study of language in general.

Where there is discussion of linguistics in this work, the reference is to mainstream or so-called 'core' linguistics, for which I take the writings of Saussure and Chomsky as representative. Given the diversity of recent developments in linguistics, it is not possible to qualify each generalisation, but the 'systems theory' view of language remains a very powerful influence within the discipline, even where the realist assumption is made that no two speakers speak exactly the same language. Specialist topics in forensic linguistics and applied sociolinguistics of law are not covered in this work, except where they relate to the meaning and interpretation of legal language/texts and the role of 'ordinary language' in the legal context. Forensic linguistics is concerned with how linguistics can be applied in an evidential or expert witness capacity, or in defence of the language rights of groups who are especially disadvantaged by the language culture of the legal process. It deals with issues such as legal interpreting and translation; the comprehensibility of legal documents, of jury instructions and of police communication with suspects and the general public; issues of age, gender, race within the discourse of the legal system; discourse analysis of the language of judges; plagiarism and the authenticity of documents. Many of these areas are specialisations in their own right, such as forensic phonetics and acoustics in speaker identification. There exist a number of excellent textbooks in this area, and the reader is referred to the further reading section at the end of the book.

Where general terms such as 'law', 'judge' or 'statute' are used, the context should be understood to refer to common law jurisdictions. 'English law' is a term of art which covers the legal system of England and Wales: Scotland is a separate jurisdiction with distinct legal terminology and procedures. It is important to keep in view the diversity of legal cultures, traditions of legal theory, and the anthropological question of the nature and boundaries of law, even if these issues lie largely outside the scope of this book. On this point the anthropologist Mary Douglas (1921–2007) offers this cross-cultural observation: 'A theory of justice has to be balanced between theories of human agency, on the one hand, and theories of community on the other' (Douglas 1987: 126).

The book is organised as follows. A short introductory section, 'Parables of Language and Law', presents underlying conceptions of language within the Western tradition, evoking ideas which resonate through discussions of law and language. Part I (Theoretical Frameworks) offers a general but highly selective survey of relevant theoretical domains; Part II (Selected Topics) offers discussion of more specific areas, namely dictionaries, legal control of interpretation and representation, and trademark law. Part III (Key Issues) presents 'bite-size' discussions of theoretically contentious issues. The conclusion (Part IV) looks at the comparative semiotics of language, law and money in terms of 'fixity' and 'motion'. The appendices provide further discussion materials and a selection of classroom-style exercises. The reference section is preceded by a brief guide to further reading.

Introduction: Parables of Language and Law

In Genesis (II: xix), this account is given of the origin of human language:

> And out of the ground the Lord God formed every beast of the field, and every fowl of the air; and brought them unto Adam to see what he would call them: and whatsoever Adam called every living creature, that was the name thereof.

In William Blake's (1757–1827) painting *Adam Naming the Beasts* (1810), the Adam figure gazes forwards, right arm raised in a gesture of benediction, his left hand caressing the serpent's head, as the animals file pass behind him. This evokes a moment of linguistic perfection, in which Adam assigns labels to the world without even needing to gaze upon it, a process innocent of interpretation and dispute. The names are natural names, and the things are given in nature by God. At Babel, this innocence is shattered (Genesis XI: i–ix):

> And the whole earth was of one language, and of one speech. And it came to pass, as they journeyed from the east, that they found a plain in the land of Shinar; and they dwelt there. [. . .] And they said, Go to, let us build us a city and a tower, whose top may reach unto heaven; and let us make us a name, lest we be scattered abroad upon the face of the whole earth. And the Lord came down to see the city and the tower, which the children of men builded. And the Lord said, Behold, the people is one, and they have all one language; and this they begin to do: and now nothing will be restrained from them, which they have imagined to do. Go to, let us go down, and there confound their language, that they may not understand one another's speech. So the Lord scattered them abroad from thence upon the face of all the earth: and they left off to build the city.

The attempt to understand human linguistic diversity and the existence of mutually incomprehensible languages has been one of the primary challenges of the Western intellectual tradition. The Babel episode offers an explanation in terms of divine punishment. At Babel, language was dramatically set adrift; it entered time and history, and the vicissitudes and contingencies of the human realm. Babel signifies that the human condition is one of perpetual linguistic and conceptual disorder, and that attempts to establish regimes of cooperation organised through language must struggle to master that disorder.

Harris and Taylor (1989: 44) make a link from the building of the Tower of Babel to the 'builder's language' imagined by Ludwig Wittgenstein (1889–1951) in the *Philosophical Investigations*. In imagining this language, Wittgenstein was illustrating Augustine's account of language learning (Wittgenstein [1953] 1978: 2). As a child Augustine had learned the names attached to objects in the following manner: 'When they (my elders) named some object, and accordingly moved towards something, I saw this and I grasped that the thing was called by the sound they uttered when they meant to point it out.' From the choreography of body and voice around the objects, 'I gradually learned to understand what objects they signified', and then how use those names 'to express my own desires' (Wittgenstein [1953] 1978: 3).

> Let us imagine a language for which the description given by Augustine is right. The language is meant to serve for communication between a builder A and an assistant B. A is building with building-stones: there are blocks, pillars, slabs and beams. B has to pass the stones, and that in the order in which A needs them. For this purpose they use a language consisting of the words 'block', 'pillar', 'slab', 'beam'. A calls them out; – B brings the stone which he has learnt to bring at such-and-such a call. – Conceive this as a complete primitive language.

This language, while it might be said to consist of a set of names, is actually a set of commands, or rather resists reduction to either of these labels. Interestingly, even this minimal primitive language is used in a hierarchical society. A legal theorist might ask: where is the law, or what is the nature of the sovereign power, that requires that B must do as A says? The sovereign within legal theory is frequently an off-stage force which animates the legal universe and is not directly exposed to the gaze.

An essential feature of the builders' language is that it is 'non-reflexive', that is, it does not refer to itself. A modern theorist might express this by pointing to the lack of 'meta-linguistic' resources in the language: there is no conceptual space for the 'negotiation of meaning'. The builders' language is an endlessly recycled set of name-commands, and does not accrue a shared memory of past interactions: it has no history. The builders' world is a totalitarian one in which language, command and obedient act are perfectly coordinated. Therein may lie a clue to its hold over the builders: perhaps authority lies in the language itself and there is no need of law, since in the imaginary domain of this primitive language, there is no room to think outside its categories and therefore no escape from the compulsion it exercises.

The Adamic language is a form of language that lies outside that coercive domain but also outside history, and it is not clear whether this ideal space can be found, or recreated, in our fallen communicational order. The entry of language into history is thus understood as a fall from an innocent relationship to a world of things where naming was not contaminated by coercion. This ideal haunts modern theorizing about language. At Babel, human cooperation is possible because of that shared language, which means that humans by their joint endeavours can dream of touching the divine. In Wittgenstein's 'language game' of building (which both stands for, but also intentionally misrepresents, the boundless family of 'language games' that make up ordinary language), coercion is the central element that ties the names to things, and that coercion is enacted through language as a system of commands.

An alternative reading of the expulsion from Eden and the confusion of Babel is one of liberation into authentic identity, either of the group or the individual. In the section immediately preceding the Babel episode, the sons of Noah and their sons in turn divide up the earth after the flood: 'every one after his tongue, after their families, in their nations' (Genesis X: ii). Conceptual order is provided by cultural and linguistic diversity. As between languages there may be disorder or at least difference; within each language there is coherence and a world of cultural meaning, a 'world view'. The linguist Einar Haugen (1906–94) entitled a book on bilingualism *Blessings of Babel* (1987), and the blessings he evokes are those of ordered ethno-linguistic diversity, not of disorder and chaos. On this view, order and meaning are found at the level of a people (*ethnos*) and its culture, and the coherence of language is found in its role as constituting that culture.

The liberation of language from things was a potential source of creative energy for the individual. For Samuel Taylor Coleridge (1772–1834), a symbol 'always partakes of the Reality which it renders intelligible; and while it enunciates the whole, abides itself as a living part in that Unity, of which it is the representative' (Coleridge 1816: 36–7). In an 1800 letter to William Godwin (1756–1836), Coleridge wrote 'I would endeavour to destroy the old antithesis of Words and Things: elevating, as it were, Words into Things and living things too' (cited in Richards 1968: 12). A further way to understand Babel as liberation is thus to suggest that it was language itself that was liberated at Babel, as it developed autonomy and power of its own, and was now set free from its natural bond to things. Human beings were destined to struggle against its hold over their imagination, but those who accepted the challenge could seek to harness and shape its dynamic disorder into a higher, meaningful order.

The liberation of language from things brought with it the danger that 'language unbound' could establish its own worlds of meaning, its own forms of life, and induct human beings into them. Humankind would be confined by shackles of which it was only dimly aware. Language was a second-order reality, a perhaps necessary but unreliable witness to the nature of world.

Many philosophers have thus seen it as their task to interrogate language, and, by unmasking the distortions of language, to maintain a conceptual link between language and reality, so as to anchor language as far as possible in the world of the real.

The view that words were a second-rate substitute for things was satirised in Jonathan Swift's *Gulliver's Travels*, where scholars in the Grand Academy of Lagado resolved that 'since words are only names for things, it would be more convenient for all men to carry about them such things as were necessary to express the particular business they are to discourse on' (Swift [1726] 1960: 150). In the Western tradition, love of language and of its ability to serve the imagination ('logophilia') co-exists with fear and mistrust of language and its autonomous power ('logophobia'). One form this logophobia has taken in the modern West has been the cooption of Eastern philosophy as therapy for the perceived sclerosis of language and thinking. In Jack Kerouac's novel *Dharma Bums*, the narrator meets his mentor, Japhy, after spending time meditating in the woods (Kerouac 1959: 15):

> But now I wanted to tell him all the things I'd discovered that winter meditating in the woods. 'Ah, it's just a lot of words', he said sadly, surprising me. 'I don't wanta hear all your word descriptions of words words words you made up all winter. Man I wanta to be enlightened by actions.'

Words are a secondary and inferior supplement to actions, they are second-rate pseudo-actions.

Fear and mistrust of language frequently go together with fear and mistrust of law ('jurisphobia'). Law is the tower that language built. The opening paragraphs of Charles Dickens's (1812–70) *Bleak House* describe a fallen world. London is drowning in a sea of fog and mud, and 'at the very heart of the fog, sits the Lord High Chancellor in the High Court of Chancery'. There the lawyers were (Dickens [1853] 1971: 50),

> mistily engaged in one of the ten thousand stages of an endless cause, tripping one another up on slippery precedents, groping knee-deep in technicalities, running their goat-hair and horsehair warded heads against walls of word; and making a pretence of equity with serious faces, as players might.

In his introduction to the novel, the critic J. Hillis Miller reads the jurisphobia of *Bleak House* not primarily as a call for social reform but as the expression of the universal condition of humanity. Language and interpretation are the essence of the fall: 'The villain is the act of interpretation itself, the naming which assimilates the particular into a system, giving it a definition and a value, incorporating it into a whole.' Interpretation is the 'original evil' (Miller

1971: 22, 34). This fallen state is 'irremediable'; language alienates the person, and personal names 'assimilate him in terms of something other than himself'. The social sickness is a symptom of 'the ineradicable human tendency to take the sign for the substance' (Miller 1971: 3–4). The categories of language, like social institutions, do violence by forcibly assimilating the individual into an alien symbolic order (Miller 1971: 22). J. Hillis Miller sees law as a pathology of language. *Bleak House*, he argues, is 'woven of words in which each takes its meaning not from society outside words, but from other words' (Miller 1971: 30).

This way of reading the novel undercuts its surface meaning as a work of social criticism. When the novel's narrator observes that '[t]he one great principle of the English law is, to make business for itself', and that this is the key to understanding law as a 'coherent scheme' rather than 'the monstrous maze the laity are apt to think it is' (Dickens [1853] 1971: 603), this appears to make reference to social reality outside the novel. This suggests faith in the novel as moral map, and therefore in the ability of language to represent not only the world as it is, but, by implication, the world as it should be. Orwell, who wrote that 'if thought corrupts language, language can also corrupt thought', none the less believed that 'the decadence of language is probably curable' (Orwell [1947] 1972: 367). Orwell's critique of language was informed by belief in its 'realist' potential, that is, its ability to represent the world.

The moral of Babel is that, on being expelled from the God-given domain of truth and representation, language entered the domain of human responsibility in which 'there is no connection between word and world unless we put it there' (Hogan 1996: 9). Once it is no longer underwritten by divine authority, the ability of language to depict reality or provide points of shared orientation is constantly in question. There is no single authority which stands outside language and controls it, nor is there a consensus as to how to describe and characterise the world. This raises the question of whether human cooperation through language is only conceivable as a form of coercion, whether it is only through the exercise of power that order can be imposed on the conceptual chaos of language and its relation to the world. Similar issues arise in relation to secular law and the nature of law's authority, once it is no longer justified by reference to divine authority. With both language and law, theorists have none the less tried to locate a single source of order, regularity, coherence, authority or sovereignty. Alternatively, foundational claims have been attacked as being in bad faith, as fictions or myths which maintain a false autonomy, or mask an underlying indeterminacy.

Part I

Theoretical Frameworks

1 Legal Theory and Language

In the 1997 film *Cube*, directed by Vincenzo Natali, characters find themselves trapped in a maze of interlocking rooms, in which there is no consistent orientation of up and down, and a series of puzzles and deadly traps awaits. The characters come into conflict over their interpretation of what is going on and what, if anything, can be done about it. This parallels somewhat the experience of following legal theory through its debates about language and interpretation, a field which has been described as 'awash in fancy theories' (Alexander 1995: 1081). The central issue in legal theory has been the question of whether judges 'make' law rather than simply 'find' it, a debate which Chafee (1947: 405) traces back to *Langbridge's Case* of 1345. The question is now posed more in terms of the political and ideological role of judges within constitutional theory. What follows is a brief survey of legal theory, offered as an aid for the reader who wishes to read further, with commentary on how different approaches tend to understand the role of language.

Natural law and legal positivism

Natural law theorists reject attempts to define law independently of morality for the purposes of philosophical or jurisprudential analysis, and see law as properly understood to be a teleological system which aims to bring about a just society (Bix 2002: 776). The term 'natural law' implies a set of ethical standards which exist before and outside actual existing legal systems and which have independent force in relation to them. These 'true and valid standards of right conduct' (Finnis 2002: 3) are available to the exercise of human reason, either as inherent in the foundations of humanity as an ethical species or as an expression of the divine ordering of the universe and of ethical commands laid down by God. Natural law theorists subsume law under morality, and argue that human beings have the ability to distinguish right from wrong. A 'natural law theory of interpretation' has been described as one where 'there is a right answer to moral questions, a moral reality' and 'the interpretative premises necessary to decide any case can and should be derived in part by recourse to the dictates of that moral reality' (Moore 1985: 286).

Legal positivism is generally associated with Jeremy Bentham (1748–1832), John Austin (1790–1859), Hans Kelsen (1881–1973) and H. L. A. Hart (1907–92). The 'pure theory of law' of the Austrian philosopher Kelsen defined law as an autonomous, normatively grounded domain, which was neither a set of moral rules, nor reducible to sociological categories. For positivists, moral questions are not irrelevant to law, and the separation is intended primarily as a methodological one: it is necessary to distinguish between law as it 'is' ('positive law') and law as it 'should be' (Hart 1983), the so-called 'separation thesis'. There is, however, a tension between describing the way law 'is' and prescribing the way it 'ought to be' running throughout legal theory. For example, studies of statutory interpretation may focus on how judges actually interpret authoritative legal texts or how they should (or should not) interpret them, but any descriptive assessment of the decisions of a particular judge will almost inevitably analyse judgments in terms of their coherence or other patterns of reasoning, and will take the form of an implicit or explicit critique: 'the threads of "is" and "ought" are interwoven in most theories of statutory and constitutional interpretation' (Greenawalt 2002: 271).

Formalism and realism

Formalism can be defined as the view that legal decisions reached by judges are highly constrained by law. Formalism was not a school of legal thought, but was associated with the nineteenth-century ideal of law as a formal and autonomous science with defined axioms and determinate modes of reasoning. In current legal theory 'formalist' is best understood as a polemical label for the automatic or logically closed application of legal rules, or the belief that the application of legal rules should ideally proceed in this fashion: 'That the judge can, or ought to, arrive at his decisions exclusively by a process of logical inference from explicit premises always has been, and must be, a fiction' (Hayek 1982, 1: 116–17). A close look at jurisprudential discussions reveals no clear definition (Stone 2002), and formalism is generally defined by its opposite, as in Cornell's formulation (Cornell 1992: 12; Stone 1995: 41):

> the very idea of a rule as a force that pulls us down the track through each new fact situation, determining the outcome of a particular case, is false. Therefore, no line of precedent can fully determine a particular outcome in a particular case because the rule itself is always in the process of reinterpretation as it is applied. It is interpretation that gives us the rule, not the other way round.

The reference here is to Wittgenstein's *Philosophical Investigations* ([1953] 1978: 85):

> Whence comes the idea that the beginning of a series is a visible section of rails invisibly laid to infinity? Well, we might imagine rails instead of a rule. And infinitely long rails correspond to the unlimited application of a rule.

Formalism is associated with the 'case method' under which law students were taught a specialised form of analysis and specific modes of reasoning with reference to decided cases. The original promoter of this method was the dean of the Harvard Law School, Christopher Langdell (1826–1906). This method represents an exercise in training of professional perception, in distinguishing the legally relevant from the extra-legal. For critics of legal education, this reinforces a set of myths about what the law is and how it functions, and a legal training is viewed negatively as a training in what *not* to see (Kennedy 1983; Goodrich 1987b: 200). There is, however, no necessary connection between the case study method and the idea of law as autonomous science (Carrington 1995).

Oliver Wendell Holmes (1809–94) is sometimes understood as an early exponent of 'legal realism', a trend in American jurisprudence associated with a sociological understanding of law and a rejection of strong claims about law's autonomy (Holmes [1881] 1967: 5): 'The life of the law has not been logic: it has been experience.' It was argued that the legal materials did not constrain or determine legal decisions, especially in cases heard at the appellate level. One much quoted statement is Holmes's assertion in *Lochner v State of New York* (1905): 'General propositions do not decide concrete cases' (at 76). Holmes also offered a critique of legal language, deploring the 'evil effects of the confusion between moral and legal ideas' (Holmes 1896/7: 458). The law was 'full of the phraseology drawn from morals' and this led to a confusion between the domain of law and the domain of morality: 'the mere force of language continually invites us to pass from one domain to the other without perceiving it, as we are sure to do unless we have the boundary constantly before our minds' (Holmes 1896/7: 459–60). For Holmes, the uncoupling of law and morality had as its corollary that the lawyer and judge of the future would be a technocratic expert: 'For the rational study of law the black-letter man may be the man of the present, but the man of the future is the man of statistics and the master of economics' (Holmes 1896/7: 469). The greater the faith in the technocratic, social engineering potential of sociology and social science, the more attractive the argument that law should submit its rule-making to sociological scrutiny. Holmes lamented in particular the 'divorce between the schools of political economy and law' (Holmes 1896/7: 474).

Formalism was often pejoratively labelled 'mechanical jurisprudence'. The more radical position within legal realism rejected any possibility of applying law deterministically, as the materials of law were inherently contradictory. Roscoe Pound (1870–1964) argued that the scientific approach to adjudication was fundamental, since it removed from the system the individual and possibly idiosyncratic values of the judge (Pound 1908: 606). But Pound rejected the idea that science meant deductive science (Pound 1908: 608). Law should not be scientific 'for its own sake', but as a means to an end, and that end lay outside of law in the effect of law on society. It was neither the 'niceties of internal structure' nor 'the beauty of its logical processes' that were important in law, but the results that were achieved in terms of justice (Pound 1908: 605–6).

For realists, judges had their own individual 'mental background' and were subject to 'forces which they do not recognize and cannot name [. . .] inherited instincts, traditional beliefs, acquired convictions' behind the mask of law (Cardozo 1921: 12–13). Judges were often primarily reacting to the case as a personal and social narrative. The legal process was more than a mere mechanistic 'judicial slot machine', with 'the facts being inserted in one end of the machine and the decision, through the use of mechanical logic, coming out at the other end'. This image was drawn from the German jurist Rudolf von Jhering (1818–92) (Frank [1930] 1970: 221, 223; Duxbury 2007: 29fn.). There was no 'law behind the law', no coherent system which underlay the whole of law and dictated its rules (Frank [1930] 1970: 284).

At the heart of realism is a critique of language. Law is enthralled by its own language, and has lost sight of the distance between legal terminology and sociological reality. What Pound saw as the nadir of mechanical jurisprudence was a style of interpretation which treated words themselves as offering legal solutions. This involved what the philosopher of pragmatism, William James, had termed a 'primitive kind of quest' for the magic formula. In law, word magic sought the key to a case 'in the shape of some illuminating or power-bringing word or name'. Conceptions were no longer seen as 'premises from which to reason' but as solutions in themselves (Pound 1908: 620):

> Current decisions and discussions are full of such solving words: estoppel, malice, privity, implied intention of the testator, vested and contingent – when we arrive at these we are assumed to be at the end of our juristic search. Like Habib in the Arabian Nights, we wave aloft our scimitar and pronounce the talismanic word.

Pound is not attacking specialised legal vocabulary itself, but rather the treatment of that vocabulary as self-sufficient, as if it provided self-contained legal answers to legal questions. Paradoxically, mechanical jurisprudence finds its ultimate expression in primitive 'word magic', where human control and will are surrendered to an external agency, language, understood as having its own autonomous source of power and energy. Felix Cohen in a famous essay spoke of 'logomachy', 'word-jugglery', the tendency to 'thingify' legal terms, within 'theological jurisprudence' (Cohen 1935; Waldron 2000).

The diversity of the realist tendency is shown by the fact that realists have been seen as advocates of the policy-making cost–benefit analysis found in contemporary law and economics, as well as having anticipated the Critical Legal Theorists' embrace of radical indeterminacy. Formalism, understood as a strict adherence to the language of authoritative legal texts, has been revived as 'textualism' within US jurisprudence (see Scalia 1997). Schauer defends formalism understood as 'decisionmaking by rule', and argues that adjudication should follow a theory of 'presumptive formalism' (1988: 547).

Liberal rule of law ideology

The liberal understanding of law involves belief in the relative autonomy of law, with law as (imperfectly but importantly) impersonal and impartial, and fidelity to the text of law and to the rule of law as fundamental principles. Liberal left, feminist and socialist critiques overlap to a degree with mainstream liberalism, analysing law critically in terms of its impact on, or representations of, women, and its reflections of class and race interests, but looking to law reform and the granting of rights as part of a wider programme of progressive social change. Fidelity to procedure, and to the special rights that procedure creates (e.g. the right not to be detained without legal authority, the right to know the substance of a charge), is key to the liberal understanding of the rule of law. Liberal constitutionalism, with its respect for the rule of law as an intrinsic social value and moral good, is arguably the point at which natural law theory and liberal legal positivism meet. The idea of 'natural justice' is both a value of liberal law recognised by judges as a substantive rule of law, and a reflection of secularised natural law ideology, as in Lon Fuller's emphasis on 'procedural correctness' (Fuller 1969). Hogan (1996: 194–5) argues that interpretation in law and other disciplines is centrally concerned with 'our behavior as ethical agents', and that ethics must be informed by 'Enlightenment ideals of clarity and rationality, a concern for truth, an advocacy of intellectual freedom'.

Legal language is viewed as (relatively) autonomous and, while imperfectly certain, as providing a generally stable system of signification with which law operates. It is recognised that this transparency is mainly available to legal insiders. Judges are viewed as highly constrained by the legal materials, though they must arbitrate where the texts they have to interpret do not offer a unique solution, in so-called 'hard cases' (Greenawalt 2002: 277): 'Given the conventions of natural language and law, many statutory provisions, cast in fairly precise terms, do require one understanding in context and exclude others.' If language is the (relatively) transparent medium of law, then the fundamental dilemmas are non-linguistic: the proper limits of state power, balancing social interests, maintaining social order, assigning liability, and so on. Theorists who see language as a relatively stable system for communicating ideas ('the transmission of meaning from mind to mind by material'; Finnis 2002: 38) or for describing the world tend not put language at the heart of the moral and policy dilemmas confronting law. Bix (1993: 178) argues that 'language has, for the most part, been a false focus for legal theory', and that linguistic questions 'have been used as an excuse for decisions that are more properly attributable to political – or at least policy – decisions' (Bix 1993: 178). For Finnis, language is 'never truly fundamental', though it is a factor in the limitations of law, characterised by 'under-determinacy' and vagueness 'inherent both in our purposes and in the language by which we may try to articulate and promote them' (Finnis 2002: 38).

A liberal theory of law seeks to evaluate how the autonomy and alienation of law from the 'everyday' as an achievement necessary for fairness and impartiality balances with the sociological and psychological impact of law on ordinary citizens. The legal process in criminal law can be viewed as a complex sequence of choreographed events. On one level it involves a sequence of events in time: the questioning of a suspect, then arrest, charge, indictment and arraignment, bail proceedings, trial, verdict, sentencing hearing, proceeding to possible appeals, probation, and so on. It also involves a parallel set of formalities for the circulation and transit of documents, with strict control of linguistic forms, formulations and reference to names, places, times and dates, with a regime of documentary and evidentiary order, and set time periods for key events, with legal supervisory mechanisms operating on law itself, including the presumption of innocence, the right to be charged with an offence known to law, the right to legal representation, the right to copies of documents, the right to the rights implicit to the procedure itself, etc. For a first-time arrestee it is a bewildering and disorienting experience of an alien world with its own ritual density, units of time, forms of language, and criteria of relevance. In Garfinkel's terms, the arrestee undergoes a series of 'degradation ceremonies' which separate them progressively from the legitimate social order (Garfinkel 1956). Civil law is no less complex or alien, but the central dramatic element found in serious criminal cases, the direct 'grip' of state power on the personal fate of the defendant as a physical body (as well as legal subject), is absent.

In terms of rule of law ideology, the opacity of legal language to outsiders reflects its commitment to formal consistency, its 'proceduralism'. The ritual language of law represents a formal buffer between state power, majoritarian morality, religious dogma and the individual citizen. Even if proceduralism is not honoured by state actors (e.g. when police officers fail to follow rules governing the control and questioning of suspects), or is unevenly distributed because of inequities in access to legal expertise, it remains an ideal of secular law. On this view, the ritual density of legal language reduces the transparency of law to the addressees of law, but the benefit for this cost is that the same density also slows, dissipates and monitors state action, requiring it to translate any action into the language and rituals of the legal system, breaking it down into a multitude of micro-steps, and thereby setting a series of barriers between political power and individual citizens. One way to understand the importance of proceduralism is to observe law at work in its absence. Historically, proceduralism can be seen as part of the achievement of secular law as an autonomous system, one which applied a 'civic and political' conscience independent of religious authority and private belief (Saunders 1997).

Radical approaches to law

Marxism

At the heart of many radical critiques of law are various versions of Marxism. A simple way to explain the Marxist view of law in liberal democracies is that law operates as a reflection of class interests and the capitalist system. Lawyers, especially judges, are members of the ruling class, and the processes, language and ritual trappings of law, with its defence of private property interests, are a veil behind which economic interests operate. Marxists reject ideas of the integrity and autonomy of law. Underlying economic relations, and the contradictions in the capitalist order, are reflected in the arena of law, though how to characterise such relationships is controversial in Marxist theory, as many Marxists reject 'vulgar' economic determinism. Political revolution would either transform law or ultimately lead to its disappearance as an autonomous category of social control, along with the disappearance ('withering away') of the state.

Marxist-derived theories of law emphasise the intersection of 'commodity fetishism' with law: just as capitalism replaces 'use-value' by 'exchange-value' represented through an abstract universal system of exchange, namely money, so law abstracts away from qualitative differences between individuals to define them as abstractly as holders of economic, political and legal interests (Milovanovic 1983: 358). Law's generality or abstraction is thus part of a wider mystification of human relationships, in which highly abstract systems of signs (semiotic systems) are naturalised as commonsense assumptions about property, value and social relations (Marx 1889: 41–2):

A commodity appears, at first sight, a very trivial thing, and easily understood. Its analysis shows that it is, in reality, a very queer thing, abounding in metaphysical subtleties and theological niceties. So far as it is a value in use, there is nothing mysterious about it, whether we consider it from the point of view that by its properties it is capable of satisfying human wants, or from the point that those properties are the product of human labour. [. . .] The form of wood, for instance, is altered, by making a table out of it. Yet, for all that, the table continues to be that common, every-day thing, wood. But, so soon as it steps forth as a commodity, it is changed into something transcendent. It not only stands with its feet on the ground, but, in relation to all other commodities, it stands on its head, and evolves out of its wooden brain grotesque ideas, far more wonderful than 'table-turning' ever was.

Under capitalism, 'the productions of the human brain appear as independent beings endowed with life, and entering into relation both with one another and the human race' (Marx 1889: 43). This leads to the Marxist ideas of 'inversion', whereby ideas are wrongly seen as 'cause' and social reality as 'effect'. This gives rise to 'false consciousness', a disjunction between the beliefs or self-narratives that individuals, groups or societies adhere to overtly and the actual forces and underlying factors that shape their development.

Language and linguistics have emerged in recent years as a key topic for Marxist and post-Marxist theory (see Harpham 2002: 69ff; Holborow 2006). Marxist philosophies of language would agree on the relevance of the 'social' as a category for language, and reject ideas of the autonomy and self-sufficiency of language as a transparent system for the exchange of ideas. Like commodities, words and ideas circulate with apparently stable and well-grounded meanings and values, but to understand language we need to contextualise it, and the more deeply language is contextualised, the more its stability and transparency appear problematic. The materialist understanding of history as proceeding from concrete social forms to increasingly abstract ones is reflected in an understanding that words with time acquire new, increasingly abstract meanings and metaphorical associations (Jones 2001: 239). For the literary critic Raymond Williams (1921–88), words were 'condensed social practices, sites of historical struggle, repositories of political wisdom or domination' (Eagleton 1998: 317–18). Contemporary 'hypercapitalism', a global system of electronic exchange and information trading in which currencies themselves are the primary traded commodity, is constituted by an economy of knowledge. This involves the 'linguistification of value', 'the commodification of language and thought', a political economy of language, thought and technology where 'language in the strictest sense – spoken or written words – is the ultimate coordinating element in which social perceptions of value are created, modified, and mediated' (Graham 2006: 51, 59, 57). Thus language is 'the only analytical entry we have' (Graham 2006: 65). In the global knowledge economy, the ultimate fetishised object is language itself.

Marxism derives from capitalism a fascination with the concept of 'circulation'. An ideal system for market economists is the maximally efficient circulation of goods and money in free exchange; for the Marxist, free circulation is a phantasm of ideology, and values that appear free and natural are loaded with hidden or unrecognised meanings. For the Marxist, the ideal underlying contract law of 'freedom of contract' between autonomous, independent and voluntaristic economic agents (e.g. employers and workers) is illusory (Mensch 1981): 'Real markets are never just machines for instantaneous transactions among economic agents equally knowledgeable and equally able to await the next offer or withdraw from the current course of dealing' (Unger 1983: 67). Thus, words circulate as if in an open market of the exchange of ideas, but are in reality loaded with historical, contextual and ideological meanings, and are realised as inequalities in exchange transactions. A recognised category of language ('educated accent') may symbolise something about its source, or a recognised social category such as style of clothing (e.g. business suit) or ethnicity/race may lend authority to (or detract from) a request for discretionary action by someone with administrative authority. Marxists reject the view that that in liberal democracies language operates as a free and unfettered medium of exchange. Goodrich's statement that 'a critical linguistic orientation [. . .] suggests that the separation or isolation of questions of law and legality from wider considerations of discursive processes as a modality of power and of inter-group or class relations is hollow ideologically' (Goodrich 1987a: 81) would be shared ground between Marxists, critical sociolinguistics and what has been termed 'Critical Legal Studies' (CLS).

Critical Legal Studies

CLS draws on both Marxist and feminist approaches, and reflects the broad intellectual preoccupations of cultural studies, as well as the politics of race and law, now a topic pursued under the heading of Critical Race Studies (see below). CLS represents a radical politics of law which is suspicious of liberal reformism, rights discourse, and any assertions of law's integrity, autonomy and internal coherence: 'Positivist philosophy of law has hitherto been a closed discourse' (Goodrich 1987a: 211). CLS is defined by a tension between an activist political agenda and a critique or 'interrogation' of language and text, with strong links to psychoanalysis, poststructuralism and literary deconstruction, with the idea of 'indeterminacy' at the centre. Deconstructive writing can be understood as 'performative' of its distrust of language, rationality and 'logocentricism': the idea that language can act as the foundation for ordered systems of meaning and belief.

CLS rejects the liberal view of language as a transparent and neutral system of stable signification and law's facade of certainty and predictability, viewing its underlying structures as profoundly indeterminate. But it is not always clear within which explanatory framework this indeterminacy is located, whether it is a property of language itself, arises as an interaction between language and context, or is simply a sub-category of general human perceptual subjectivity. One view is that CLS extends the legal realist critique of adjudication as indeterminate to a critique of language itself (Leiter 2003). However, Kelman (1987: 13) associates linguistic indeterminacy with legal realism and views CLS as making a distinct claim about the indeterminacy of 'justificatory schemes'.

A radical feminist critique of law views law as deterministically enacting patriarchal values, and as reflecting 'male' understandings of property, authority and 'women's place'. It views the state as 'male jurisprudentially, meaning that it adopts the standpoint of male power on the relation between law and society' (MacKinnon 1989: 163). Law speaks the 'language of the father', and is in this sense a secular expression of monotheistic, text-based, 'logocentric' religion, with 'Law' replacing a 'God the Father' as a transcendent and unquestionable authority, and as the ultimate interpreter and adjudicator. The idea of law as displaying integrity or autonomy is rejected, and feminists see in law's adversarial, rule-based culture, and even its claim to 'evenhandedness' (Conley and O'Barr 1998: 61), a reflection of its patriarchal nature. West (1988) sees law's protection of individual autonomy and framing of freedom as an ability to escape undesired connections with others (the right to be let alone) as reflecting law's male character: 'the Rule of Law does not value intimacy – its official value is autonomy' (West 1988: 58). CLS and feminist legal theory reject the liberal understandings of the public-private distinction, and sees all interpersonal, social and public spaces as contested and contentious. Possible slogans for CLS include 'law is politics', 'law is politics all the way down' (Tushnet 1991: 1526), 'law is politics by other means' (Hutchinson 2004: 279), 'law is interpretation' (Cornell 1987: 149), or, perhaps, 'law is the politics of interpretation'.

Postmodernism applies the idea to law that the 'grand meta-narratives' of Western thought (liberalism, Marxism, capitalism) have lost their persuasive power, and a pluralist, relativist, polycentric world of surfaces is evoked (Donaldson 1995). Postmodernity is inhabited by interacting, simultaneously closed and open-ended systems which escape direct human control, and these reflect back attempts to gaze through their surface into their imagined 'depths' (Goodrich 1990: 212):

> we should recognize that, as a language, law does not refer to any anterior realm of legal things; it refers simply to the system of legal notation, to other signs of law, to other legal texts.

The individual self as agent or subject disappears from view: 'As it is deconstructed, broken down into component systems which are all trans-subjective, the self or subject comes to appear more and more as a construct: the result of systems of conventions' (Culler 1986: 78). A fundamental, underlying dilemma for both reformist and radical theories of law is that activism and appeals for individual or group recognition by law require relatively stable categories. Deconstructive and postmodern anti-foundationalism may be radical if directed at hegemonic discourse, but also undermine consciousness-raising or the focusing effect of politicisation (Wicke 1991; Frug 1991).

Critical Race Theory

Critical Race Theory (CRT) in law takes up many of the same themes as CLS and feminism, including the interrogation of ideas of autonomy and objectivity. CRT sees law's history as haunted by race, and looks at law's construction of property and ownership in the context of slavery, offering a narrative of law and history which focuses on exclusion, segregation and expulsion (both literal, in terms of land claims, social spaces and migration, and symbolic, in that law's narrative excludes alternative experiences, voices and modes of story-telling). CRT sees different narratives as socially constructed distinct realities, and therefore contests dominant, 'essentialising' narratives of race and identity. Racial categories are 'products of social relations', they are 'categories that society invents, manipulates, or retires when convenient' (Delgado and Stefancic 2001: 7).

CRT raises the fundamental issue of the tensions and contradictions between 'perspectivism' ('an approach characterized by an emphasis on how it was for a particular person at a particular time and space'; Delgado and Stefancic 2000b: xvii) and outsider status ('[b]eing an outsider or "stranger" may *enhance* opportunities for gathering information and perceiving certain facets about a given situation'; Kennedy 1989: 1795, emphasis in original). To argue for the importance of outsider viewpoints is not necessarily to endow the outsider with 'presumptively insightful' qualities (Kennedy 1989: 1795), and is logically distinct from universalism, the claim that a particular viewpoint is objective and has general validity across different contexts and experiences. Balkin (1987: 1157–8), discussing Jacques Derrida's (1930–2004) concept of justice as non-deconstructable (Derrida 1990), notes that legal understanding never allows us 'to understand situations or the persons affected in all their uniqueness', as their experience is filtered through legal categories. However, 'the requirement that law be impartial demands that we not speak the language of a particular party, but in a language that is neutral and fair. [. . .] Legal justice strives for an impartiality that is also impersonal', yet this neutral language is doubly false to the parties in a dispute, and 'doubly falsifies the situation by denying or obscuring the uniqueness and singularity of each side'. If however the state is understood as both party to a dispute and mediator (as it is explicitly in the criminal law, albeit on behalf of the 'people', the Crown and so on), then the law can be understood as speaking a partial language, that is, its own.

CRT rejects the liberal ideal of a 'colour-blind' law as intrinsically conservative of a racially inequitable status quo. CRT experientially based narratives should, however, not be understood to exclude policy-driven analyses of law. Within the politics of American academia, the CLS position that promotion of greater rights through legal reform was primarily an extension of control and a form of cooption through hegemony was challenged by CRT on the basis that rights, while in some sense flawed legal fictions, represented potentially transformative forms of recognition for minority groups: 'many minority lawyers cling to *rights* while white lawyers in the Critical Legal Studies left are quick to throw them away' (Delgado and Stefancic 2000b: 41; Williams 1987). Critics of CLS accused it of merely 'trashing' legal doctrine and of failing to develop a positive vision (see Fischl 1992).

Right-radical approaches to law

The assumption is often made that the recognition of indeterminacy and attacks on liberal ideologies of autonomy are politically radical, by which is understood a leftist, Marxist-derived form of political progressivism. Historically, 'anti-individualist', 'anti-capitalist', 'anti-humanist', 'anti-Enlightenment', 'anti-universalistic' and 'anti-rationalist' are also labels for strands in European fascist thought, with its revolt against bourgeois social norms and the mechanical, 'soulless' alienation of modern life (Wolin 2004). The attack on 'logocentricism' (the fetishisation of the authority of the word) was a feature of radical inter-war German philosophy. The power of word and text over the social order was seen as reflecting a Jewish or Judaeo-Christian 'nomocracy' (patriarchal rule by the text of law), within which a rational modernity stifled the vitality and life-force of the Germanic race. Anti-logocentricism in European fascist thought reflected a cultic search for vital social forms, in which the stale language of modernity is broken down and reanimated in etymological play. Logophobia, the hermeneutic attack on the 'unworldliness' of Platonism and the apparent stability and worn-out 'presence' of language, struggles with a deferred logophilic sense that language must be remade authentically in Martin Heidegger's (1889–1976) 'house of being'.

Radical-right German political philosophy associated Enlightenment universalism with the forced induction to modernity following the Napoleonic conquest of Europe and was deeply hostile to the imposition by Napoleon of legal codes granting civil rights to Jews. Deep in the European 'political unconscious' and its racial theorising was a rejection of the Jews as the ultimate stateless, rootless, urban 'moderns'. In fascist ecology Jews were the ultimate 'humans' in their alienation from nature and 'normal' human diversity (Hutton 2005). A rejection of the 'Enlightenment' dream of the rational, self-regulating rule of law was a feature of inter-war radical-right legal thinking, as exemplified by the German jurist Carl Schmitt (1888–1985). Schmitt saw Hans Kelsen's legal positivism as reflecting the 'Enlightenment project', one which sought the subordination of human society to an impersonal rule of law. The autonomy of law on this view is one of the pathologies of modern state rationalism. For Schmitt, positivism concealed the true sources of legal power and sovereignty; for Kelsen, law is a 'self-sustaining' legal order, grounded in the *Grundnorm* or 'basic norm', so that it appears to run automatically: 'Now the machine runs itself' (Dyzenhaus 1994: 10), a picture of law 'from which 'human beings have almost disappeared' (Cotterrell 2003: 104). However, Cotterrell (2003: 108) stresses that, unlike that of Schmitt, Kelsen's vision of law is shaped by 'hostility to all forms of autocracy'.

The modern intellectual ancestor of both left- and right-radical thinking in law, as well as modern scepticism about language as a system of neutral representation, is the work of Friedrich Nietzsche (1844–1900) ([1873] 2000: 56):

> What then is truth? A movable host of metaphors, metonymies, and anthropomorphisms: in short, a sum of human relations which have been poetically and rhetorically intensified, transferred, and embellished, and which, after long usage, seem to a people to be fixed, canonical, and binding. Truths are illusions which we have forgotten are illusions; they are metaphors that have become worn out and have been drained of sensuous force, coins which have lost their embossing and are now considered as metal and no longer as coins.

Law and economics

Economic understandings of law, represented by the 'law and economics movement', reject the liberal-positivist notion of the autonomy and coherence of law, but equally oppose interventionist and reformist policy-driven changes unless they can be shown to promote the efficient allocation of resources. Regulation or intervention must be justified by its promotion of market efficiency: 'law should be structured so as to promote competitive markets' (Mercuro and Medema 2006: 96). Social actors are viewed as fundamentally rational in their assessment of their own interests: 'economic agents are rational maximizers – that is they make purposeful choices so as to pursue consistent ends using efficient means' (Mercuro and Medema 2006: 102). Law therefore finds right answers by applying a principle such as 'wealth maximisation' systematically, rather than applying vague and subjective notions such as 'justice', 'fairness' or 'equality'. Law and economics theories are often characterised as 'consequentialist' or 'utilitarian', that is, they look at outcomes, rather than abstract moral or legal principles, to establish norms of adjudication.

Proponents of the law and economics view argue that there are principled ways to model the assignment of legal liability, taking into account 'externalities' (such as pollution, insurance rates) and the 'transaction costs' of the legal process itself, and the way in which liability falls on various parties, including the state. In tort law, liability is assigned by defining a standard of negligence and risk of harm or damage that an ordinarily reasonable and ordinarily prudent person might reasonably foresee. 'Reasonable foreseeablity' is a legal fiction which must be applied by the judge (or a jury) to distinguish between consequences for which the negligent person is liable and other consequences, often in an apparently arbitrary way (*Palsgraf v Long Island Railroad Co*

(1928); Stone 1995: 69–80). The law and economics view suggests that rational economic criteria, rather than a fictional apparatus of legal concepts of causality, proximity and remoteness, should be applied.

In Richard Posner's view, the autonomy of law is a veil for the 'poverty of doctrinal analysis as a tool for solving the problems of the legal system' and the 'artificiality of many of the law's doctrinal distinctions' (Posner 2001: 3, 46). Law as legal or doctrinal discourse is incoherent, and economics and cost–benefit analysis can 'reveal a deep structure of law that has considerable coherence' and show 'the porousness of the boundaries that separate law from other forms of social control' (Posner 2001: 40, 46). The law and economics view offers both descriptive analysis and an agenda for reform, what Posner terms 'a positive and a normative programme', but both these derive 'from a single theory of human behavior' (Posner 1988: 1).

The traditional objection to such economic models is their highly reductionist nature and their perceived commodification of legal and moral dilemmas. This reductionism, however, provides law with a rational and unifying external criterion, one which, it is argued, offers insights into all areas of law, including free speech issues and sexual morality. Posner (1983: 16) points out that censorship of publications can be done at source ('advance censorship') or after publication ('post-publication criminal punishment'). One can distinguish more generally between legal regimes that control and supervise the inception of a process in advance (*ex ante*) or those which intervene only when informal social practice and dispute resolution break down after the fact (*ex post*), and look at the implications of the balance between these two in any regulatory system. The legislator may also use words such as 'fair' or 'reasonable' in drafting statutes (see for example the use of 'fair' in the Consumer Credit Act 2006 Ss 19–22), and this represents an *ex ante* determination that *ex post* judgments are needed to fill in the law's substantive content.

Friedrich von Hayek's (1889–1992) market-oriented philosophy of law denies precisely that judges or any other organizing agents are in a position to make the judgments that law and economics requires. The ideal is that of a judge-made legal order where the judge works by 'piecemeal tinkering' or what Hayek terms 'immanent criticism', operating as an instrument of the 'evolution of thought', so that the judge maintains (Hayek 1982, 1: 118–19)

> a going order which nobody has designed, an order that has formed itself without the knowledge and often against the will of authority, that extends beyond the range of deliberate organization on the part of anybody, and that is not based on the individuals doing anybody's will, but on their expectations becoming mutually adjusted.

Posner's judge would be, for Hayek, too much like a central planner.

In law and economics terms, the ritual proceduralism and linguistic density of law are a transaction cost. They are an obstacle between a dispute and its resolution, and should be assessed in terms of their overall contribution to social arbitration and control. In civil law, parties may decide that the high transaction costs of law outweigh its benefit as a neutral adjudication system, but this may be an overall benefit, promoting informal arbitration mechanisms, or preventing parties going to court over every commercial disagreement. In criminal law, police officers do not arrest every jay walker and miscreant motorist, and can only pursue a limited number of lines of investigation when faced with a whole social field of mundane criminality. The transaction costs of a criminal investigation trial are high, when compared with legal systems where the police have the power to arrest and impose imprisonment as an administrative sanction.

The dense proceduralism of law imposes a high burden on the state in terms of resources, in that it must maintain a high standard of formal fidelity to the rules and formulations of law. This means that the state must maintain large numbers of professional lawyers, and fund a complex judicial system. The high transaction cost of state action, however, also imposes a similar burden on the defence. The presumption of innocence, which is an additional transaction cost for the state, may not offset the substantial gap in resources and legal expertise available to ordinary defendants, thus favouring the wealthy. Further, victims of sexual crimes often see going to law as exacting too high a personal and emotional cost. In many civil law contexts, the transaction costs for large multinational companies with their own legal divisions are relatively low, giving them privileged access to law. This is notoriously the case with the libel laws in the United Kingdom. Law's proceduralism is rarely equally distributed, often favouring the state, or large multinationals operating in jurisdictions where the legal system is underfunded.

There is no law and economics approach to language as such, but it offers a realist critique of much traditional legal terminology, law's reliance on legal fictions, and subjective and inconsistent use of terms like 'fairness' and 'justice'. Its emphasis on rationality and transparency to objective analysis makes it unreceptive to ideas of indeterminacy (see Posner 1988: 209–68), especially if we think of indeterminacy as involving the inability in principle of a system to assign value to a sign. This would mean that language as a sign system is characterised by chronic 'market failure', that is, it is constituted by discourse exchanges for which no clear values or meanings can be assigned.

Another way of looking at language within a law and economics framework is from the point of view of before the fact (*ex ante*) and after the fact (*ex post*) determinations. The *ex ante* view of language is that its basic meanings or values need to be fundamentally determined by the system in advance of the context in which words are used, and the addressee is primarily the decoder or receiver of the message, otherwise communication cannot proceed. This is the view promoted within mainstream linguistic theory. The *ex post* view is that it is primarily the addressee or the reader within a particular contextual situation or the community of readers within a social context who assign values, as in Fish's concept of 'interpretative community' (Fish 1980: 321). Deconstructive methods empower certain kinds of reader over the text ('the critic as meaning-creator'; Fiss 1982: 762) and over the author, since it is the deconstructive reader who recognises and pulls at the stray thread which will unravel the whole textual garment.

A law and economics model would see language as a market, and the best allocation of interpretative authority would be one that works best for individual transactions or exchanges set against a general social context where a set of shared expectations and conventions may reduce transaction costs. Everyday exchanges are conducted under an assumption of approximate symmetry in interpretative authority. Law, however, imposes strict rules on witnesses in court proceedings, and prevents them from merely 'telling their story'. This reflects law's *ex ante* control not only over the assignment of meaning, but of the process whereby meaning and truth for the purposes of law are arrived at. The transaction cost for the witness is high, and in informal social exchanges an attempt to enforce this dramatic asymmetry in authority would generally lead to a rupture in social relations, or would be evidence of a highly coercive relationship. But asymmetry in the context of cross-examination is defended with reference to a claim for the clarity, consistency, systematicity and balance that this achieves, as a benefit for the achievement of justice in the individual case, and as a benefit for law and society as a whole. A further example of a non-legal asymmetrical context is found in luxury goods stores, where in exchanges between shop-assistants and customers there is allocation of exclusive interpretative authority to the customer: 'The customer is always right.'

Luhmann v Habermas: autopoiesis and law

In the autopoietic theory of Niklas Luhmann (1927–98), law is understood as a self-referential, self-reproducing system, rather than a form of social integration (Luhmann 2004: 143); it is 'self-constituting, self-referring and self-describing' (Beck 1994: 406–9). Autopoiesis is a term derived from evolutionary biology, referring to systems that reproduce themselves autonomously: 'law produces by itself all the distinctions and concepts which it uses [. . .] the unity of law is nothing but the fact of this self-production, this "autopoiesis"' (Luhmann 2004: 70). As a social system, law is constituted by acts of communication, which cannot be reduced to the conscious, willed acts of the individual people who are members of the institution. Systems create their own realities and their own languages, their own processes and modes of classification, such as the binary classification 'legal/illegal'. This idea of law is summed up in the slogan 'law thinks' (Teubner 1989).

One crucial question raised by a systems theory approach to law is the nature of law's interaction with whatever lies 'outside' the boundaries that law draws for itself. The central notion here is that of law as 'operative closure'. Closure does not mean total isolation, but refers to the autonomy of the internal, self-referring communicative order. Biological systems have 'intensive causal links' with their environment, but these must be mediated, as the environment is highly complex and undifferentiated. In evolutionary terms, systems acquire internal complexity which is not reducible to links to the 'outside' but based on selection and categorisation. This form of autonomy Luhmann terms 'informational' or 'semantic' closure (Luhmann 2004: 80). This high degree of internal complexity, self-reference and self-modification determines how the law evolves, but to survive law must also be 'irritated, stimulated, disturbed and faced with changes in the environment' (Luhmann 1988: 335). In addition, there exist links in the form of 'structural couplings' between law and other systems such as economics and politics.

There is an absolute boundary between law and non-law, but law in its own systems of self-reference includes systems that recognise or represent the external world to law. External factors and forces may act upon law contingently to cause the reorganisation of aspects of the internal system. One consequence of Luhmann's view is that there is no way to assess accurately or control the direction of change, as there are no 'macrosocial steering functions' (Habermas 1996: 49). Since social sub-systems are highly distinct and autonomous, there is no overall way to deal purposefully with global environmental degradation, even though these systems may be resonating with anxiety and alarm (Luhmann 1989). Luhmann's theory of the autonomy of law has been linked to positivism ('[a]n inference about norms cannot be made from facts'; Luhmann 2004: 352), but the systems approach, and Luhmann's bracketing out of individual autonomous agency and motivation from law, have also led to comparisons with Foucault (Borch 2005; Habermas 1996: 47). Nobles and Schiff (2006: 230) describe Luhmann's systems theory as 'a post-modern theory', in that it is anti-foundational, but unlike deconstruction 'systems theory engages with the absence of foundations, and seeks to account for the manner in which modern society functions in their absence'.

By contrast, the philosopher Jürgen Habermas is concerned with the legitimation of law in democratic societies where traditional sources of authority are discredited. He seeks to elaborate an ideal of democratic participation, one in which the 'public sphere' plays a central role. He rejects what he terms Luhmann's 'radical objectivism' (Habermas 1996: 470):

> Subjects who constitute their own worlds or, at a higher level, intersubjectively share common lifeworlds, drop out; consequently, all intentional integrating achievements disappear from view.

Habermas argues that systems theory cannot offer a coherent view of how social sub-systems interact, and how they impact and act though the ordinary 'lifeworld' of members of society, without assuming some underlying 'general social communication' (e.g. ordinary language) which is at odds with the 'architectonic of systems theory' (Habermas 1996: 53ff).

The theory of the democratic legitimacy of law is grounded in a special understanding of language and discourse. This public sphere is imagined as an ideal speech situation, characterised as a non-coercive, free and equal space in which participants are committed not to their private narratives or instrumental goals, but to a communicative order governed by a mutuality and intersubjectivity. This sphere is independent of the market and of administrative rationality, and devoid of the feudal pomp and display of the traditional 'theatre of the state', being a sphere comprised of the public reason of private citizens (Peters 1993). What Habermas terms the 'lifeworld', the layered, everyday, face-to-face world of family, social practice and taken-for-granted belief, sustains the public sphere: 'The lifeworld forms both the horizon for speech situations and the source of interpretations, which in turn reproduces itself only though ongoing communicative actions' (Habermas 1996: 23). This lifeworld is threatened with colonisation by systems that have become detached from it, such as economics, mass media and the consumer-welfarist modern state: 'the imperatives of autonomous subsystems make their way into the lifeworld from the outside – like colonial masters coming into a tribal society – and force a process of assimilation upon it' (Habermas 1987: 355). The lifeworld cannot itself withstand direct conscious scrutiny, as it is based on accumulated assumptions and norms experienced as unproblematic. The linguistic ideal underlying Habermas's theory is one of a committed, engaged, intersubjective dialogue between consensus-oriented individuals drained of egocentricism.

Where does law fit into this picture? It might be argued that law is one of the primary systems engaged in colonizing the lifeworld; alternatively, law might be one social sub-system in which aspects of the ideal public sphere are found. An explicit application of Habermas's philosophy to the language of the law can be found in Philips (2002). For Habermas, the objectivity of the judge-interpreter, 'founded on the requirement or practice of justifying decisions by reasons, reflects in reality the intersubjectivity of the citizens constituted as a community of interpreters' (Philips 2002: 140). A legitimate legal system is one where law is grounded in the intrinsically consensual, cooperative and intersubjective lifeworld. Law is legitimate to the extent that it fits with the goals and norms that emerge in a public sphere authentically grounded in the lifeworld, and to the extent that citizens can feel themselves to be the ultimate authors of law. However, social sub-systems inevitably develop their own highly specialised language and forms of life, far removed from the ordinary communicative practice and norms of the lifeworld: 'Such systems develop their own codes, as the economy does with money and the administration does with power' (Habermas 1996: 354). Law is the integrating factor that links the lifeworld to these systems (1996: 354):

Through the legal institutionalization of steering media [. . .] these systems remain anchored in the society component of the lifeworld. The language of the law brings ordinary communication from the public and private spheres and puts it into a form in which these messages can also be received by the special codes of autopoietic systems – and vice versa. Without this transformer, ordinary language could not circulate throughout society.

In a postscript, Habermas explains that law (1996: 448):

fulfills socially integrative functions; together with the constitutionally organized political system, law provides a safety net for failures to achieve social integration. It functions as a kind of 'transmission belt' that picks up structures of mutual recognition that are familiar from face-to-face interactions and transmits these, in an abstract but binding form, to the anonymous, systemically mediated interactions among strangers.

For law to have the quality of democratic legitimacy, it must not simply be plucked out of the air. If human rights are understood merely as imposed by a sovereign legislator, then those to whom these rights are addressed 'would not be able to understand themselves as its authors if the legislator were to discover human rights as pregiven moral facts that merely need to be enacted as positive law' (Habermas 1996: 454).

Law is in effect the institutionalisation of the ideal discursive qualities of the public sphere, so that 'the very forms of communication that are supposed to make it possible to form a rational political will through discourse need to be legally institutionalized themselves'. What Habermas terms 'the discourse principle' is transformed into a 'principle of democracy', but at the same time law must create the private autonomous status of the legal person, without which there is no medium 'for legally institutionalizing those conditions under which citizens can first make use of their civic autonomy' (Habermas 1996: 455). This means that positive law represents a restriction on how people's lives are regulated, in that 'paradoxically they are no longer free to choose the medium in which they can realize their autonomy' as 'legal subjects'. In simple terms, they cannot determine the language of law, but in a democratic system are offered a guarantee that law is grounded in accountability to the lifeworld (Habermas 1996: 455).

The legitimacy of law and of the legal code is not derived top-down from the sovereign or a higher moral law but 'only from a procedure of presumptively rational opinion and will-formation', so that 'the only regulations and ways of acting that can claim legitimacy are those to which all who are possibly affected could claim assent as participants in rational discourse'. This 'discourse principle' in which citizens test out which rights they would accord each other to operate ('self-legislation') must be anchored in the medium of law itself. As legal subjects 'they must legally institutionalize those communicative presuppositions and procedures of a political opinion- and will-formation in which the discourse principle is applied'. The legal code 'must be *completed* through communicative and participatory rights that guarantee equal opportunities for the public use of communicative liberties'. What this means is that the discourse principle 'acquires the legal shape of a democratic principle' (Habermas 1996: 458).

Philips (2002: 178) finds in Habermas a defence of the specialised language of law. Parties involved in a conflict of values 'must jointly shift to the more abstract level of moral reasoning and agree on rules for living together that are in the equal interest of all' (Habermas 1998: 432, cited in Philips 2002: 178):

> If there is an irreconcilable conflict of values instead of a conflict of compromisable interests, then the parties must jointly shift to the more abstract level of moral reasoning and agree upon rules for living together that are in the equal interest of all. That is just one of many examples of interdiscursive relations. What matters here is that these relations are not dictated from the perspective of a superdiscourse. Rather, they emerge from the logic of questioning within a given discourse, with the result that the good is privileged over the expedient and the just over the good.

Habermas seeks to ground law in the ideal of a lifeworld free of coercive asymmetries. He sets this against Luhmann's evocation of a world in which systems run autonomously without reference to human agency and beyond direct human control. However, Lenoble (1998: 37–81) argues that Habermas offers 'a view of linguistic communication that utterly fails to take into account its inherent undecidability'. Harpham (2002: 195–202) sees Habermas as simply choosing to ground his universal ethics in an ideal language or discourse, one fundamentally oriented towards the intersubjective seeking of consensus and understanding. What we call 'language' or discourse is amoral and without an intrinsic ethical order to which we can appeal.

Within Habermas's model there is a danger that legal language and quasi-legal proceduralism will colonise or 'juridify' the lifeworld. This would mean that the democratic mutuality between the lifeworld and law, which sustains law by maintaining its link to the ideal speech situation latent in the lifeworld, would be undermined. Law would take on the systems-like autonomy and objectivist power evoked by Foucault's concept of discourse. A Foucaultian twist to Habermas's model is to ask where we could in theory stand so as to be able to grasp the extent to which the lifeworld is colonised by law, but this is a question for Foucault as much as for Habermas.

Conclusion

The fundamental issue at stake in legal theory is the notion of law's 'autonomy'. The liberal view of law as autonomous, consistent, internally cohesive and ordered is paralleled to a degree by the linguist's view of a language as a stable structure which is constituted as an internally coherent and ordered conceptual system. The liberal view of law is also dependent on the possibility of language performing, to a high degree of accuracy and transparency, the task which law sets for it, and putting its stability and transparency at the service of the rule of law's requirement for fidelity to the language of the law. Mechanical jurisprudence is a negative characterisation of the principle that there should be a high degree of fidelity to the language of law. This ideal of fidelity is one of the pillars of the liberal theory of the rule of law: in being 'true' to the language of law, judges restrain themselves from transgressing the bounds of their constitutionally assigned role. The liberal view of law and the view of languages as stable and transparent systems thus form two separate yet intertwined strands in a theory of social cohesion.

The autonomy of law within liberal jurisprudence is held to reflect its impartial distance from the language, categories of thought and prejudices of ordinary social life. Thus for those who accept this vision of law, and who also have faith in the ability of language as a stable and transparent system to meet this task, mechanical jurisprudence re-emerges as an ideal, the noble dream of predictability and impartiality, rather than the nightmare. For defenders of legal integrity, fidelity to law implies restraint and abstinence in the face of the temptation to politicise adjudication. However, the nature of this distinction between fidelity to the text of law and interstitial law-making is at the heart of debates in legal theory concerning the nature of adjudication. Radical criticism of law rejects arguments for law's autonomy, seeing them as a veil for special interests. For critics of law, its boundaries and distinctions do not inhere in the legal materials and are drawn either arbitrarily or strategically in the covert service of ideology. None the less, the understanding of adjudication as constrained by fidelity to law cannot be easily discounted: it represents a very powerful interpretative framing device with deep roots in the culture and practice of law.

2 Systems Theory, Normativity and the 'Realist Dilemma'

Introduction

This chapter looks at the concept of 'system' as applied to the study of language, and the methodological and theoretical dilemmas that this raises. A system is an abstract model, and a systems theoretical model involves a complex, interlocking set of representations. Systems theory approaches are fundamental to the natural sciences, as well as to economics, social science and linguistics, and draw on a wide range of theoretical sources, from biology and evolutionary theory to philosophy and semiotics, in order to represent categories such as mind, language, law or society itself. A systems model strives for maximal explicitness and terminological and conceptual coherence. This creates a tension between systems-internal criteria and the credibility of the system as a 'realistic' representation of law, the mind, society, and so on. Any systems theory model is vulnerable to a realist challenge, since by definition a systems theory is an abstract formalisation or systematisation set against the complex, multidimensional, inchoate nature of its environment or 'reality'. A systems theory may claim to discern an underlying order in the social phenomenon, or may be rejected as projecting its own, internal, fictive order onto external reality. This chapter explores the nature of linguistics as a branch of systems theory, the bracketing out of normativity from linguistics and its inclusion within ethnomethodology, and the methodological dilemmas to which systems theories give rise. The fundamental challenge represented by systems theories is that they tend to marginalise, or completely deny, the relevance of social actors' subjectivity and control over social meanings. In its extreme form, this implies that social actors 'do not know what they are doing', and their lived experience is an 'epiphenomenal' or contingent rather than constitutive feature of social interaction.

Description and prescription in linguistics

Linguists see language as governed by rules. Sentences are deemed to 'follow' or 'violate' a linguistic rule, and theoretical models have a high level of internal complexity and abstractness, including meta-rules, or rules about rules ('rule-ordering'). Linguists' rules are intended to capture significant generalisations about language structure, and are deemed 'descriptive' in the sense that the language system exists prior to, and independently of, the observations of the linguist. This descriptive posture is often contrasted with so-called 'prescriptivism'. In the disciplinary culture of linguistics there exists a general dislike of those who set themselves up as having authority over language and over ordinary users ('lay speakers'). A prescriptive approach is one that lays down standards of correctness for users of the language to follow, and as a corollary, also declares certain usages to be incorrect and therefore to be avoided (Milroy and Milroy 1991: 1):

> Prescription depends on an ideology (or set of beliefs) concerning language which requires that in language use, as in other matters, things shall be done in the 'right' way.

Prescriptivism is associated by linguists with authoritarianism, and with social prejudices such as the stigmatisation of certain pronunciations or accents in employment contexts (Milroy and Milroy 1991: 4). Prescriptivism is perceived as irrational, as it ascribes values to what are inherently arbitrary forms, such as ascribing superior value to 'I haven't any money' as opposed to 'I ain't got no money' (Hill 1954: 396).

Underlying the attack on prescriptivism is an ideology which regards language as a natural or quasi-natural entity, one which is the shared and equal property of its speakers, and which should change naturally, without the conscious interference of its speakers. While language use may vary across domains and in relation to social categories such as gender, ethnicity and class, no group can claim superiority in its use or particular authority over it. Any such claim to authority is not grounded in intellectual insight or rationality but derived from social status and power and reflects snobbery and elitism. However, linguists who take an interest in social issues – as opposed to pure systems linguists – tend to condemn prescriptivism where they see it operating so as to reflect or reinforce social inequality, and support it when it intervenes to create usage practices that symbolically empower marginalised groups. This might be thought of as prescriptive 'affirmative action', aimed at countering the ideological distortions that circulate about language.

Proposing a more general term, 'verbal hygiene', Cameron has argued that the prescriptivism condemned by linguists is just one of many ways in which particular values are read onto or into language, and that a society without 'verbal hygiene' of any kind is inconceivable: 'making value judgments on language is an integral part of using it and not an alien practice perversely "grafted on"' (Cameron 1995: 3). If we take Cameron's insight seriously, then linguistic prescription in its wider sense involves ascribing value, controlling or attempting to control, claiming or assigning authority, contesting labels and categories, and a multiplicity of everyday, mundane linguistic practices. In effect Cameron rejects the idea that there exist individual systems known as 'languages' which can be meaningfully characterised independently of the values attached to them. This criticism involves the classic 'realist' rejection of an abstract systems model as distorting the fundamental reality of the object of study.

Given that so much of the authority of the law is manifested through language and control of language, there is a tendency for linguists to distrust the law as an institution, and legal language as an elitist code. Law, in Cameron's terms, is a massive system of verbal hygiene. The law prohibits statements that are made to mislead in commercial transactions (misrepresentation) or in advertising (trade descriptions); it renders certain utterances or acts of publication illegal by defining protected forms of confidentiality (official secrets, private data, certain commercial information), and it requires other forms of utterance, disclosure or publication, such as requiring information in exchange for state services (welfare benefits), declarations that accompany tax or other forms, mandating cooperation with the official Census. The law regulates the media through licensing and censorship; it allows access to the court system to protect public reputations against unfounded attacks; it protects ownership in creative products through copyright, and brand identity through trademark protection and the prevention of 'passing off'. The law may forbid certain forms of threatening, aggressive or obscene language, or place controls on inflammatory utterances calculated to incite violence or hatred of particular groups, or forbid certain forms of political utterance such as treason. In some jurisdictions there may be also extensive language planning provisions, including rights to use or be given information in certain languages, or rights of access to official bodies through designated languages. The legal system itself constitutes an enormous body of linguistic regulation to which all those involved in it, or who interact with it, are subject.

A banal yet fundamental example of prescription is law's assumption of privileged access to the legal effect of labels attached to situations. The fact that a document has been stamped in red 'confidential' does not necessarily mean that a court will recognise and protect its confidentiality. Calling an agreement a 'contract' or a landlord–tenant agreement a 'lease' does not mean the courts will accept these labels as determinative of legal status. In such cases judges see their role as looking past the labels ('form') to the legal reality beneath or behind the label ('substance'). This is prescriptive in that it disallows or invalidates a particular linguistic label or usage as being inappropriately matched to the facts of the situation as the law determines them to be.

The linguistic prescription of law can be further illustrated in relation to names. There are powerful non-legal (family, social and cultural) norms about how names are given, what names are appropriate and desirable, how names change on marriage, and so on. Names have social values attached to them, and social values exist in relation to (often contentious) behavioural norms.

Extra-legal norms may be just as powerful as legal ones in their control of behaviour. Naming is a formal 'speech act' of prescription, but it is at one end of a continuum that includes teasing with temporary nicknames, and indeed any mundane act of characterisation, describing or labelling. Defamation law, for example, monitors acts of public labelling or characterisation. In most common law jurisdictions the law recognises the right of individuals to use any name they choose, provided the name chosen does not itself breach any other laws (e.g. a name expressing a racist sentiment), and provided the name is not used for the purposes of fraud. There are, however, legal controls on the use of names in the commercial sphere (company law, trademark law, domain names, etc.), and internet domain names are a rich source of conflicts. The United States has an Anticybersquatting Consumer Protection Act 1999, and UK courts have protected trademark proprietors from speculators who bought up relevant domain names with the intention of selling them (*British Telecommunications Plc & Ors v One In A Million Ltd & Ors* (1998)).

The intersection of everyday normativity with legal prescription arises in what might be termed 'civil suicide' cases. In Britain in 1995, a disgruntled customer changed his name by deed poll to 'Yorkshire Bank are Fascist Bastards' (Cicutti 1995). A similar tactic was in evidence in the Australian case *Re Mr Prime Minister John Piss the Family Court and Legal Aid Applicant and Minister for Foreign Affairs and Trade* (2000). There the court upheld an official decision not to issue a passport in the name 'Prime Minister John Piss the Family Court and Legal Aid'. In that case, a linguist testified to the effect that 'the structure of the name used by the applicant tends to cause a processing problem for speakers and hearers'. The linguist referred to evidence which 'shows that the name is frequently abbreviated or changed by those processing it as confirming that tendency', and 'in her opinion the attempt to use the grammatical string of words used by the applicant "falls outside the empirically defined bounds of acceptable linguistic behaviour"'. The court did not accept that being difficult to process was a relevant criterion, nor did it agree with the linguist that 'the fact that the construction is a possible political slogan disqualifies it from recognition and acceptance as a name, from an empirical point of view'. The court recognised 'a person's right to use his name to make a political statement'. Ironically, the court was less prescriptive than the linguist: it did find, however, that 'prime minister' and 'piss' were offensive in different ways, in the context of a passport. This use of the personal name as a weapon draws on the special cultural status and patterns of circulation of names to attack their target, but also enacts a form of civic suicide or symbolic self-disfigurement, in which a fundamental element of established social identity is erased and the bearer of the name enters social interactions defined by the mark of their anger.

If we seek to understand law as a set of prescriptive language practices, then a theory of language which brackets out, or is hostile to, prescriptivism is at least *prima facie* problematic. As we go about our social business we do not normally reflect on the continuing but latent legal dimension to every social act or context. Similarly, as we speak, write and listen, we are not constantly aware of contested labelling and the normativity of language. The attack on prescriptivism within linguistics obscures a key social fact: all language use is potentially or latently monitored, contested or regulated by virtue of the fact that it can be represented as a form of behaviour, a judgment, 'making a statement'. Law is in this respect no different in essence from any other form of language use, except that it habitually operates at a level of higher foregrounding or linguistic self-consciousness than so-called 'ordinary language' usage, and the authority that it brings to bear is backed ultimately by coercive state power. The linguist's descriptive rule is an abstraction away from a social practice embedded in the multidimensional normativity of the social world. Taylor (1997: 140, emphasis in original) writes: 'If language has a form, it is precisely because it is a normative activity, an activity that matters to its participants because they *make* it do so. The perspective from which linguistic form appears is not statistical, biological, chronological, logical, or psychological: it is a moral and political perspective.' This would align linguistics with other disciplines, since normativity is fundamental to systems theoretical models of social interaction and law.

Language as system

To understand the bracketing out of normativity from language, we need to look at the intellectual roots of linguistics. The history of modern linguistics is closely bound up with questions relating to the autonomy and internal coherence of its object of study, human language, and with the related claim of linguistics to be an autonomous science with its own specialised disciplinary knowledge. Like any form of analysis, linguistics seeks to make general statements, and in so doing it must – like law – operate a process of labelling or characterisation, a set of procedures for processing a social phenomenon by criteria of relevance and evidential reliability into categories on which linguistics can operate and analyse. At its most basic level linguistics seeks to identify the basic units of language and the rules which govern their combination and use. Ferdinand de Saussure (1857–1913), whose *Course in General Linguistics* is viewed as the founding text of modern linguistics, concluded that to ground an autonomous discipline one needed to identify an autonomous object of study. Without it, linguistics would be committed to studying language from several points of view at once, as both a static state and an object in perpetual flux, and as a social, psychological, historical product, as well as a social institution. This would render the object of study 'a muddle of disparate, unconnected things' (Saussure [1916] 1983: 9). Given that language taken as a whole 'has no discernible unity', the only solution was that (Saussure [1916] 1983: 9–10):

The linguist must take the study of linguistic structure as his primary concern, and relate all other manifestations of language to it. Indeed [. . .], linguistic structure seems to be the one thing that is independently definable and provides something our minds can satisfactorily grasp. [. . .] The structure of a language is a social product of our language faculty. At the same time, it is also a body of necessary conventions adopted by society to enable members of society to use their language faculty.

Saussure distinguished between 'synchrony' (the language as state) and 'diachrony' (language as an evolving, historical phenomenon), and privileged the former as providing the only systematic vantage point and a point of view from which the language system is static. This was also the point of view of the ordinary speaker of a language: 'Only by suppressing the past can he [the linguist] enter into the state of mind of the language user' (Saussure [1916] 1983: 117).

Saussure denied that words were names of things, that language was a 'nomenclature' (Saussure [1916] 1983: 97ff), and insisted on the mutually defining nature of linguistic signs in a structured system: 'a language is a system of pure values'. Different languages divided up conceptual space differently, and there was no direct relationship between concepts and things in the world. Nothing was given in advance, and concepts, that is, the meanings of words, were mutually defining. In asking what the meaning of 'red' is, we need to distinguish it from the other elements of the system, that is, in the first instance the other colour terms. Different languages divide the spectrum of colour up differently, and we do not capture the meaning of 'red' by pointing to a piece of red material. In the same way, it makes no sense to explain what the meaning of 'one' is in mathematics by pointing to a single orange.

Saussure saw a close parallel between linguistics and economics, since both dealt with, and distinguished, historical evolution from contemporary values in the system. However, 'pure' ('arbitrary') linguistic values were contrasted with economic values: the value of a piece of land had a relation to 'the income derivable from it' ([1916] 1983: 116). The *Course* pointed out that values always involve exchanges of two kinds ([1916] 1983: 159–60). The first involves the exchange of an item for something dissimilar (as in the exchange of a five-franc coin for a loaf of bread). Here the value is expressed in how much of something different one can get. Secondly, there are exchange values within the system, so that the five-franc coin can be exchanged for five single franc coins, or an amount in another currency (e.g. a dollar). The parallel with language went as follows (Saussure [1916] 1983: 160):

Similarly, a word can be substituted for something dissimilar: an idea. At the same time, it can be compared to something of a like nature: another word. Its value is therefore not determined merely by that meaning for which it is a token. It must also be assessed against comparable values, by contrast with other words. The content of a word is determined in the final analysis not by what it contains but by what exists outside it. As an element in the system, the word has not only meaning but also – above all – a value.

This places each word and its meaning within a system of variable exchange values. The value of a word is not anchored in a relationship to real things, since words are not direct labels of objects, nor is it simply to be understood as its conceptual 'content'. Each word is, like a unit of currency, variable and dependent on other systems of reference; as the system evolves, so does the value of each unit. So while we can think of each word as a form with an associated meaning, there is nothing fixed about this relationship, since it is determined by, or constituted by, wider sets of exchange relationships.

Saussure's linguistic system was not itself subject to any individual or collective will, and by virtue of being a pure medium it escaped the conscious control and analysis of its speakers. Speakers of a language can be said to 'know' it, but they have no reflexive awareness of its nature. The language system (*langue*) itself cannot be directly changed by acts of individual agency. Speech (*parole*) contains individual changes which may be at some point incorporated into the system as undirected acts coalesce into a system change. This is presented as a description of how language works, but it is perhaps better understood as an idealised vision of language, in which sovereignty over it is genuinely shared among the speakers. Unlike systems for distributing economic or political value, there is no inequality in the ideal language system, and no single individual or group of individuals can merely by acts of will control or cause fundamental changes to that system. A language is a system of perfectly decentralised control.

Saussure offers a 'contractarian' account of social order, in which instances of communication are guaranteed or underwritten by language as a general and shared social fact. As in the ideal contract, the model is symmetrical: it offers a speaker–hearer neutral model of language and communication. Structuralism presents conceptual or cultural structures as autonomous and stable, and invoking the repetitive instancing of underlying norms (linguistic, cultural) to explain human behaviour. Following Saussure, linguistics is interested in the systematic description of underlying semantic knowledge of linguistic meaning, and of pragmatic knowledge of the 'shared cognitive environment' (Toolan 1996: 184) that allows communication to proceed and interactants to find order in communicative practice. Other problems with communication are assessed against this background of shared rules and assumptions. Since the semantic and pragmatic codes are shared by the speaker and hearer, their communications are symmetrical and reciprocal. A given utterance reflects the intended meaning of the speaker, and this is accessible by the addressee. Since the linguistic system is not required to represent reality directly, the system itself constitutes a total, self-contained conceptual order, an autonomous and self-referential Adamic language.

A parallel exercise in linguistic reductionism was undertaken in the 1920s by the American linguist Leonard Bloomfield (1887–1949), albeit in the different intellectual climate of behaviourist psychology. For Bloomfield, linguistics proceeds under the assumption that in 'certain communities successive utterances are alike or partly alike' (Bloomfield 1926: 154). Bloomfield considered the case of 'I'm hungry' said either by a hungry stranger at the door, or by a child who has eaten, but who wishes to delay bed-time, commenting: that '[l]inguistics considers only those vocal features which are alike in the two utterances, and only those stimulus-reaction features which are alike in the two utterances'. The two utterances 'The book is interesting' and 'Put the book away' are from this point of view 'partly alike' (Bloomfield 1926: 154). Understood outside linguistics 'these similarities are only relative', but 'within it they are absolute'. This identity was a 'fiction' which in the historical study of language 'is only in part suspended' (Bloomfield 1926: 155). Saussure had made a similar point in relation to successive utterances of the same word (his example was 'Messieurs') in the course of a speech: 'We feel that in every case it is the same expression; and yet there are variations of delivery and intonation which give rise in the several instances to very noticeable phonic differences – differences as marked as those which in other cases serve to differentiate one word from another' (Saussure [1916] 1983: 150–1).

In the modern history of linguistics, the most famous statement about idealisation was made by Noam Chomsky in *Aspects of the Theory of Syntax* (1965). Chomsky sought to characterise the linguistic competence of the native speaker which was the subject matter of linguistics (Chomsky 1965: 3–4):

> Linguistic theory is concerned primarily with the ideal speaker-listener, in a completely homogeneous speech-community, who knows its language perfectly and is unaffected by such grammatically irrelevant conditions as memory limitations, distractions, shifts of attention and interest, and errors in applying his knowledge of language in actual performance.

Chomsky distinguished linguistic competence (the idealised underlying knowledge of a language) from performance (the actual linguistic behaviour of the speaker of a language): 'Only under the idealization set forth is performance a direct reflection of competence' (Chomsky 1965: 4). Grammar involves processes which exist 'far beyond the level of actual or even potential consciousness' (Chomsky 1965: 8).

Linguistics and systems theory

Languages for Saussure are internally cohesive and self-defining autonomous systems which offer only mediated representations of external reality. Words are not names of things; words do not refer directly to objects in the world, and do not change as a direct result of outside forces. Languages cannot be directly acted upon, and language systems are not integrated into the temporal flux of human experience. This parallels precisely Luhmann's discussion of law as an autonomous system. However, Luhmann's systems theory incorporates the dimension of time, since its focus is not on a set of formal structural relations, but on the self-reproduction of the system (Luhmann 1986: 174):

> Social systems use communications as their particular mode of autopoietic reproduction. Their elements are communications which are recursively produced and reproduced by a network of communications and which cannot exist outside of such a network.

A communication event within the system – viewed as transitory – incorporates a temporal dimension into the system 'in so far as it determines the state of the system that the next communications has to assume' (Luhmann 2004: 144). On the other hand the system achieves invariance where a given meaning is recognised as the same as a previous one, though it must both 'confirm the reused meaning and demonstrate that the meaning can also apply in a different context', which leads to a 'surplus of references, which can be shown in direct experience, and which render any concrete fixed definition of meaning impossible' (Luhmann 2004: 144). Legal norms are 'a structure of *symbolically* generalized expectations' (Luhmann 2004: 146, emphasis in original). Internal communication within law involves the achievement of stable expectations over time.

Simply put, Luhmann's system achieves stability and self-reference over time (which means that time itself must be represented to the system by the system), whereas Saussure's idealisation of the linguistic system abstracts away the dimension of time, as does Chomsky's. Chomsky's adherence to systems theory led to the radical distancing of his model of linguistic competence from the derivative and unsystematic social phenomenon 'language'. Languages in the everyday sense of the world were 'not real world objects', but 'artificial, somewhat arbitrary and perhaps not very interesting constructs' (Chomsky 1986: 26). They make up the linguistic 'noise' that lies outside the internally complex and coherent system. Chomsky's radical adherence to systems theory is shown by his resistance to the grounding of linguistic competence in evolutionary biology. Like Luhmann's autonomous law, Chomsky's autonomous model of linguistic knowledge has internal forms of organisation that do not mimic, reflect or interact with features of the linguistic environment (termed by Chomsky 'performance'). The fundamental driving force behind Chomsky's model is the search for absolute systems autonomy. Thus Chomsky puts the hypothesised 'language organ' outside natural selection (Dennett 1995: 384–93): in mainstream evolutionary theory, individual and group variation is at the heart of natural selection. Chomsky finds autonomy in the biological essence of universal humanity, in a systems version of the Adamic language: Chomsky's language system is an endowment of nature, but not the product of biological processes.

Linguistics: 'not for turning'?

The fundamental dilemmas of modern linguistic theory arise in relation to its reliance on the idea of languages as autonomous, structured codes. Without this idealisation, Saussure's logic applies, and there is no clear subject-matter on which to found an autonomous discipline. Mikhail Bakhtin (1895–1975) focused his criticism on Saussure's symmetrical model of communication, which he argued portrayed speaking and listening as separate, autonomous but symmetrical acts, with the listener understanding 'passively'. In 'real and integrative understanding', the speaker 'does not expect passive understanding that [. . .] duplicates his own idea in someone else's mind' (Bakhtin 1986: 69). This inability to represent the shared, 'dialogic' nature of interaction, and indeed of multivocal or heterogeneous literary works such as novels, follows from Saussure's exclusion of time and self-reference from the system. Bakhtin concedes that '[s]uch scientific abstraction is quite justified in itself, but under one condition: that it is clearly recognized as merely an abstraction', otherwise it is simply a fiction (1986: 69–70).

Linguistics, the discipline which in Saussure's *Course* produced the founding text of structuralism, has until recently stayed largely aloof from the cross-disciplinary 'linguistic turn' of the mid-twentieth century, in which language itself became the primary object of academic investigation. Linguistics has remained largely impermeable to developments in literary and cultural studies, in particular to the anti-foundationalism and critique of disciplinary autonomy found in the works of Michel Foucault (1926–84). Likewise, there is no parallel in mainstream linguistic theory to debates about indeterminacy within legal theory. The major exception to this has been some branches of the study of discourse, in particular the sub-fields of critical linguistics and critical discourse analysis (see for example Talbot et al. 2003: 2). There Bakhtin is incorporated into the study of class, genre and discourse, and Foucault is understood as a progressive or radical commentator on discourse, power and control.

Within the linguistic turn, language was a central concern of poststructuralism, deconstruction and postmodernism. Poststructuralism denied that autonomous limits could be identified to languages and texts, and saw disciplinary boundaries as revealing zones of conceptual instability. Autonomy and stability would be understood as achievable only through the suppression of indeterminacy and the marginalisation or expulsion from the system of elements that threaten its coherence. Derrida's deconstruction represents a strong reading of Saussurean structuralism, unraveling Saussure's model by pushing to the limits of its logic its theory of the sign (Derrida 1976). For Saussure, the value or meaning of each term can only be defined by a relational contrast with other terms in the sub-system, and thus all terms are defined by their place within the whole system in relation to all others. The final determination of meaning is always deferred. It follows that the system itself is indeterminate, and its attempt at definitional closure unattainable. Saussure described the relationship between 'signifier' (linguistic form) and 'signified' (linguistic meaning) as 'arbitrary', but this interdependence and mutual determination are seen by Derrida as a further site of instability and inversion, which can be broken open to allow a linguistic 'free play' (see Derrida 1974).

For deconstruction, following Freud, the identification of what is marginal or repressed in a model or text is often the key to the diagnosis of a textual pathology. In bringing to the surface repressed and marginalised meanings, deconstruction potentially performs a therapeutic function. Terms or concepts which are opposite or ideologically contradictory on the surface may be in collusion or dialectic interaction in a particular text. Oppositions where one term is privileged over another can be shown to be interdependent, and within particular texts subject to interaction. Indeterminacy implies movement: relationships between texts, readers and contexts are in motion, and there is no one point of view or interpretative position from which a single meaning can be assigned. Examples of privileged or hierarchical oppositions would be presence versus absence, speech versus writing, reason versus madness, the ideal of the rule of law versus the state of nature. In the case of Saussure's *Course*, the primary targets of deconstruction are these ideas of order, autonomy and system themselves.

More direct critics of linguistics deny that there is a stable, transparent system which underwrites and maintains social communication and that linguistic order underwrites social order. The idealisations of linguistics 'establish the fixed code as the core concept of linguistic theory and so allow the linguist to proceed on the assumption that languages are systems of fully determinate signs', whereas 'the human condition is such that all signs, whether linguistic or not, are intrinsically indeterminate' (Harris 1998: 61). Deleuze and Guttari (1988: 100–1) declare that '[s]ince everybody knows that language is a heterogeneous, variable reality, what is the meaning of the linguists' insistence on carving out a homogenous system in order to make scientific study possible?' For Bourdieu, the radical separation made between internal and external linguistics means that 'one is condemned to looking within words for the power of words, that is looking for it where it is not to be found' (Bourdieu 1991: 107).

Reflexivity, ethnomethodology and systems theory

While mainstream theoretical linguistics remained closed to debates about the nature of social order, the study of conversation and discourse was strongly influenced by trends in sociology (ethnomethodology, conversational analysis) and philosophy (pragmatics). These approaches remained within the systems theory framework, but explicitly incorporated normativity, time and reflexivity into their models of human interaction. 'Reflexivity' is a key term in contemporary social science, and for that reason extremely hard to define (Holland 1999). It can mean the formal quality of a rule or system or formal programme that it is 'self-referring'. In constitutional law, for example, there is debate about whether and how a law can entrench the conditions for its own amendment or repeal (Hart 1983: 170–8). Language is reflexive in that it can be 'turned back' upon itself, and includes a complex vocabulary for talking about, or referring to, itself. Reflexivity does not always connote self-awareness or insight, and systems theory models attribute reflexivity to systems such as law without necessarily implying subjective insight into the nature of the system on the part of social actors. However, reflexivity can also be used to refer to self-awareness or self-consciousness. Reflexivity in social science implies that researchers become conscious of their own position as situated actors working towards an understanding of social order, and further, incorporate into their models the impact of their research methods upon either society in general or the individuals and groups they are studying.

In ethnomethodology, a branch of sociology which involves the fine-grained, micro-contextual study of daily interaction, especially conversation, reflexivity is a term used to capture the normative quality of social interaction and the inseparability of social action from normative practical reasoning. Reflexivity 'refers to the simultaneous embedded and constitutive character of actions, talk and understanding'. Social actors 'have a sense of the field of action, explicitly reason about the field of action, and act in the light of such understandings and reasonings in ways that variously affect (reproduce or change) the field of action' (Pollner and Emerson 2001: 121). Ethnomethodologists see participants in social action working to produce and maintain order, rather than that order being external to, and existing prior to, their behaviour. Order is an 'accomplishment' of their interpretative practices. Participants are seen as both 'orienting to' a presumed order and simultaneously maintaining and creating the fabric of the world-known-in-common. The aim of ethnomethodology is to uncover norms of tacit reasoning, and illuminate everyday, mundane rituals, strategies and procedures for maintaining social order against a shifting, taken-for-granted set of local rules and commonsense knowledge. Rituals of everyday interaction include greetings, requests, apologies, refusals and conversational closings: these involve local (contextual) practical reasoning, and strategies of self- and mutual monitoring, action sequencing (speakers apply a system of turn-taking') and repair (self- and other-correcting), as well as the assigning of accountability by tacitly or overtly appealing to norms and rules in cases where 'procedural trust' is violated or social order is disrupted.

Ethnomethodology draws on ideas of proceduralism ('a *procedural* sense of common or shared'; Schegloff 1992: 1298, emphasis in original) and seeks to elucidate understanding as a set of a strategic and situated practices. Schegloff sees the theory as wrongly focusing only on 'interpretative procedures' (1992: 1298):

> The general stance [. . .] appears designed to disavow access to any deter-
> minate structure or character of a real world input – whether from the
> physical world or from the conduct of other social actors – and to focus
> on interpretive procedures as, in effect, the sole locus and source of inter-
> preted order.

For Schegloff, this view suggest a systems theoretical-like divorce between environment and system, since social actors are oriented above all towards each other and must seek to attain and maintain an ongoing sense of order in the absence of direct access to real 'input' from the conduct of others. Against this, Schegloff sees intersubjectivity as an alternative or supplementary stance, taking the conduct of others not as 'in effect, random or inaccessible to affirmative inquiry', but 'together with interpretative procedures, coshaping an appreciated grasp of the world'. This intersubjective understanding must then be defended by interactants against misunderstandings and other break-downs. Since 'virtually anything in the talk can be a source of misunder-standing', the potential for a more fundamental collapse of interactional order must be defended against. If a source of misunderstanding escapes the multiple possibilities to repair a breakdown, then 'the potential for trouble' for the 'institutional superstructure is vast' (Schegloff 1992: 1337). Schegloff steps back from a complete elimination of shared subjectivity from the system, since that would leave participants defenceless against a collapse of the communi-cational order.

A key concept in ethnomethodology is 'accountability'. According to Garfinkel, it is a fundamental feature of social order (Garfinkel 1967: 33):

> The policy is recommended that any social setting be viewed as self-
> organizing with respect to the intelligible character of its own appear-
> ances as either representations of or as evidences-of-a-social-order. Any
> setting organizes its activities to make its properties as an organized
> environment of practical activities detectable, countable, recordable,
> tell-a-story-aboutable, analyzable – in short, *accountable*.

Accountability includes attributions of responsibility for actions and utter-ances; further, the concept is intended to capture the quality of everyday discourse that it proceeds on the basis that participants publicly display and construct mutual moral accountability in the way they interact, so that, for example, use of categories and acts of labelling or describing are treated as accountable to norms which have a latent moral dimension. People who are queuing for a taxi are not just performing a particular category of social action, they are able to label it as such and also derive a set of local norms for judging the conduct of others. Nor is this label 'queuing for a taxi' simply the neutral name of the activity. Harvey Sacks (1935–75) formulates this by saying that there is no room in interaction to 'just name': 'any doing of naming is also formulatable as doing something else' (Sacks 1992a: 544). Naming is also accountable.

Garfinkel distinguishes between natural and classical accountability. The first is the general, taken-as-background quality of everyday discourse that we can if necessary explain what we are doing and why. An example of the latter is the explicit 'recounting-as-accounting' of an incident or a case by a subordinate to a superior. Law would involve both classic and natural accountability. While law's institutional practices are much more explicitly and consciously accountable, for ethnomethodology no system of rules can autonomously govern behaviour. Ongoing contextual filling in of the gaps and reorienting of rules means that behaviour always escapes the determinism of a formal set of rules. Social actors make their own sense of what is reasonable, feasible and sensible, including adding in their own moral calculations and operating a parallel system of 'discretion' alongside the formal rules. Institutional practices can never be exhaustively formalised (Gregg 1999: 359):

> We modify rules unconsciously to render them applicable to contingency and experience. We do so in a naive attitude that rules are guiding our behaviour when in fact our behaviour is guiding our use of rules. In turn, those rules define that behaviour, thus allowing us to maintain a naive attitude toward those rules, believing that we are simply applying them when in fact we are changing them.

Rules, including legal rules, do not interpret themselves, they have an inevitable 'et cetera aspect' to their generality, which requires or licenses 'practices whereby persons make what they are doing *happen* as rule-analyzable conduct' (Gregg 1999: 363, 371; see also Garfinkel 1968: 220), and the giving of reasons for an action cannot exhaust the explanatory possibilities. This also implies that judges' explicit accounts of what they are doing in law are not definitive within the system.

Ethnomethodology (and its offshoot, conversational analysis or CA) at times seems to present social interaction in objectivist terms, as a machine which compulsively seeks order for its own sake, in which social actors, like Sisyphus, are condemned to labour for ever. While not automatons or 'judgmental dopes', they can only gain flashes of local and temporary reflexive insight, as the underlying order is disturbed and then repaired. Here is a highly 'systems-oriented' description of turn-taking and repair (Sacks et al. 1974: 724):

> The compatibility of the model of turn-taking with the facts of repair is thus of a dual character: the turn-taking system lends itself to, and incorporates devices for, repair of its troubles; and the turn-taking system is a basic organizational device for the repair of any other troubles in conversation.

There is more than a hint of Wittgenstein's compulsive builders here, though the social actors depicted by ethnomethodology are reflexive order builders: they are not building a Tower of Babel, but rather are constantly engaged in the building, maintaining and defending of social order itself.

Sacks formulated the analyst's task as trying 'to construct the machinery' that would produce the occurrences being studied and the inferences that interactants draw. Sacks's evocation of an 'inference-making machine' in adjudication might seem to bring us back to the idea of mechanical jurisprudence. However, he does not suggest that the judicial inference-making machine is infallible, and quotes at length from an arbitration judgment in an employment dispute. Rather the machine operates regardless of the quality of the input from reality to produce a 'proposed order' out of what from another point of view is 'simply a coagulation of random events' (Sacks 1992b: 125). The debt to systems theory in this formulation is clear, since systems theories distinguish in the same way between the internal normative order of the system (Luhmann's view of law's code as the binary 'legal/illegal') and the 'noise' or 'disorder' of its environment.

Conclusion

Linguistic structuralism, with its view of language as an autonomous system of sub-systems, is one of the intellectual pillars of modern systems theory. The subjectivity of the speakers, the dimension of time, local and historical context and a direct relationship to reality have been radically excluded in the service of methodological purism. The systems nature of Saussure's model of language has escaped clear notice, because the academic study of language can draw on, and has been re-embedded in, social and political concepts, and culturally salient practices such as writing. Linguistics represents the most radical form of systems theory, since it excludes the interdefining dimensions of time, normativity and reflexivity from the core system. Time is fundamental to reflexivity, and reflexivity is a central feature of normative behaviour. To be normative, the system has to allow for more than one possible response to a given system-state, where the evolution of a system over time cannot be predicted. Time is therefore central to Luhmann's radically objectivist theory of law. Luhmann's autonomous law maintains order by its high degree of closure to external social reality, and its contingent interactions with that reality are not systematically representable within the system of law. As in evolutionary biology, change is not managed by an overseer or capable of being directed towards any particular goal. Ethnomethodology offers a microsystems theory view of human interaction, in which disorder or 'social noise' is constantly held at bay by reflexively constituted normative order. Social actors do not have a determinate external reality to relate to and from which they can draw a source of stability and shared reference. In its absence, the task is to maintain and constantly remake or 'repair' coherence and social order. Social actors must work with whatever contextual strategies and interpretations are reflexively at hand to create and recreate order.

The history of linguistics since Saussure can be seen as a series of attempts to reconnect the systems model to social, psychological or neurological reality, without relinquishing the idea of language as a system itself, and the disciplinary autonomy and authority that it sustains. For example, models have been developed which seek to incorporate linguistic variation and change within a systems view of language. Attempts by the discipline of linguistics to connect to law have relied on an association of systems theory with scientific status, and in some cases lawyers and courts have accepted this authority (Ainsworth 2005/6; Solan and Tiersma 2005: 13ff). However, this is problematic, if it constitutes an attempt to apply a systems theory model. Legal questions that involve determining the ordinary meanings of words are contextual, interpretative and normative questions. Logically, they are not representable within the system, and potentially open up statements made by linguists in the forensic contest to realist challenge. Campos (1995: 973) makes this point in terms of a context-neutral model (linguistics) being applied to a context-sensitive set of problems (law): 'Textual meaning always occurs in the context of, and indeed is generated by, the intentional semantic content of a particular utterance.' Since utterance meaning is contingent, 'you can't have a true theory of linguistic practice'. This is illustrated with an analogy (emphasis in original):

> Suppose I want to know how much the tiger at the zoo weighs. Someone tells me that he doesn't know what this tiger weighs, but that 'in general' tigers weigh 375 pounds. Of course, this may or may not prove to be helpful information. Maybe this tiger is exceptionally large or small. More to the point, such a generalization does not tell me very much about what interests me, which is just what *this* tiger weighs, not what tigers are generally understood to weigh. Now suppose my informant were to insist that in some sense he has *already* told me what I want to know, because all tigers have two weights: 375 pounds (their theoretical tiger weight) and N pounds (the particular and hence variable weight of any individual tiger).

The notion of system-sentence meaning, which is at the heart of the linguist's understanding of semantics, cannot offer any interpretative help to the reader who wants to know what a particular sentence means in a particular text (Hutton 1995). Golanski (2002) argues that law and linguistics pursue different objectives derived from different theoretical positions, and that this limits the possibility of linguistics playing a major role in law. In addition, linguistics offers a plethora of competing systems models. The study of meaning within linguistics, semantics, is 'confused, fragmented, and underdeveloped', and this raises doubts about 'whether linguists should be regarded by the courts as experts on meaning in ordinary language' Goddard (1996: 269, 270). The legal effect of any determination of meaning will in any case always remain a matter for the legal process and the judge: 'Rules on expert witnesses are likely to continue to be a matter defined in ways which reinforce rather than query the court's authority in the matter of what utterances mean' (Durant 1996: 207).

For the linguist interested in law's search for meaning, the ideal would be that descriptive objectivity in relation to language could be put at the service of the normative objectivity of the law. If law itself at a particular juncture recognises the need for a descriptive answer to a question of meaning, then this act of framing the interpretative question offers the linguist at least a potential role within the interpretative practices of law. Linguistics represents language as speaker-neutral and context-neutral and this may be on occasion just the construct of language that the law requires. However, for the systems linguist, this objectivity is not logically available for contextualisation. Roger Shuy, reporting on his involvement as a linguist in a number of trademark dispute, reports that the linguist for the other side, who self-identified as a 'theoretical', that is, Chomskyan, linguist, stressed that any opinion he might offer derived 'from his stance as a native speaker of English, not as a professional linguist' (Shuy 2002: 104).

These problems can be understood in Luhmann's terms as the impossibility of direct communication between systems. For Luhmann, the language of law is an autonomous sub-system which cannot be directly mapped onto, or compared with, 'ordinary language', just as law in effect has its own understandings of causality, intention, insanity and morality. Following this systems logic, the term 'ordinary language' is just a label for the undifferentiated and uncategorised linguistic environment ('noise') of law. For the systems theory of language, law is likewise merely part of the undifferentiated environment, and within its own systems theoretical framework, language can be seen as autopoietic (Nobles and Schiff 2006: 22). Within a systems theory approach to law, the entire legal system can be understood as 'a semiotic system of signs' in which different actors and agents communicate both internally among themselves and with society at large (Kevelson 1988). But the 'real' relationship between that internal communicative order and the social environment is paradoxically not representable within the system itself.

Jackson's theory of law as internal 'narrative coherence' is founded on an understanding that legal language 'itself constitutes the object through its own discourse' (Jackson 1988: 193). Following Saussure and the semiotician Algirdas Greimas (1917–92), Jackson insists on the non-referential character of the language of law. However, in an attempt to escape this closed hermeneutic circle, he looks to 'integrity', and to 'trust in people' as an alternative to trust in 'the relationship between what they say and some external reality' (Jackson 1988: 192–5). But this rather unconvincing move merely serves to dramatise the dilemmas that the systems model creates, and their vulnerability to realist challenge.

Arguing that 'it is not within the brief of linguistics to make useful theories' (2003: 10), Widdowson argues that it is the very 'remoteness and partiality' of descriptions offered by linguists that make them revealing: 'If linguistics could provide us with representations of experienced language, it would be of no interest whatever' (Widdowson 2003: 7). Discussing Luhmann's systems theory of law, King (2006: 52) writes that the theory's 'usefulness' might paradoxically lie 'precisely in the *uselessness* of the theory as a blueprint for the improvement of social systems and those who try to make his theory useful in this way may well be contributing to the theory's ultimate *uselessness*' (emphasis in original). One way to deal with the 'realist dilemma', therefore, is to accept that it represents a challenge which cannot be answered, and to rely instead on the paradoxical insights to be gained through a rejection of the possibility of representing 'experienced language'.

3 Philosophy, Law and Language

Introduction

Political philosophers concerned with the nature of law have seen language as one of the key elements in the formation of political collectivities ruled by law. But language as law's medium has also been seen as a potential source of instability and uncertainty, and legal theorists and political philosophers have differed widely in their assessment of the importance and role of language in law. If law is a part of the social contract between citizens and the sovereign, and language is the medium for the recording of law and for its explication, then the terms of that contract, and language in general, become the primary medium through which social order is created and maintained. The medium of language conjoins the private world of individual thought with the realm of social exchange, and ordered society is made possible by the creation of a reliable and stable medium of exchange. Just as a reliable instrument of commercial exchange, a currency, must underlie commercial transactions, a stable and transparent medium for the exchange of ideas must underlie social and political life. The importance of a currency lies in its ability to mirror the values that underpin commercial exchange; language must similarly allow for the accurate expression of the ideas and values that constitute society.

Philosophy, language and social order

The central philosophical and political anxiety in relation to language has been that language is liable to fail as a transparent medium of exchange and thereby obtain mastery over its speakers, becoming a cause of social divisiveness, manipulation and obfuscation. The power of language to create worlds of the imagination, the force of metaphor in creating false analogies, and the potential domination of language over thought all led to fears that language could be corrupted and manipulated. Political crises were also crises of language; political decline was accompanied by a loss of linguistic value. Political philosophers therefore saw language as part of the social contract, a medium of exchange for ideas in which parties should ideally match their thoughts exactly with their words and display fidelity to their public and agreed meanings.

Francis Bacon (1561–1626) argued in his *New Organon* that the human mind had a fragile grasp of reality and was prone to the influence of four kinds of *idola* or 'idols' ('illusions' or 'fallacies'; see editors' note, Bacon 2000: 18fn.). The first category, 'idols of the tribe', was 'founded in human nature itself', as 'all perceptions, both of sense and mind, are relative to man, not to the universe', and human understanding is 'like an uneven mirror receiving rays from things and merging its own nature with the nature of things' (Bacon [1620] 2000: 41). 'Idols of the cave' arise due to the influence of factors idiosyncratic to any given individual: 'each man has a kind of individual cave or cavern which fragments and distorts the light of nature'. The 'idols of the marketplace' were illusions with an origin in social relationships, arising through 'human exchange and community' whereby the mind was thrown into confusion by the power of words (Bacon [1620] 2000: 42).

> Men associate through talk; and words are chosen to suit the understanding of the common people. And thus a poor and unskilful code of words incredibly obstructs the understanding. The definitions and explanations with which learned men have been accustomed to protect and in some way liberate themselves, do not restore the situation at all. Plainly words do violence to the understanding, and confuse everything; and betray men into countless empty disputes and fictions.

The fourth were the 'idols of the theatre', in that 'all the philosophies that men have learned or devised, are, in our opinion, so many plays produced and performed which have created false and fictitious worlds' (Bacon [1620] 2000: 42).

For Thomas Hobbes (1588–1679) the 'general use of speech' is 'to transfer our mental discourse' into 'verbal' form; it makes 'the train of our thoughts' into a 'train of words' (Hobbes [1651] 1998: 21). Speech then transmits what would otherwise have been private thoughts, and private thoughts enter the public or social sphere in linguistic or verbal form. There were four special functions of language, each of which, however, had corresponding abuses, the first involving self-deception (Hobbes [1651] 1998: 21):

> when men register their thoughts wrong, by the inconstancy of the signification of their words; by which they register for their conceptions, that which they never conceived; and so deceive themselves.

In addition to this self-deception, words could be used to deceive others when used 'metaphorically', which Hobbes explains as 'in other sense than that they are ordained for'. Thirdly, people use words wrongly 'when by words they declare that to be their will, which is not'. Finally, language could be used to chastise and 'grieve' others, since humans used words as weapons in the way that animals used horns and teeth. But the exception was where a superior used language to chastise 'one whom we are obliged to govern', for 'then it is not to grieve, but to correct and amend' (Hobbes [1651] 1998: 21). For Hobbes, language does not of itself guarantee social order, and requires what amounts to good faith on the part of its users, and if necessary correction by the sovereign. In the absence of that good faith or social control of public language, social disorder is inevitable. The linguistic part of the social contract is a continuing mutual relationship of dependency between members of a community.

The idea that language creates a public medium of exchange for what would otherwise be private is fundamental to the political philosophy of John Locke (1632–1704). Like Hobbes, Locke did not see language as intrinsically stable and viewed it as subject to abuses of various kinds (Locke [1690] 2001: 403):

> Besides the imperfection that is naturally in language, and the obscurity and confusion that is so hard to be avoided in the use of words, there are several wilful faults and neglects which men are guilty of in this way of communication, whereby they render these signs less clear and distinct in their signification than naturally they need to be.

It was a difficult but necessary task to find a remedy for these ills, given that speech was 'the great bond that holds society together, and the common conduit, whereby the improvements of knowledge are conveyed from one man and one generation to another' (Locke [1690] 2001: 420). Locke recognised the limits of possible reform and the limits of control, so that to 'require that men should use their words constantly in the same sense, and for none but determined and uniform ideas, would be to think that all men should have the same notions, and should talk of nothing but what they have clear and distinct ideas of' (Locke [1690] 2001: 420).

Locke drew an analogy between a market in the exchange of words and ideas and the commercial market, so that someone who 'puts not constantly the same sign for the same idea, but uses the same words sometimes in one and sometimes in another signification' was like someone 'who sells several things under the same name'. However, the 'market and exchange must be left to their own ways of talking' (Locke [1690] 2001: 417). Locke put great faith in definition as a kind of disciplining of meaning in the public sphere: '[w]ithout the possibility of stipulative definition – however unsatisfactory, provisional, or exacting in exactitude – there would be no guarantee that all exchange of views was not, as Locke puts it, "nothing but so much insignificant noise"' (Harris and Hutton 2007: 27; Locke [1690] 2001: 330).

Philosophers have sought various means to overcome the fear of control and manipulation by language. One strategy has been to ground the concepts of language in an operational method, so that the language of science can be shown to be grounded in public, observable and repeatable practices. Bacon argued for a fusion of the application of reason with the experimental method. A second strategy is to declare what words mean and seek to enjoin language users to remain faithful to those meanings, making use of 'stipulative definition' (Harris and Hutton 2007). Taking stipulative definition to its logical conclusion, philosophers have posited ideal universal languages from which the contingent features that weaken languages as a means of communication and for the representation of reality have been stripped. A famous example is John Wilkins's *Essay towards a Real Character and a Philosophical Language* (1668). Elements of these strategies run through all the law's dealings with language.

There is, however, an inevitable tension between a pragmatic language of law, which deals in the causes and effects of legal language in the 'real world', and an ideal language of law, in which coherence and consistency are achieved by a separation from the categories and experiential language of the world. Another way to frame this is to see law as a form of translation in which everyday language and concepts are analysed or converted into legal language, as law mediates between different languages and different social groups. White (1990: 230) writes that translation is 'both an art of recognition and response, both to another person and another language'. The greater the perceived gap between the language of law and social reality, the more law is vulnerable to the charge that its language is a set of fictions which refer to entities of its own invention.

Bentham's concern with the language of law led him to dismiss many fundamental legal concepts as the names of fictitious entities. Bentham famously considered the notion of 'natural right' as 'nonsense on stilts' (see Bentham [1795] 2002). Terms such as 'duty', 'right', 'power', 'title' were abstractions, and such terms needed to pass through a definitional test in order to determine whether they had empirical content. Ideas must ultimately derive from the senses and traditional methods of definition were useless and abstract terms had meaning only when expressed 'in terms calculated to raise images either of substances perceived, or of emotions; – sources, one or other of which every idea must be drawn from, to be a clear one' (Bentham [1776] 1988: 108fn.):

> The consequences of any Law, or of any act which is made the object of a Law, the only consequences that men are at all interested in, what are they but pain and pleasure? By some such words then as pain and pleasure, they may be expressed: and pain and pleasure at least, are words which a man has no need, we may hope, to go to a Lawyer to know the meaning of.

A word like 'obligation' was a fiction, but it could be related to everyday experience by a process of contextualisation and translation. First it could be put in a sentence such as 'X is under an obligation to pay Y £10', and then this sentence should then be translated into one or more sentences 'where the word "obligation" does not appear' (Hart 1982: 130). Bentham in his 'Essay on Logic' added a third element to this, that of 'archetypation', which involved revealing the underlying imagery. In the case of 'obligation':

> the emblematic or archetypal image is that of a man lying down with a heavy body pressing upon him, to wit in such sort as either to prevent him acting at all or so ordering matters that if he does act it cannot be in any other direction or manner than of the direction or manner requisite. (Bentham 1843: 247, quoted in Hart 1982: 131)

The tension between the need for the language of law to relate meaningfully to the world and its search for internal coherence and consistency is fundamental to Bentham's thinking on law. Bentham was deeply hostile to the ideology of an evolving, pragmatic common law – for him this was personified in the English jurist Sir William Blackstone (1723–80). Bentham perceived it as a muddle, and described the 'after-the-fact' or *ex post* quality of much common law adjudication as 'dog law': '[w]hen your dog does anything you want to break him of, you wait till he does it, and then beat him for it' (Bentham [1782] 1970: 185; Lobban 1991: 116).

In his attack on Blackstone, Bentham produced this diatribe against legal language and the resistance of common lawyers to law reform (Bentham [1776] 1988: 21fn.):

> A large portion of the body of the Law was, by the bigotry or the artifice of Lawyers, locked up in an illegible character, and in a foreign tongue. [. . .] Fiction, tautology, technicality, circuity, irregularity, inconsistency remain. But above all the pestilential breath of Fiction poisons the sense of every instrument it comes near. The consequence is, that the Law, and especially that part of it which comes under the topic of Procedure, still wants much of being generally intelligible.

Blackstone (1756: 3) had written that the interpretation of law involved inquiring after 'the will of the maker', which could be ascertained from 'the Words, the Context, the Subject-matter, the Effects and Consequence, or the Spirit and Reason of the Law', and this also gave rise to equity 'or the Correction of that wherein the Law (by reason of its Universality) is deficient'. Blackstone's judge-centred view of law contributed to a relative lack of anxiety about language: judges, as 'living oracles', were repositories of knowledge and experience (1765–9, I: 69). Bentham was by contrast a strong supporter of the rational reform of law through a complete and systematic codification which he termed a 'Pannomium' (Sullivan 1994). Bentham's faith in codification implies a superior confidence in the ability of language to carry rational meaning when contrasted with Blackstone's faith in the judge and equitable discretion.

In John Austin's (1790–1852) 'command theory' of law, in which law represents the will of a political superior or sovereign (Austin 1832: 11), law is a mode of coercive communication of the desires of the sovereign to the subjects of law. If law is to represent those desires, the language of law must both be adequate to express them, and adequate for them to be understood by the addressees of law. A command is defined as '(1) A wish or desire conceived by a rational being, that another rational being shall do or forebear. (2) An evil to proceed from the former, and to be incurred by the latter, in the case the latter not comply with the wish. (3) An expression or intimation of the wish by words or other signs' (Austin 1832: 11). Commands could be express if 'signified by words' or tacit if signified by other 'signs of desire' (Austin 1832: 29). Like Bentham, Austin was concerned with clarity of terminology, including that of the word 'command' and 'laws' (Austin 1832: 6, 21), and in his elaboration of the basic theory of law also drew on the language of logic ('unrivalled for its brevity, distinctness and precision'; Austin 1832: 12).

Austin, like Bentham, rejected the expression 'natural law', since only the laws ordained by God could be spoken of 'without metaphor' (Austin 1832: 2). Again like Bentham, he recognised that words like 'right' needed to be carefully and circumspectly defined, since 'the strongest and wariest minds are often ensnared by ambiguous words' (Austin 1832: 305fn.), and he deplored the 'proneness of German philosophy to vague and misty abstraction' (Austin 1832: 371fn.). This mistrust of abstraction led to an insistence that general terms like 'public good' should be understood as referring to the 'aggregate enjoyments of the single and individual persons who compose that public' (Austin 1832: 115). If this concept was misused, and the good of individual persons were scarified 'to the good of those persons considered collectively', then this would be a sacrifice to a 'mere name' and these interests would be 'victims of a barren abstraction, of a sounding but empty phrase' (Austin 1832: 116). Austin's basic approach is to attach precise meanings to terms like 'command' and other key terms, so as to avoid a clash with 'the current of ordinary speech' (Austin 1832: 11), but to 'strip them of a certain mystery, by which that simple meaning appears to be obscured' (Austin 1832: 19). Law fundamentally is or should be a rational mode of communication using a maximally rational and precise instrument.

In the modern era, language became more directly the focus of intense philosophical scrutiny. Philosophers of science termed 'logical positivists' sought to clarify the relationship between sentences or propositions and reality, by distinguishing meaningful from meaningless statements and by stripping away misleading surface linguistic structures to reveal whether there was an underlying, properly verifiable statement or not. In an extreme form this approach branded any metaphysical statement, for example any religious statement such as 'God is love', as nonsense, since there was no way to verify it (Ayer 1936). Logical positivism, like its intellectual successors, viewed language as a potentially disruptive screen or lens between the observer and reality, and it was thus necessary to interrogate surface language forms to test their transparency as a window on, or representation of, reality.

Many apparently intractable philosophical disputes could be shown to be simply arguments about words, with nothing of practical consequence hanging on the outcome of the debate. The view of language as a map and reality as the territory was central to a popular intellectual movement termed General Semantics, which both reflected and spoke to fundamental practical and intellectual concerns in American society (Korzybski 1948; Hayakawa 1974). General Semantics viewed language as potentially misleading as to the nature of reality, and saw unthinking language use as leading to entrenched habits of mind and a dangerous belief that those habits directly reflected reality. Consequently there was a need to reform language constantly to make it a better guide to reality and to raise consciousness about the dangers of being misled by language and by mistakes as to the level of abstraction (simplification) of concepts with which one is dealing. This movement, with its distrust of abstractions, was not without influence on legal thinking: 'It is the lawyer's business to master words; the risk that the law runs is that they master him' (Schaefer 1958: 118). The attack on 'mechanical jurisprudence' by legal realists was very much in the spirit of General Semantics (Probert 1959).

Logophobia in various forms pervades discussion of the language of law: 'All languages threaten to take over the mind and to control its operation, with all this implies for one's feelings, for one's sense of self, and for the possibilities of meaning in one's actions and relations' (White 1987: 1966). White objects to the use of the term 'concept', in particular because to talk about concepts rather than words is 'to take a step in the direction of talking as if words have no force of their own, as if they are transparent or discardable once the idea or concept is apprehended' (White 1987: 1968). Talk about concepts also 'tends to nominalize, and hence to reify, everything', so that the noun dominates over the verb and the adjective, so that 'the principle of life that is found in the active verb' is lost: 'Imagine a language that emphasized the verb instead of the noun and copula; our thought would be full of a sense of movement, life, and change, of actors engaged in action' (White 1987: 1971). This can lead to the intellectual confusion exhibited by the lawyer 'who thinks that the world comes in legal categories' (White 1987: 1971). Bentham by contrast put his faith in nouns, preferring 'verbal substantives' to verbs: it was clearer to say 'to make application' than 'to apply' (Ogden 1951: lxxxvi). The legal philosopher H. L. A. Hart's mistrust of 'the growth of theory on the back of definition' reflects the twin influences of Bentham and ordinary language philosophy (Hart 1954: 37).

The linguistic turn in philosophy as a turn to law

Since the 1940s, many disciplines and areas of academic inquiry have undergone what has been termed a 'linguistic turn'. This phrase has a number of possible meanings, and indeed one could trace a number of such 'turns' back through Western intellectual history. In post-World War II intellectual developments it was instanced in so-called 'linguistic philosophy' or 'ordinary language philosophy'. At its most general the linguistic turn has involved focusing on language and issues of conceptual clarity in delimiting intellectual puzzles. Richards (1968: 231) argued that 'all objects we can name or otherwise single out' are 'projections of man's interests', and the study of the 'modes of language' was therefore 'the most fundamental and extensive of all inquiries'. A key text was Thomas Kuhn's *The Structure of Scientific Revolutions* (1962), which pictured the history of science as involving competing but incommensurable 'paradigms' or discourses.

In law and legal theory the phrase 'linguistic turn' could be applied to any number of opinions and theoretical positions. Williams (1945–6: 72) argued that, given the 'imperfections of language', jurisprudence was 'badly in need of semantic analysis'. Legal historians such as J. G. A. Pocock put language at the centre of their inquiry, which meant 'starting with the language and working outwards', looking within a general politics of language at the 'meanings it can be said to have borne', rather than starting with the assumption that language simply reflects an indeterminate social reality (Pocock 1971: 36). The linguistic turn in legal theory could be seen ambivalently as either a retreat to a new and formalistic 'law as language' analysis of legal concepts as a closed system, or an opening up of law to the study of communication, semiotics, and the study of organisational behaviour and everyday interaction such as is found in ethnomethodology (Shapiro 1981).

Ordinary language philosophy sought to 'unpack' traditional philosophical questions, often phrased in definitional terms, for example 'What is the good?', by looking at the different ways in which the word was used, and the shades of meaning it could exhibit in different linguistic contexts. It saw itself as a rational inquiry into the reasonable limits of language, and evinced a mistrust of abstractions and grand claims for truth. Bertrand Russell (1872–1970) pejoratively characterised linguistic philosophy as one 'which cares only about language, and not about the world' (Russell 1959: 15). J. L. Austin saw ordinary language philosophy as drawing on time-tested linguistic distinctions, in that the 'common stock of words' at our disposal 'embodies all the distinctions men have found worth drawing, and the connexions they have found worth marketing, in the lifetimes of many generations' (Austin 1956: 8). This concern with ordinary language leads to a particular focus on distinctions, on the boundaries between concepts, as reflecting 'the inherited experience and acumen of many generations of men' (Austin 1956: 11). Ordinary language works well 'for practical purposes in ordinary life', even though 'even ordinary life is full of hard cases' (Austin 1956: 11). Language usage is understood as an exercise in correct characterisation of situations, and guidance to correct characterisation is found by paying careful attention to established usage. A corollary of this model of language is an emphasis on relative uniformity of usage – differences in usage are held by Austin to be generally traceable to an underlying difference in how a situation has been imagined (Austin 1956: 9–10), rather than to what a linguist might call variation in the linguistic system itself. Law, with its extraordinary demands, does violence to the distinctions of ordinary language (Austin 1956: 12).

Wittgenstein's writings have been highly influential within the philosophy of law, and debates over the nature and status of rules have made widespread use of the phrase from the *Philosophical Investigations*, 'form of life'. This phrase, with its roots in linguistic philosophy, echoes through general and philosophical discussions of the language of the law, as in James Boyd White's affirmation that 'the law offers an especially interesting form of life' (1987: 1963). One simple (if not necessarily Wittgensteinian) way to understand the term 'form of life' within law is to look at practices that endow words, sentences and comments with relatively certain or stable meanings. For example, many business or trades employ so-called 'standard form contracts', and these acquire over time an established status within the relevant trade such that the courts are unwilling to interfere with them. In *Schroeder Music Publishing Co Ltd v Macaulay* (1974), Lord Diplock stated (at 1316): 'The standard clauses in these contracts have been settled over the years by negotiation by representatives of the commercial interests involved and have been widely adopted because experience has shown that they facilitate the conduct of trade.' Given the detailed legal analysis to which such contracts are subjected over time, a body of law arises 'giving many of their terms legally predictable meanings' (Sealy and Hooley 2005: 20).

For White, law as a form of life works in its most characteristic moment, the legal hearing, 'by testing one version of its language against another, one way of telling a story and thinking about it against another, and then by making a self-conscious choice between them'. Law is 'an institution that remakes its own language and it does this under conditions of regularity and publicity that render the process subject to scrutiny of an extraordinary kind' (White 1987: 1963). In this way the structure of the legal process 'entails remarkable possibilities – little realized in the event – for thinking about and achieving that simultaneous affirmation of the self and recognition of the other [. . .] essential to the ethical task of a discoursing and differing humanity' (White 1987: 1963). In an ideal sense, the legal hearing is committed to 'a momentary equality among its speakers' and 'the recognition that all ways of talking, including its own, may be subject to criticism and change' (White 1987: 1964). Evans (1988: 19) sees this concept as offering a solution to the 'problem of classification', by avoiding the extreme positions of both the realist and the nominalist. Wittgenstein's motto that 'to share a language is to share a form of life' is interpreted as saying that 'there are different ways of developing and structuring our basic discriminatory capacities' and that human beings possess 'the innate capacity to develop, given appropriate education and encouragement, the capacity to make discriminations in common ways' (Evans 1988: 19).

Wittgenstein's concept of a form of life evokes language as creating and sustaining its diverse realities through social practice. A related idea is that of the 'language game', one which represents linguistic behaviour as straddling both competitive and cooperative forms of life. An example of a language game is the word 'game' itself. Wittgenstein asks us to see that we cannot find one single underlying essence to all these activities we call 'game', the core meaning of the word 'game'. We are dealing with 'a complicated network of similarities overlapping and crisscrossing: sometimes overall similarities, sometimes similarities of detail' (Wittgenstein [1953] 1978: 32) Wittgenstein is generally seen as attacking the essentialist view that we need to look 'behind' language to find some clearer, better-defined set of concepts, rules or entities. In this sense, the language games of traditional philosophy also potentially mislead us into believing in a world of explanatory essences which it is the job of philosophy to bring into clearer view. The concept of 'form of life', while it is sometimes presented as a form of 'soft' sociology, is actually the site of extreme tension in Wittgenstein's writing. It is caught between the acceptance of language as creating and sustaining meaningful social worlds and the fear that the 'grammar' of language will lead philosophers to build edifices of nonsense: philosophical problems arise when 'language goes on holiday', when 'language is like an engine idling' (Wittgenstein [1953] 1978: 19, 51). For law, however, this is the crux of the matter, since the boundary between language 'at work' and language 'at rest' is often at stake in the interpretative politics of a particular case. For the deconstructionist, by contrast, language is always potentially 'at play', and this again is not an idea that law can formally assimilate into its own self-understandings.

The social contract of language

There has been constant interaction between philosophy and law over questions of rule, norm and the contractual nature of communication. Austin's speech act theory (Austin 1962), with its notion of felicity conditions for speech acts, reflects this modern philosophical turn to law. Western philosophy had been preoccupied to such an extent with language as a representational system for reality that when J. L. Austin published his *How to Do Things with Words* (1962), it was hailed as an intellectual breakthrough. Austin pointed out that language involved acts ('speech acts') which in part constitute – rather than simply reflect – social reality. The representation of states of affairs was only one of the many functions of language. Austin divided utterances into performatives and constatives; performatives accomplish or enact some action, and the clearest examples of these are the 'explicit' performatives which often appear in legal or ritual contexts and take the form of 'I [hereby] X', where X is the present simple tense. Constatives describe what is the case or state facts and can be seen as true or false.

Austin's core example of a performative was a linguistic act such as 'promising'. A promise is not a description of the world, but a social 'speech act' which imposes an obligation on the speaker: 'I promise to visit you on Wednesday' can also be expressed formally as 'I hereby promise to visit you on Wednesday.' Another common example was the speech act of apologising, so that 'I apologise for ruining your evening' can be expressed as 'I hereby apologise for ruining your evening.' Austin argued initially that performatives are special in that in uttering them one does things, and one does not merely say things or report states of affairs; performatives achieve their effect or result in a change in actions because there are specific conventions linking the words to institutional or institutionalised procedures. They do not describe the action, they actually perform the action. These 'performative' speech acts include those with legal effect, such as 'I name this ship the *Bismarck*', 'I now pronounce you man and wife', 'I sentence you to three years in prison.' The speech act of promising is understood in quasi-contractual terms and set against a set of felicity conditions. If felicity conditions are not fulfilled, the speech act 'misfires' or is 'insincere'. Austin's speech act theory thus offers a rewriting of tacit social rules in quasi-legalistic terms.

In the course of working out his argument, Austin came to see that stating facts or asserting that certain things were or were not the case were also actions. Thus all utterances perform a speech act of some kind; stating facts is also 'performative', so we can see constatives as a sub-category of performatives. All utterances including constatives have what Austin terms 'illocutionary force' (Austin 1970: 251, italics in original):

> Besides the question that has been very much studied in the past as to what a certain utterance means, there is a further question distinct from this as to what was the *force*, as we call it, of the utterance. We may be quite clear what 'Shut the door' means, but not yet at all clear on the further point as to whether as uttered at a certain time it was an order, an entreaty or whatnot. What we need besides the old doctrine about meanings is a new doctrine about all the possible forces of utterances.

Austin uses the term 'perlocutionary effect' to cover the non-conventional results of an utterance, that is, the effect of the utterance in the context, 'such effects beings special to the circumstances of the utterance'.

The insight that language was not only or primarily a means of representing states as true or false drew on a legalistic understanding of discourse as establishing mutual obligations and relationships, and performing socially significant acts which change the state of the social world. Participants bind themselves to future action ('promising'), recognise fault ('apologising'), advise, warn, convince, deter and oblige. In society as in law, language is fundamentally social action.

This legalism or contractualism emerges clearly in Paul Grice's (1913–88) model of human communication or theory of pragmatics. Grice elaborated the so-called cooperative principle (CP): 'Make your contribution such as is required, at the stage at which it occurs, by the accepted purpose or direction of the talk exchange in which you are engaged' (Grice 1975: 46). Grice argued that the assumption of a cooperative orientation is fundamental to understanding. If a remark seems to lack relevance or coherence on a literal level, we look first to interpret it on a metaphorical or other non-literal level before assuming the absence of a cooperative spirit (aggression, hostility, insanity). Grice's theory of pragmatics relies on four basic maxims of interaction (1975: 46):

> *The maxim of quantity*: (1) Make your contribution as informative as is required (for the current purposes of the exchange). (2) Do not make your contribution more informative than is required.
> *The maxim of quality*: Try to make your contribution one that is true. (1) Do not say what you believe to be false. (2) Do not say that for which you lack adequate evidence.
> *The maxim of relevance*: Be relevant.
> *The maxim of manner*: Be perspicuous. (1) Avoid obscurity of expression. (2) Avoid ambiguity. (3) Be brief (avoid unnecessary prolixity). (4) Be orderly.

Grice did not intend this system as a set of recommendations, in the way that a guide to good table-manners teaches polite eating within a particular culture. He argued that an implicit set of maxims underlies everyday interactions, and that people use these assumptions in making sense of what is said, particularly in the case of utterances which seem to be literally nonsensical or unconnected to the previous talk. Human beings search for coherence in what is said because they operate with an assumption that a cooperative spirit underlies human interaction, and that cooperation is realised in the maintenance of coherence or relevance. Something that is meant, but is not said, is termed an *implicature*.

Parties are enjoined under a consensus model of conversation to calculate the degree of relevance which the addressee of a remark is expecting and to which therefore he or she is entitled. Underlying human interaction is a contract, a shared agreement as to how conversation should be conducted. Breaches of contract are sanctionable, but may be permissible to make a particular conversational point. Speech act theory and Grice's theory of implicature both seek to explain how, given the gap between literal and intentional meaning, interactants none the less make sense of verbal exchanges in the context. The literal meaning of the words used (the meaning of the sentence) does not account for the force or implication intended in the utterance. Taking what somebody says literally, that is, interpreting what they say according to the dictionary definitions of the words used, can in some contexts be seen as offensive, humorous, sarcastic or, of course, unduly 'legalistic'.

Time and the framing of rules

The linguistic-juridical turn in philosophy has meant an intense focus on the status of rules and norms. Philosophers such as Rawls (1955) and Searle (1964) have distinguished two kinds of prescriptive or normative rules, namely 'regulative' and 'constitutive' rules. Regulative rules act on behaviour which goes on independently of the rules and whose existence is not dependent the rules. Constitutive rules actually create the conditions for that behaviour to take place or within which that behaviour is meaningful as social action. An example of a regulative rule is a traffic rule concerning where parking is allowed and at what times, or an instruction about how the plate is to be held when drinking soup. The rules of organised sports are often cited as examples of constitutive rules, since there is no activity 'playing chess' independently of the rules of chess. Many of the rules of the legal process itself are constitutive rules, such as the rules governing the conduct of a trial, or the rules that deter-mine whether a printed text is a copy of a lawfully enacted statute or simply a piece of paper with writing on it. Law in some sense may constitute society; it certainly regulates it in myriad ways. Constitutive rules are also regulative, in that in creating the framework against which actions are meaningful, they also lay down rules regulating those actions. The rules constituting the legal process or a sport also assign responsibility for interpreting and applying the rules.

The distinction between regulative and constitutive rules can be understood as dependent on the point of view and time-frame of relevance adopted by the observer. Parking a car is an activity which may plausibly be seen as regulated rather than constituted by the parking regulations. But to see the rules of parking as regulative rather than constitutive depends on taking a narrow view and isolating the activity from its wider legal embedding in land law, object ownership, and the entire battery of legal rules concerning cars and driving, as well as legal sanctions available for breach of parking regulations. While the rule on the sign in the street may merely regulate rather than constitute people's actual parking behaviour, the category of parking can be presented from a broader angle as to a very high degree constituted by law, just as scoring a goal in football is constituted by the rules of the game. In this sense how we understand a rule is dependent on how much of the background, context and history we treat as taken-for-granted. If we relegate to the background the context and history of traffic regulation and car ownership, then we can see a traffic sign as regulating instances of parking behaviour. If we include all these elements into our account, then an act of parking is constituted at least in part by the rules that govern it. Similarly, if we treat the rules of football as taken-for-granted, then the referee as the personification of the rules is regulating, not constituting, the game.

The characterisation of rules as regulative or constitutive can be understood as dependent on a point of view of what was placed in the foreground and what was taken-for-granted background. Thus to treat a rule of parking a regulatory is to adopt a narrow focus and confined time-frame. To treat the rule of parking as substantially constituting the parking behaviour is to adopt a much wider angle and a historical time-frame. The 'framing' of a rule as regulatory involves maximising the taken-for-granted background, and minimising the content of the foreground. In other words, the rule emerges as a description because of an idealisation away from its multiple embeddings and reflexive qualities. If by contrast the foreground is maximised, we have the situation in which the 'taken-for-granted' is reduced to a corresponding minimum. If there are no agreed background assumptions, the social world grinds to a halt. Law is on occasion in danger of grinding to a halt over language: in dealing with the assignment of meanings to words or interpretations to texts it is constantly faced with a dilemma over where to find/draw the line between the taken-for-granted background and the under-scrutiny foreground.

Conclusion

The philosophy of language, to the extent that it turned away from the relationship between language and the world (and it should be stressed that this has been far from universal in the discipline), embraced anti-foundationalism in a postmodern turn (Rorty 1979) or sought coherence and order in the everyday social contract that underlies communication. On the social contract view, utterances are understood as social acts, and semantic order cannot be said to inhere in language itself, or in the relation of words to a stable external reality. Rorty (1982: xviii) sees philosophy as having reached the end of the Platonist and Cartesian dualist road. Anti-foundationalist pragmatism 'lets us see language not as a *tertium quid* ["third thing"] between Subject and Object, nor as a medium in which we try to form pictures of reality, but as part of the behavior of human beings'. On this view, 'the activity of uttering sentences is one of the things people do in order to cope with their environment'. Paradoxically, however, law itself often looks to legal language to be precisely what this linguistic-juridical turn denies it to be, namely a system of objective representation which stands outside social action and provides a set of categories and classifications against which social acts are measured.

4 Issues in Legal Interpretation

Authority and interpretation

Questions of language and the law arise in a general anthropological context of social life regulated by authoritative linguistic formulae. Belief systems that centre on sacred or canonical texts, such as Judaism, Christianity and Islam, have complex traditions of textual interpretation, as do societies historically organised around a hierarchical bureaucracy, such as China. The secular law found in modern societies is part of much larger human reflection on 'the rule of rules' (Alexander and Sherwin 2001) and it would be a mistake to presume that societies organised around texts transmitted orally have radically different concerns. All societies have rules laid down to guide human behaviour, texts or precepts (both oral and written) that have authority over human conduct and regulate human affairs, and specialised forms of linguistic usage that bind those who fall within its domain, as well as authority figures who interpret rules and precepts and mediate in disputes.

Secular law reflects the assumptions of a post-Reformation and post-Enlightenment world. The Protestant Reformation embodied a profound textual revolution. In simple terms it had the consequence of allocating power to interpret the Bible in a non-definitive way between the specialist priest-class and the laity. This simultaneously lowered the status and textual authority of the priest and raised that of the laity under the banner of the 'priesthood of all believers'. Protestantism, in promoting the translation of the Bible into the vernacular, in moderating or setting aside the power of institutional hierarchy, emphasised individual faith and reason. The authority of the Biblical text rested on a belief in the possibility of unmediated access to its meaning, and Bible study integrated this sacred text into the daily life rhythms of the faithful. Protestantism came to encompass a wide spectrum of responses to the question of hierarchy, the need for guidance and leadership from ministers, issues of ornamentation, the form of religious observance, the level of sacredness ascribed to the space set aside for religious activities, and the desirability of plain personal style in clothing, speech, and so on. For some Protestant groups the text itself was an authority from which there could be no appeal to human interpretation. The emphasis on unmediated access to religious truth, however, also led some Protestant groups to provide a lesser role for the Bible, since the text, like the priest, can be seen as standing in the way of direct experience of the divine. The same logic is often applied by radical critics to law.

Protestantism posited an underlying shift in the base of religion from the semiotics of awe and mystery to transparency, egalitarianism and plain meaning. When set against the hierarchical certainties of Catholicism, Protestantism can be understood as introducing a dynamic of scepticism with regard to authority over meaning and interpretation, and a corresponding set of doctrines aimed at containing that doubt. Secular law remains on both sides of the symbolic culture wars of the Reformation. It rules by hierarchy, awe and ritual, and by persuasion, reason and transparency. The dynamic of sceptical inquiry into religious authority led to questions about the source of political and legal authority and shaped a parallel constitutional development in uncertainties in the allocation of power between the Crown, Parliament, the judiciary and the people.

Under the democratic theory of the rule of law, law derives its constitutional role ultimately from the legislature as the representative of the people. Judges are bound to respect the higher legitimacy of the legislature, and citizens are obliged to obey the law, because on this social contract view the citizens are law's ultimate authors. If judges make law, or are seen to make law, then this social contract is broken. One can dismiss this model as a legal fiction, and it is indeed fictional to ascribe direct agentive intent to the people to produce highly complex tax regulations or delegated legislation. In this sense ideals of democratic sovereignty, while they suggest a 'bottom-up' derivation of power, owe much to pre-modern systems of monarchical power. The symbolism and ritual of law and its absolute powers in many areas of social life have led radical critics to associate modern law with pre-modern absolutism, as in Foucault's understanding of modern law as in effect a 'juridical monarchy' (Hunt and Wickham 1994: 43). The immunities and privileges of judges and their powers as the representatives of law (symbolised in the British context as the 'Crown') exist in tension with their constitutionally subordinate position to the legislature, and to the understanding of law as also binding and limiting judges.

In legal theory, common law judges are sometimes seen as having an inviolable jurisdiction derived from 'natural justice' or, more narrowly, from 'equity', and this exists in tension with the doctrine of legislative supremacy. The taboo on judicial legislative activity is thus balanced by another ideology, namely that judges have an independent jurisdiction which derives from the unchanging principles of reason and justice. This contentious and part-mythological jurisdiction potentially sets judges against law, understood as a set of formal rules, and against the sovereignty of Parliament, since the doctrine of an untrammeled sovereignty can be regarded as residual of monarchy, not an expression of democracy. This is a residue of a once powerful view of

English history in which the Norman invasion had ended a golden age of Anglo-Saxon freedoms. One profound principle of the feudal system of the Normans was that all land was held by the Crown, which symbolically reduced all others to different levels of subjecthood, and the spread of hegemonic, centralised law, swallowing customary law and creating a uniform system of control. While this myth of the 'Norman Yoke' imposed on free Anglo-Saxons no longer has political relevance in this form, its Romantic nationalist narrative of the Norman conquest, and the imposition of feudal land tenure and a tax system which was to be served by the information gathered in the Domesday Book, resonates with postcolonial and Foucaultian critiques of law and common law today. It has continuing relevance in the context of indigenous rights and aboriginal land claims within common law jurisdictions, where the judge may be asked to declare the limits of the common law itself in relation to a pre-existing and incompatible social order.

Legal rules concerning interpretation are an assorted mixture of conventions, maxims, principles and authorities. A higher court may overturn the decision of a lower court, and the legislature can enact laws to correct what is seen as an erroneous judgment, but there is no mechanism of direct enforcement for legal rules of interpretation. The powers of judges are those assigned to them in a particular constitutional order, but as noted judges themselves have historically laid claim to autonomous realms of authority, and the edges of judicial authority have been subject to historical shifts and uncertainty. The landmark case of *Marbury v Madison* (1803) established or affirmed the right of the United States Supreme Court to declare a statute unconstitutional. In the context of English law, the so-called 'Factortame' cases raised questions about the powers of judges to disapply national law where it conflicted with European Union law (see *R v Secretary of State for Transport, ex p. Factortame Ltd* 1991). However, the most fundamental power held by common law judges is jurisdiction over the process of interpretation itself, which explains why judicial interpretation is the focus of such intense critical scrutiny. Judges sit at a junction in the system where the abstract democratic powers of the legislature, derived in constitutional theory ultimately from the people, meet again those people as individuals in the flesh who are now the direct subjects of law.

For some commentators, legal interpretation is an example of shared, reflexive *praxis*, in which internalised norms, formal and informal institutionalised feedback and professional self-discipline ensure objectivity and non-partisan independence. The shared socialisation in law of judges means that judicial interpretation 'is not a function of a single judicial or lawyerly mind, acting alone'; it is collective or 'community-bound' and the interpretative criteria are 'elaborated intersubjectively, among an interpretive community that is constituted by fidelity to law'. These criteria are public and available as justification for a decision (Wendel 2005: 1190–1). Against this view there has arisen a substantial body of analysis which maps the decisions of the contemporary United States Supreme Court directly onto the political orientation of the judges (Tobin 2007). This way of reading judicial decisions is particularly salient in the public culture of the United States, reflecting the key role of the legal system and the Constitution in arbitrating divisive social issues.

Any normative system such as law which sets itself up as an authority over language, and which employs its own language experienced as remote and foreign to the everyday linguistic experience of lay members of society, is vulnerable to demystifying, debunking or deconstructive attack. One example of such demystification is the plain language movement in law, which re-enacts the Protestant Reformation in proposing a translation from the high sacred language to vernacular or colloquial 'plain' or 'transparent' language (see Barnes 2006; Cutts 1996). In questioning a hierarchy of interpretative authority the argument for plain language offers a secular rendering of the Protestant notion of the 'priesthood of all believers'. The plain language approach replaces an arcane or esoteric sacred text which requires priest-like intermediaries with an appeal to a timeless, context-free and transparent language. The same general approach would argue for a radical simplification of legal procedure, and for transparency and comprehensibility of process.

It is hard to object to the principle of more easily comprehensible legal language. Law binds by the authority of its words, and, famously, ignorance of it is no excuse (*ignorantia legis non excusat*). Law deems those subject to the law to know the law, that is, to have what the law calls constructive notice (knowledge that is implied or assigned by operation of law) of its content. Morrison comments that lawyers 'engage in and live the myth that each person knows the law because it is in English' (Morrison 1989: 285). This is one of many legal fictions that sustain law: the ritual promulgation of the statute creates textual language which is binding over all who fall within its domain. Yet the texts of law are unbounded and unknowable in their totality and it is the operation of the legal process itself which provides a degree of determinacy. Law is thus retrospective to a degree rarely acknowledged, since the precise category and degree of criminal responsibility or the existence and extent of a civil obligation is often only clarified by the legal process itself.

However, one fundamental problem for the plain language argument in its more radical forms is that, even if the language of a legal text is (or appears) comprehensible and clear to a non-specialist reader, its legal effect is not, and cannot be simply 'read off' the surface of the text. A plain language statute, for example, as interpreted by successive layers of case law commentary, requires a specialist reading to determine, or at least estimate, its legal effect when set against a particular factual matrix. If we take the famous example 'No vehicles in the park' (Hart 1994), the fact that this rule is written in plain English did not prevent a vast jurisprudential literature growing up to comment on and explain it.

While accepting that the density of legal language represents the mystification of political and ideological authority, the radical critic (e.g. from
Critical Legal Studies) is no less sceptical of plain language as an ideal
premised on the existence of a stable set of signifier–signified relations, transparent in the same way to the legal interpreter and to all addresses of law. This
suggests that law when expressed in the medium of plain language is self-
sustaining, self-justifying and self-explanatory, that law can show and explain
fully its own forms of reasoning and rationale. The radical critic distrusts the
'priest-caste' of professional legal interpreters, but is equally sceptical of the
notion of an autonomous language that can 'speak directly for itself' and
mean what it says in the same way to all addressees. This form of attack seeks
to demystify not only privileged legal authority over language, but the authority and stability of language itself. The radical critic is constantly reinserting
or foregrounding 'time', 'context' and the diversity of law's addressees into
discourses that are viewed as erasing or containing these sources of instability
and delegitimation.

Dilemmas of legal interpretation

Like many secular systems law is caught between its commitment to change,
reform and its own vitality as a living institution, and the need to validate its
practices by showing that they have stood 'the test of time'. Common law has
its own foundation myths of origin and historical authority. One aspect of the
temporal semiotics of law is an ideology of time as validating legal principles.
Repetition and quotation give authority to words, endlessly embedding and
re-embedding them in the fabric of law, and blurring the distinction between
a habit and a rule. Maxims that are quoted over many centuries acquire a high
degree of authority by virtue of this repetition. Within the culture of judgments, maxims and textbook pronouncements that stand for centuries have
proved their worthiness by virtue of their very survival and adaptability to the
changing legal context. They are 'memes' in the evolution of law (Dawkins
1976).

Yet because the common law also understands itself as in its deepest structures timeless and unchanging, it has the moral authority to repair its own
fabric constantly, to apply it pragmatically by working constantly to free
society from what Lord Denning referred to in *Liverpool City Council v Irwin*
(1976) as 'the dead hand of the past' (at 332). In a self-consciously scientific
or rational jurisprudence, the survival of a rule is not enough: 'Every one
instinctively recognizes that in these days the justification of a law for us
cannot be found in the fact that our fathers always have followed it'; the most
important task for a true science of law is 'the establishment of its postulates
from within upon accurately measured social desires instead of tradition'
(Holmes 1898/9: 452).

Within common law ideology, fidelity to the language of law is often presented as the essence of the rule of law, and the plain meaning of a text framed as a defence against arbitrary official action. In an English war-time case which concerned the Home Secretary's right to order the detention of someone on grounds of national security, Lord Atkin dissented on the grounds that the House of Lords had concluded that all that was required for the Home Secretary to have reasonable grounds for detaining someone was that he believed he had reasonable grounds (*Liversidge v Anderson* 1942, at 245):

> I know of only one authority which might justify the suggested method of construction; 'When I use a word,' Humpty Dumpty said in a rather scornful tone, 'it means just what I choose it to mean, neither more nor less.' 'The question is,' said Alice, 'whether you can make words mean different things.' 'The question is,' said Humpty Dumpty, 'which is to be master – that is all.' [. . .] After all this long discussion the question is whether the words, 'If a man has' can mean 'If a man thinks he has.' I am of the opinion that they cannot, and the case should be decided accordingly.

However, 'hard cases' by definition involve more creative reasoning by judges. In *Spartan Steel & Alloys Ltd v Martin & Co* (1973), a power cut caused by a contractor's negligence led to the electricity supply to a steel company being cut off. The question arose as to whether, in addition to damage to metal in production and loss of profits that would have arisen from the sale of the metal, the company could also claim the 'pure economic loss' of profits caused by the shut-down of production. The final part of the claim was denied. Lord Denning, however, set aside attempts to analyse the problem in conventional legal terminology (at 37):

> The more I think about these cases, the more difficult I find it to put each into its proper pigeon-hole. Sometimes I say: 'There was no duty.' In others I say: 'The damage was too remote.' So much so that I think that the time has come to discard these tests which proved so elusive. It seems to me better to consider the particular relationship in hand, and see whether or not, as a matter of policy, economic loss should be recoverable, or not.

As Stone (1995: 72–3) points out, Denning, in electing to frame the case in terms of where the economic loss should fall, set aside what he presented as obscurantist legal language in favour of a 'loudly declared realism and transparency'. However, Stone (1995: 73) asks why the principle declared by Denning was not intended to be given 'the same normative reach in every other case'. In maintaining the distinction between physical damage and pure economic loss the judgment remained within the guidelines of traditional tort doctrine. As with many interpretative moves, its generality was designed to fit the case at hand.

A case where questions of change, statutory language and the common law arose was in relation to the so-called 'marital rape' exemption, under which a husband was deemed to be not capable of committing the crime of rape against his wife (*R v R* 1992). The original authority for this rule was found in legal textbooks (Hale 1736; Hume 1797). This principle was challenged in the 1989 Scottish case, *S v H.M. Advocate*, where Lord Emslie rejected the idea that a wife by marriage submitted herself 'irrevocably to sexual intercourse in all circumstances'. However, the English courts were faced with the Sexual Offences (Amendment) Act 1976, S 1(1)(a). A man was guilty of rape if he had 'unlawful sexual intercourse with a woman who at the time of the intercourse does not consent to it'. The general consensus was that, in a meaning derived from ecclesiastical law, 'unlawful' meant 'outside marriage'. In *R v R* (1992), the leading judgment in the House of Lords by Lord Lane in effect set the word 'unlawful' aside (at 611):

> The only realistic explanations seem to us to be that the draftsman either intended to leave the matter open for the common law to develop in that way or, perhaps more likely, that no satisfactory meaning at all can be ascribed to the word and that it is indeed surplusage. In either event, we do not consider that we are inhibited by the Act of 1976 from declaring that the husband's immunity as expounded by Hale no longer exists. We take the view that the time has now arrived when the law should declare that a rapist remains a rapist subject to the criminal law, irrespective of his relationship with his victim.

Further, the entire concept was based on a fiction (at 611):

> the idea that a wife by marriage consents in advance to her husband having sexual intercourse with her whatever her state of health or however proper her objections (if that is what Hale meant), is no longer acceptable. It can never have been other than a fiction, and fiction is a poor basis for the criminal law.

Fidelity to law in *R v R* (1992) meant something more than fidelity to the language of law, and the court drew in essence on a myth of a timeless and just common law, paradoxically declaring the rule to be a fiction, that is, one that had never properly existed, and at the same time abolishing it.

While radical critiques of law have pronounced logophobic tendencies, the fear and mistrust of language in a milder form is also a central feature of mainstream legal discourse itself, and arises within a framework of an ideal fidelity to legal language (Frankfurter 1947: 546):

Words are clumsy tools. And it is very easy to cut one's fingers with them, and they need the closest attention in handling; but they are the only tools we have, and imagination itself cannot work without them.

The place of definition within law is deeply controversial (Harris and Hutton 2007: 133–95). Statutes are often criticised for failing to define key terms, yet reliance on definitions is often self-defeating, setting off a regress of explanation. The special meaning given by the definition in the statute is always in danger of contamination by the 'ordinary' or 'intuitive' meaning. In his *Commercial Law*, Roy Goode, noting the centrality of legal construction (interpretation) to many areas of the law, argues that those whose business it is to 'work with words' in this way 'soon acquire an appreciation of the limitations of language' (Goode 2004: 21). The meaning of a word is dependent on context and 'the purposes for which its meaning is required to be elucidated' (2004: 21). Goode goes on to specifically address the question of definition (2004: 21): 'One of the great myths propagated by lawmakers is that everything can be made clear by definition', but words and phrases could only 'be defined only in terms of other words or phrases', and so on. The 'excessive use' of definitions in modern legislation often served to 'obscure rather than illuminate the meaning'. However, the legislature was sometimes willing to concede that 'certain words are wholly indefinable': 'Thus the word "possession" appears in innumerable statutes, but Parliament has wisely chosen not to attempt a definition.' In a particular case, the choice between literal and liberal definition of a word or phrase 'may involve little more than value judgments' (Goode 2004: 22). That is to say, for Goode, an interpretative dilemma may not involve any strictly *linguistic* questions at all.

It is worth stressing that general statements about language and interpretation often have a decisive primary context in the 'interpretative politics' of the case, that is, in what we could call the 'framing' of the interpretative issue. The critique of language may have a particular place in framing the legal issue at stake in a particular case (Byles J. in *Stevens v Gourley* 1859, at 112):

The imperfection of human language renders it not only difficult, but absolutely impossible, to define the word 'building' with any approach to accuracy. One may say of this or that structure, this or that is not a building; but no general definition can be given; and our lexicographers do not attempt it.

But this apparently general statement was in its context a ground-clearing exercise, not a statement of the futility of definition. It created the space for the judge to offer a sketch of a definition:

Without, therefore, presuming to do what others have failed to do. I may venture to suggest, that, by a 'building' is usually understood a structure of considerable size, and intended to be permanent, or at least to endure for a considerable time. A church, whether constructed of iron or wood, undoubtedly is a building. So, a 'cow house' or 'stable' has been held to be a building, the occupation of which as tenant entitles the party to be registered as a voter. On the other hand, it is equally clear that a bird cage is not a building, neither is a wig-box, or a dog-Kennel or a hen-coop – the very value of these things being their portability.

In this case, a contractor built a shop which was elevated off the ground, in an apparent attempt to evade planning regulations. In spite of the judge's comments about the impossibility of making general definitions, the definition was then subsequently considered and applied in other cases, for example in a burglary case, *B and S v Leathley* (1979). B and S had been convicted of stealing goods from a freezer container on a farm, and appealed against their conviction for burglary. It was held that the container was 'a structure of considerable size and intended to be permanent or at least to endure for a considerable time' and was therefore a building within S 9 of the 1968 Theft Act.

Law cannot plausibly be seen as a bounded social category, and the language of law therefore draws on, and circulates among, multiple domains. The divide between legal language and non-legal language has always been fluid, with law drawing on 'ordinary language' metaphors, and legal language and metaphors diffusing into many other domains, for example literary language. Law impacts on the imagined public space of language through the overlapping circulation of legal and non-legal language. The apparent speeding-up of the diffusion of legal language can be seen in part as a symptom of the interactions of law, public administration and regulation (Morgan and Yeung 2007). For example, the origins of the phrase 'fitness for purpose' appear to be in consumer law (e.g. Sale of Goods Act 1893, S 14), but the phrase is now widely used in the United Kingdom across a whole range of domains, in particular in relation to quality assurance in the public sector. This not only illustrates the diffusion of legal language, but also is evocative of the rise of a powerful consumer model of citizenship, in which the citizen relates to the state as a consumer of public services. New classes of 'experts' such as management consultants constantly introduce new 'language games' and metaphorical frameworks which circulate through public institutions in a never-ending pursuit of the nirvana of 'excellence'. 'Due diligence', now widely used in quality assurance or audit contexts, came to prominence as a defence to liability for misstatements or omissions under S 11 of the United States Securities Act 1933, but it is attested in early nineteenth-century American legal sources.

While it may be difficult to characterise the language of the law and law's determinations as to how it should relate to ordinary language, this boundary is frequently of profound importance to the courts, and the subject of judicial commentary and debate. Judges on occasion make the claim that their interpretative practices are or should be aligned with those of ordinary language users (*Investors Compensation Scheme Ltd v West Bromwich Building Society* 1998). In the English case of *R v Caldwell* (1982), the judges disagreed over the relevance of the ordinary meaning of 'recklessness' in the legal context. Lord Edmund-Davies, dissenting, rejected an attempt to ground what had become a specialised legal term ('recklessness') in everyday usage: 'The law in action compiles its own dictionary. In time, what was originally the common coinage of speech acquires a different value in the pocket of the lawyer than when in the layman's purse' (at 23). The boundary between legal and ordinary language also potentially represents a demarcation line between the expertise of the lawyer and that of the academic linguist. Even though judges have argued for the alignment of their interpretative practices and those of ordinary language users, the boundary between legal and ordinary language, as in *Caldwell*, is often constructed contentiously in the context of a particular case; it is thus dependent on the reflexive inquiry and control of the law, rather than any external expertise.

The 'literal', 'golden' and 'mischief' rules

Law students are generally introduced to three basic 'rules' for the interpretation of statute law, namely the literal rule, the golden rule and the mischief rule, as well as an underlying distinction between literal and 'purposive' interpretation (see Evans 1988; Zander 2004: 127ff). They are thereby introduced to a way of thinking about texts as having an interior and an exterior. The history and nature of these rules resists easy summary, but the general consensus is that the literal rule became dominant in the early nineteenth century. It is generally explained as follows: 'it is the task of the court to give the words to be construed their literal meaning regardless of whether the result is sensible or not' (Zander 2004: 130). One formulation is also much quoted, that by Lord Esher in *R v Judge of the City of London Court* (1982):

> If the words of an Act of Parliament are clear, you must take them in their ordinary and natural meaning, unless that meaning produces a manifest absurdity. Now, I say that no such rule of construction was ever laid down before. If the words of an Act are clear, you must follow them, even though they lead to a manifest absurdity. The Court has nothing to do with the question whether the legislature has committed an absurdity.

This creates a double temporal taboo, that is, it forbids looking back to seek further evidence of the intentions of the law-maker (as these are most purely realised in the language of the statute itself, not in the messy, open-ended legislative process), and it forbids looking forward to evaluate the consequences of applying the language strictly to the facts of the case. Apart from the argument from fidelity to privileged language, a further claim in favour of the literal rule is that it is the most appropriate for modern, highly detailed legislation, and encourages disciplined drafting: 'the length and detail of modern legislation has undoubtedly reinforced the claim of literal construction as the only safe rule' (Lord Evershed, Master of the Rolls, preface to Wilson and Galpin 1962: vi).

Zander (2004: 131) suggests that an early formulation of the golden rule can be found in *Mattison v Hart* (1854, at 385):

> We must, therefore, in this case have recourse to what is called the golden rule of construction, as applied to acts of parliament, viz. to give the words used by the legislature their plain and natural meaning unless it is manifest from the general scope and intention of the statute injustice and absurdity would result.

The obvious object to this is the difficulty of identifying absurdity ('what seems absurd to one man does not seem absurd to another'; Lord Bramwell in *Hill v East and the West India Dock Co* 1884, at 464–5), and it is not clear how to read the pairing of 'injustice' with 'absurdity'. Does this suggest that a non-absurd injustice, or an absurd but just outcome, fall outside the golden rule?

While the focus of these rules is on statutory interpretation, they are sometimes discussed in the context of legal documents in general (*Grey v Pearson* 1857, at 106). The mischief rule as it is generally formulated (see *Heyden's Case* 1584) is, however, logically confined to the interpretation of statutes and would not be applicable without modification to other forms of legal interpretation, though it does suggest a way of framing the interpretative task. Explaining the rule, Lord Coke set out a four-step approach to a problem of statutory interpretation. The four steps are as follows: the court should first determine the state of the law before the passing of the Act, then the 'mischief or defect' which the law was not able to deal with, and thirdly the 'remedy' that Parliament had chosen 'to cure the disease of the commonwealth'. The final stage required the court to consider:

> The true reason of the remedy; and then the office of all the judges is always to make such construction as shall suppress the mischief, and advance the remedy, and to suppress subtle inventions and evasions for continuance of the mischief, and *pro privato commodo* [for private benefit], and to add force and life to the cure and remedy, according to the true intent of the makers of the Act, *pro bono publico* [for the public good].

Objections to the literal rule as the default rule of legal interpretation draw on scepticism about the existence and nature of the meaning on which it relies. It is often pointed out that words and expressions have more than one dictionary meaning, and general terms ('vehicle') have to be clarified by reference to a particular sub-meaning. Further, in the context of a courtroom battle, it is likely that there will be two meanings in competition (Zander 2004: 141–2). By contrast, a contextual and intention-referenced purposive approach has the air of modernity, as an approach within which interpretation is seen as a dynamic process, and the focus of attention shifts both back to the intent of the author of the document (even, after the English case of *Pepper v Hart* 1993, looking on occasion behind the veil of the legislative process) and forwards to the particular results of applying the rule in a particular way to particular people, and the effect of the case within the general architecture of law.

It has been argued that these three rules can in fact be reconciled into a procedure for determining the intent of Parliament (Evans 1988: 11–12):

> The mischief rule states that in order to understand the intended meaning of a rule, courts should consider what those who passed it were trying to achieve. The golden rule states that if what seems to be the normal meaning of the words give rise to an absurdity, this is a good clue that this meaning was not the intended meaning; while the literal rule states that if the normal meaning is the only possible meaning courts must stick to it.

A similar composite view of legal interpretation was offered by Blackstone: words should be understood 'in their usual and most known signification', not strictly according to the 'propriety of grammar', but in their 'general and popular use'. If meaning was none the less 'dubious', the legal context could provide an answer. If the literal meaning gave rise to an 'absurd signification', then the interpretation could deviate from it, but the final, 'most universal and effectual way of discovering the true meaning of law, when the words are dubious, is by considering the reason and spirit of it; or the cause which moved the legislator to enact it'. It was equity that offered insight into the 'the reason of the law'. This was because 'in law all cases cannot be foreseen or expressed', so there was need of a final 'power vested of excepting those circumstances which (had they been foreseen) the legislator himself would have excepted', though this liberty should not be taken too far 'lest thereby we destroy all law, and leave the decision of every question in the breast of the judge'. Law without equity was preferable to equity without law, where judges would simply be legislators (Blackstone 1765–9, I: 59–62).

For Karl Llewellyn (1893–1962), canons of statutory interpretation cannot constrain interpretation, since for every rule there was a contradictory one: 'A statute cannot go beyond its text', but 'To effect its purpose a statute may be implemented beyond its text'; 'If language is plain and unambiguous it must be given effect', but 'Not when literal interpretation would lead to absurd or mischievous consequences or thwart manifest purpose' (Llewellyn 1950: 401,

403). Winter (2001: 217) comments that for Llewellyn legal certainty must be
achieved by change in rule interpretation, that paradoxically the law must
change, so as to be seen to stand still: 'if the change on the judge's part is
keeping up perfectly [with semantic change], neither judge nor layman realizes
that any change has occurred [. . .] and legal certainty prevails. It can only
prevail through change.'

In similar spirit to Llewellyn, Hutchinson (2000: 333–42) offers a play-book
of the 'argumentative maneuvers' that underlie legal debate and judicial reasoning. Hutchinson divides these into strategies that draw on 'precedent', and
those that relate to 'policy'. Under precedent, there are four basic oppositions:
(1) literal versus purposive interpretation of meaning; (2) narrow and broad
interpretations of rules; (3) general versus detailed statement of facts, so that
the categorisation of facts is not independent of the kind of rule or principle
that is applied; (4) old versus modern authorities, so that an old rule can be
defended as having survived the test of time, or discarded as being so old that
it has lost touch with 'the realities of modern society'. Policy concerns can
likewise be shown to contain strategic alternatives. For example, a court can
defend 'strict' rules as ensuring predictability, or 'flexible' rules as allowing justice to be tailored to the facts of the case. It can apply a rule to
protect 'formal' equality, so that everyone is treated in an identical manner
under the rule, or to promote 'substantive' equality, by recognising that existing differences require that some groups be treated differently.

One issue that the mischief or 'purposive' rule raises is the range of materials that the court is entitled to consult. When the rule was first formulated,
statutes had much longer preambles which gave the judge a strong indication
of the objective of the statute. Though there were grey areas in the range of
materials that might be cited, there was a prohibition on citing the parliamentary background, in particular the debates leading to the enactment. In
English law, this grey area was dramatically widened by the ruling in *Pepper v
Hart* (1993), where for the first time the purposive approach was widened to
allow consultation of the parliamentary materials in the background to the
enactment, under certain defined circumstances.

In literary terms this might be equivalent to consulting letters written by the
author which refer to a novel in progress or records of discussions in a literary salon or other public forum. One can of course also consult a living author
over the meaning of a puzzling passage, perhaps many years after the work
has been written, but in some sense that author, although the same person, is
located differently from the original author, having experienced the response
to the work from readers, reviewers and critics, no longer having in mind the
original moment of creation, and having perhaps evolved in other ways.
Asking any speaker 'What did you mean when you said that?' in any case
invokes a particular context and occasion on which the question is asked, and
may, by its selection of an extract or a single remark, carry a particular implication for the questioner's attitude and views. In other words the relating of

that context of discussion to the original context of production requires a further act of interpretation. Parliament likewise, though constitutionally 'it never dies', evolves from day to day in terms of political profile and membership, and for many theorists is a reference point for meaning only as an ideal speaker/subject.

In the House of Lords case *Hilder v Dexter* (1902), Lord Halsbury argued that as a draftsman of the relevant statute, the Companies Act 1900, he was in the worst possible position to interpret it. 'I have more than once had occasion to say that in construing a statute I believe the worst person to construe it is the person who is responsible for its drafting.' This was because the drafter was liable to confuse 'what he intended to do' with 'the effect of the language which in fact has been employed'. At the time of drafting the drafter 'may have been under the impression that he had given full effect to what was intended, but he may be mistaken in construing it afterwards just because what was in his mind was what was intended, though, perhaps, it was not done' (at 477). However, although he abstained from giving a judgment, Lord Halsbury did offer comment on the other (unanimous) judgments, noting that 'I entirely concur with every word' and that their interpretation did indeed reflect the intended meaning of the statute: 'I do not say my intention, but the intention of the Legislature. I was largely responsible for the language in which the enactment is conveyed, and for that reason, and for that reason only, I have not written a judgment myself' (at 477–8).

This is a possibly unique meta-judgment, in which the judge delivers a verdict on the correctness of the other judges' opinions, without actually offering a judgment himself. Halsbury's position seems to be that there is a danger specific to interpretation by the drafter that the otherwise clear meaning of the statute will be obscured 'because of his exceptional stake in affairs' (Toolan 2002: 169). On close inspection, Halsbury's statements collapse into contradiction. He offers a model of restraint in respect of his right to interpret, not directly on grounds of conflict of interest, but on grounds of the subjective partiality that might arise from the dual role. He describes himself as the 'worst person' to interpret the statute, but at the same time he endorses the verdict of the court as being compatible with the intention of the legislature, being careful to avoid saying that this is also 'his' intention. Obviously this constitutes a claim of direct access to the uncontaminated meaning, that is, 'the literal objective wording of the statute, autonomous and fixed' (Toolan 2002: 169).

It might be thought that the literal rule is more or less dead, and that characterisations of purposive construction as flexible, contextual, dynamic, holistic and so on have been ultimately persuasive. In the much-discussed English case *Re Rowland* (1963), the interpretation of a will left by a couple made its legal effect dependent on whether their death was coincident or one party predeceased the other. Husband and wife disappeared together in the South Pacific, but the exact circumstances of their death were unknown. The court ruled that the plain meaning of the word 'coinciding' was not covered by these facts (see Zander 2004: 135–42). Lord Denning dissented, criticising what he characterised as nineteenth-century literalism which asked for the 'ordinary and grammatical meaning'. Denning preferred to reconstruct the intention of the testator (at 9):

> In order to discover the meaning which he [the testator] intended, you will not get much help from a dictionary. It is very unlikely that he used a dictionary, and even less likely that he used the same one as you. What you should do is place yourself as far as possible in his position, taking note of the facts and circumstances known to him at the time and then say what he meant by his words. I decline, therefore, to ask myself: what do the words mean to a grammarian?

Lord Denning also remarked: 'I have myself known a judge to say: "I believe this to be contrary to the true intention of the testator but nevertheless it is the result of the words he has used"' (at 9–10). Denning located himself in the place and time of the testator, and rejected any reference outside that frame to an impersonal or decontextual instrument such as a dictionary.

In *Investors Compensation Scheme Ltd v West Bromwich Building Society* (1998), the court affirmed that the result of a fundamental change in the construction of contracts had been 'to assimilate the way in which such documents are interpreted by judges to the common sense principles by which any serious utterance would be interpreted in ordinary life'. The 'old intellectual baggage of "legal" interpretation' had been largely discarded and interpretation should involve 'the ascertainment of the meaning which the document would convey to a reasonable person having all the background knowledge which would reasonably have been available to the parties in the situation in which they were at the time of the contract'. This meant that the meaning of a document such as a contract needed to be read against the 'matrix of fact', that is, the surrounding circumstances and expectations in which the document was embedded (judgment of Lord Hoffmann, at 912). This involved an assertion that the judge should normally attempt to mimic the ordinary non-legal approach to understanding a document, and consciously adopt an extra-legal or commonsense point of view.

This falls short of asking what the contract actually meant ('subjectively') to the parties concerned; rather it asks what a reasonable observer would ('objectively') take the document to mean. This framing of the interpretative task is not as radical as it might seem, since the 'reasonable person' remains a construct or legal fiction created by law, and it should be stressed that this discussion concerned the language of contracts and was not a discussion of statutory interpretation. It still leaves open the question of how a court is to arrive at the reasonable person's interpretation, and the sort of evidence that it might adduce and strategies it might employ in making its determination. It should be stressed that this genre of general comment is often a way of clearing interpretative space in the case at hand, or in a line of cases, rather than a binding rule of interpretation.

Policy as an interpretative tool

Judges, or commentators on judicial decisions, may also invoke 'policy considerations' in looking for a rationale, where one cannot be easily found in precedent or in the strict law of the case. These are defined as 'the social, political and economic implications of the decision beyond the boundaries of the case itself' (Manchester et al. 2000: 33). A foreseen, legally allowable outcome can be rejected as 'contrary to policy'. However, the question of what constitutes 'the boundaries of the case itself' is at the heart of modern jurisprudential debate. This issue was famously raised by the legal philosopher Ronald Dworkin (1975) in relation to the Court of Appeals of New York case *Riggs v Palmer* (1889). In that case, a grandson murdered his grandfather in anticipation that the will would be altered in a manner unfavourable to him, and then inherited under the will. This was not a question of linguistic ambiguity or vagueness; there was nothing in the relevant law that forbade this. The court ruled, however, that Elmer Palmer could not inherit.

In *Riggs*, Earl J. made this determination with a number of distinct through related arguments. He appealed to a general maxim of interpretation, namely 'that a thing which is within the intention of the makers of a statute is as much within the statute as if it were within the letter; and a thing which is within the letter of the statute is not within the statute unless it be within the intention of the makers' (at 509). If the letter of the statute fell short or exceeded the precise intention, then judges were required to 'collect it from probable or rational conjectures only' (at 409). This conclusion was buttressed by so-called counter-factual grounds, based on the thought-experiment of presenting this factual scenario to the legislature: 'If such a case had been present to their minds, and it had been supposed necessary to make some provision of law to meet it, it cannot be doubted that they would have provided for it' (at 509). In addition, the application of all laws was subject to 'general, fundamental maxims of the common law' which had been 'dictated by public policy' and which had 'their foundation in universal law administered in all civilized countries' and 'general principles of natural law and justice' to the effect that no one should profit from their own wrong-doing (at 511). There were, however, reported decisions which took the opposite view, and two judges dissented. Gray J. insisted that the court was 'bound by the rigid rules of law, which have been established by the legislature, and within the limits of which the determination of this question is confined' (at 515). There was extensive legislative control of wills, and public policy did not require this will to be set aside and another substituted: 'for the demands of public policy are satisfied by the proper execution of the laws and the punishment of the crime' (at 519). This was effectively a second, additional punishment for the murder.

Equitable interpretation

In some legal contexts formal legal rules are subject to a set of equitable rules, which are applied at the discretion of the judge. For example, an agreement which lacks the requisite formality (e.g. a contract for land of the type which should be created by deed), but on which one or both of the parties have already acted, may be enforced by the court. Equity can also be understood as a relatively free-standing set of principles, which provide for some kind of moral balancing when the strict wording of the law appears to favour a party who is in the view of the court acting immorally or in bad faith, or relying on principles to their own advantage the equivalent of which they seek to deny to the other party. In the case of trust law, the legal owner (the trustee) is distinguished from the equitable beneficiary. While on paper trustees have all the rights of the owner, trustees are constrained by equitable rules from treating trust property as their own. In *Riggs v Palmer* (1889) there was discussion of the 'equity of the statute'. The dissenting judge argued that the plain language of the statute, which stipulated that no written will should be 'revoked or otherwise altered' except as set out in the statute, had ousted the 'equitable jurisdiction' of the court. Another solution that has been proposed to this case is for the judge to uphold the will but to rule that Palmer should inherit only as a constructive trustee for identified beneficial owners, that is, heirs who would have inherited under the changed will. In this way the legal coherence would have been preserved, in that title passed to the property, but no financial benefit would have followed it.

What is meant by 'equity of the statute'? Earl J. cited this account of equitable construction as a way of linking equity with a counter-factual thought-experiment (at 510):

> The reason for such construction is that the law-makers could not set down every case in express terms. In order to form a right judgment whether a case be within the equity of a statute, it is a good way to suppose the law-maker present, and that you have asked him this question: Did you intend to comprehend this case? Then you must give yourself such answer as you imagine he, being an upright and reasonable man, would have given.

Law when contrasted with equity is primarily associated with the observance of the proper formalities, equity with the intent and moral balance between the parties. Law is often associated with writing (textuality), equity with speech (orality) and with the actual conduct or behaviour of parties between themselves. Law's relative certainty comes from its decontextualised gaze (symbolised in the blindfolded figure of justice), equity is contextual. In this sense law is stereotypically masculine, stern, faceless, patriarchal, and equity is stereotypically feminine, in that it is flexible and discretionary, concerned with individual justice for specified individuals. Equity gives remedies for particular individuals in particular cases, and as it is a discretionary jurisdiction it does not create legal precedents. Equity is also personified as an agent which 'intervenes'. Much of the original domain of equity is now also formalised (e.g. the rules regarding consideration in contract, the law of trusts), but the trend to formalisation is never absolute and equity remains an open-ended category of judicial discretion.

Law and equity correspond in this sense to the law and economics distinction between regulation *ex ante* and *ex post*. Law looks at a situation from the point of view of the rule as given in advance; equity looks at the situation from the point of view of the consequences of applying the rule to the actual situation, and asks, in some restricted circumstances, whether the result 'offends the conscience of the court' and should be set aside. This is symbolically a contrast between faceless or impersonal law (where 'justice is blind' to the lifeworld inhabited by the parties themselves) and the personified law with a conscience (where justice, as it were, removes the blindfold). The cost–benefit analysis of this in traditional terms is the trade-off between certainty and consistency as a positive value assigned to a system of norms, versus flexibility and discretion as a positive value assigned to contextual, case-specific adjudication.

Conclusion

The rules set out in legal textbooks for legal interpretation are in one sense as fictional as the constitutional ideals to which they refer. The choice of an interpretative strategy cannot be completely separated from the wider issues at stake in a particular case, and there could be no ultimate 'meta-rule' to determine which strategy is applicable. In the case of statutory interpretation the judge is faced with a text which has been created in the past and formally declared complete by the rituals of enactment or closure. In front of the court is a particular, present set of factual-legal circumstances, which have been pre-digested and labelled by the system but which require a definitive resolution in terms of the statute. Projected forwards into the future is the outcome in the particular case, with its foreseeable effect on the parties: X goes to gaol, Y is ruined financially, Z will take a share of the ownership of the marital home. In high-profile cases there is also a foreseeable reception of the outcome seen as a dramatised morality play within a wider moral or political narrative. The court's decision may be read as siding with the 'little guy' against the 'big corporation', a setback when seen against a particular social or political agenda, and so on. In 'hard cases' judges must also have in mind implications for the wider coherence and certainty of the law, not to speak of worries about the reception of a decision by other lawyers and academics, concerns about being overruled, and so on.

Modern secular law exists within a conceptual matrix where any deployment of authority is liable to be questioned or challenged on many levels, and requires justification and reasoned explanation. The contested legitimacy that attaches to the exercise of power is derived from political models which are themselves contentious. Constitutional arrangements where different forms of power are assigned to different organs of state inevitably give rise to territorial disputes over boundaries and over the right to draw boundaries. Law's authority derives from its occupation of a ritualised, quasi-sacred space in which the coercive power of the state is enacted, but modern secular law is also committed to ideals of equality and justice, attained through transparent reasoning open to the public gaze. Law may be partially hidden behind the veil of ritual and majesty but it is also the theatre of reason in action. The deployment of power also takes place as political theatre, and is subject to layers of media analysis and re-representation.

One of the ideologies of 'judge-made' law is that it evolves pragmatically and adapts to the variety of circumstances with which it is confronted. The means that the language in which the law labels the world has evolved with the cumulative experience of law, and has stood the test of time. Law should evolve in a consistent, incremental manner as the unfolding of an underlying set of established principles and modes of analysis. In this way law is both grounded in reason and as far as possible predictable. However, this intertwining of the language of law with the operations of the world requires also that law maintain its distance from everyday language and its autonomy in relation to it, otherwise its value as an objective tool of analysis will be compromised. Law therefore must stipulate what its own terms mean and maintain and protect those meanings, and also retain authority over how meanings are assigned to texts. The language of law in this sense should operate as an ideal language, one that is internally coherent, and which consists, like an ideal language of science, of terms which correspond to precisely defined concepts.

The liberal view of law sees law and its language as dialectically open and closed, with external criticism maintaining a balance between these two features of the system. Law is moved forwards by social criticism, academic commentary and democratically motivated reform of the law, but law's autonomy is necessary as a safeguard of basic rights and freedoms under the rule of law. The language of law must therefore mediate between the need for consistency, coherence and internal semantic order, and external demands for transparency, relevance and social accountability. This is an intrinsically uneven process of pragmatic compromise and 'muddling through'. Luhmann's model of law sees it as fundamentally a closed system, one which is open to its environment, society, only in unsystematic and contingent ways. Luhmann's language of the law is autonomous but non-referential; law speaks its own language to itself. Foucault's model of discourse offers a similar frame of understanding, except that the system resonates with a mixture of blindness and paranoia. Habermas likewise sees law as a closed system, but offers a model in which law is none the less systematically open, albeit indirectly, to democratic accountability. Habermas sees the autonomous language of law as nourished by the ideal features of lifeworld discourse, and is optimistic about its openness to progressive social change. Radical indeterminacy theorists see law as suffused with socio-political contestation: the autonomy that characterises law is no more than a screen behind which are hidden the true mechanisms and compulsions of law. Interpretation and legal language are therefore one of many sites of ideological contestation.

Part II

Selected Topics

5 Literal Meaning, the Dictionary and the Law

Introduction

In constitutional interpretation, 'originalism' makes the claim that 'the interpretation of the constitution should seek to effectuate, or at least be faithful to, the understanding of the constitutional provisions which can be historically attributed to its framers' (Marmor 2005: 155). This is not necessarily the same as claiming that the words should be given the meaning they had in their original context, as different sorts of historical materials become relevant in each case. In the first case, statements of intent surrounding the passing of the constitution would be relevant, for example as to what was meant by 'cruel and unusual punishment'. In the second case, contemporary dictionaries and other sources would be consulted to try to understand what was meant by words such as 'cruel' and 'unusual'. Constitutional originalism involves applying a reconstructed world view, whereas semantic originalism would require applying a reconstructed meaning. In practice, in constitutional interpretation it is hard to separate these two distinct forms of historical investigation, and semantic originalism is itself liable to blur with a contemporary plain meaning approach, since unless the text is puzzling on its face, the judge is unlikely to embark on an in-depth philological investigation. In any case, the principle of binding precedent (*stare decisis*) means that judges are rarely faced with an interpretative task involving a statutory text significantly removed in time from the present on which there are no previous relevant decisions.

Literal meaning, dictionaries and law

One overlapping area of concern between linguistics and law is the definition and status of literal meaning. Legal canons of interpretation make reference to this concept, and so do legal judgments. In law, there is a profusion of terminology in this area, which reflects both its centrality and its difficulty: 'clear' 'plain', 'literal', 'natural', 'unforced', 'meaning on its face', etc. It is also not clear which of many possible literal meanings is being referred to. On the linguistics side, there are terms such as 'literal', 'core', 'denotative', 'referential', 'decontextual', 'cognitive', 'lexical', 'invariant', 'conventional' and 'type' meaning. One strong piece of evidence for the difficulty of these concepts is the quite startling silence of academic linguists on the definition and nature of literal meaning. All these concepts taken together are best understood as relational. They are used to designate by contrast another, more abstract, less immediate, derivative, implied, inferred or secondary meaning. The classic case of this is metaphor. In lexicography, the sub-meanings of a particular word are generally organised to reflect this ontological distinction. The concrete or non-metaphorical meaning is given first, and this is also generally assumed to be the historically prior one.

In the *New Oxford English Dictionary*, 'sheep' is defined with three basic meanings:

(i) A domesticated ruminant mammal with a thick woolly coat [. . .]. It is kept in flocks for its wool or meat, and is proverbial for its tendency to follow others in the flock; (ii) A person who is too easily influenced or led; (iii) A person regarded as a protected follower of God.

This reflects the idea that concrete concepts gradually evolved higher, more abstract meanings and also a strong sense that concrete images underlie more abstract ones. But while this is appealing intuitively, it reflects largely unexamined historical and cognitive assumptions. In what sense is a rose first a concrete object, then a classification, or label for, those concrete objects, and finally a set of Romantic and emotional associations or connotations? To label a concrete object with a general term implies a profound form of abstraction, namely a class of such objects. Secondly, while we can in theory separate the literal from the metaphorical meanings of 'rose', we can equally deny that any such separation exists in all contexts. Gertrude Stein was commenting on this overdetermined Romantic meaning in her famous poem 'A rose is a rose is a rose' (Stein 1922). This plays with the loss of meaning associated with repetition (iteration) of a word, but also suggests the possibility of a new concrete meaning arising from the death by repetition of the cliché.

One tactic that courts sometimes employ when having difficulty with the meaning of an ordinary word is to consult a dictionary. For courts, dictionaries have several advantages over linguists as expert witnesses on the ordinary meanings of words. Consulting a dictionary is a familiar practice within the linguistic experience of lawyers, but asking a linguist is not. Dictionaries are created by professional lexicographers, and so can serve a court as a kind of surrogate expert witness. There is a wide choice of professionally edited dictionaries on the market, with differing definitional styles and contrasting organisation of many entries. The dictionary is also obviously cheaper and more readily available, and its point of view can be ignored if unhelpful, or a second opinion sought. Most importantly the organisation of a dictionary entry is also untainted by direct exposure to the linguistic facts of the case in their social setting. The dictionary, more so than justice itself, is blind to the moral rights and wrongs of the case, whereas an expert witness testifying as to the meaning of words at issue does so with notice or knowledge of the wider legal conflict.

In *Camden (Marquis) v Inland Revenue Commissioners* (1914), the Court of Appeal stated unequivocally that (at 649–50):

> It is the duty of the court to construe a statute according to the ordinary meaning of the words used, necessarily referring to dictionaries or other literature for the sake of informing itself as to the meaning of any words, but any evidence on the question is wholly inadmissible.

In the headnote of the case the blunt statement appears that 'expert evidence as to the meaning of ordinary English words in a modern Act of Parliament of general application is not admissible'.

The point had arisen in the case because counsel for the appellant had sought to introduce an expert from within the trade, a valuer or land surveyor, to give a definition of what was commonly meant by 'nominal rent', since the determination by the court that the lessor had been in receipt of nominal rent had triggered liability to additional taxes on the reversion of the lease. The valuer had been asked under cross-examination whether the term had a technical meaning and had answered 'yes', but there had been argument about the admissibility of this evidence. Counsel for the appellant argued that the court should seek external help as to the understanding of the term, citing Lord Blackburn in *River Wear Commissioners v Atkinson* (1877) to the effect that in construing a document (at 763):

> in all cases the object is to see what is the intention expressed by the words used. But from the imperfection of language it is impossible to know what that intention is without inquiring further, and seeing what the circumstances were with reference to which the words were used and what was the object appearing from those circumstances which the person using them had in view, for the meaning of words varies according to the circumstances with respect to which they were used.

Counsel contended that this had been approved by Lord Halsbury in *Butterley Co. v New Hucknall Colliery Co.* (1910, at 382). Counsel sought to show that the words 'nominal rent' had for land surveyors a specialised meaning, namely, 'a rent not intended to represent the true rental value'. It was an established principle that courts could take expert evidence as to the meaning of written instruments (*Shore v Wilson* 1842) and a statute was such an instrument. In *Robertson v Jackson* (1845) the words were 'in turn to deliver', which had special meaning in Algiers and 'evidence was admitted to prove what it was'. The court was bound to determine in what sense the words were being used, that is, popular or legal (though the valuer's specialised opinion would appear to be neither). Counsel conceded that the court would none the less make the determination as to whether this specialised meaning was the meaning intended in the Act.

This argument was given short shrift by the court (Cozens-Hardy MR, at 647), in a statement that would horrify the average sociolinguist:

> I thought that a modern Act of Parliament was framed in language which is intelligible to everybody, and which applies not to any local custom or consideration of that kind, but to the whole of Great Britain (and I think beyond that, elsewhere, but at any rate to the whole of England).

There was no case law justification for this in relation to the language of a statute, and it was 'really not relevant to consider what a particular branch of the public may or may not understand to be the meaning of those words' (at 647). The court was entitled to use standard reference works and authoritative dictionaries 'which refer to the sources in which the interpretation which they give to the words of the English language is to be found', but there was no rule of interpretation requiring the court to check to see if there was also an additional technical meaning (at 648). The rule was less absolute in non-statutory documents such as wills where there might be a need to 'consult literary authorities as to what is the meaning of words defining a particular class or body of men' (at 648), but it would be 'of the worst example' if the application were to succeed because of evidence given as to the meaning 'which a certain branch of the community attaches to these particular words' (at 649). Swinfen Eady LJ made clear the distinction between public statutory language and private statutes or contracts: 'It is a public Act of Parliament, and the Court must take judicial cognisance of the language used without evidence' (at 651). Bennion, in commentary on this case, calls this decision 'borderline', on the grounds that if 'nominal rent' was indeed a valuer's technical term, then 'it would have been arguable that Parliament's intention was to use it in the technical sense' (Bennion 2002: 1047).

The principles enunciated in this case rule out calling an academic linguist to testify as to the meaning of a term in a statute. To allow another class of expert to offer opinions on these questions would be to cede a central area of competence from the bench to the academic linguist. Cozens-Hardy defines two basic kinds of English, namely the public language of the statute, which may be technical legal terms or words which are common to the whole domain of the law, as this was somewhat awkwardly defined in the case: 'the whole of Great Britain (and I think beyond that, elsewhere, but at any rate to the whole of England)'. Specialised sub-group language, customary language, terms for classes of individuals and the language of particular trades which appear in wills and contracts may be the subject of expert evidence. This symbolises a deep underlying ideology of the common law, that it had replaced customary and local law and practices, and unified its domain as a single universe of meaning.

In this context, a dictum from Lord Reid is frequently cited, namely that the 'meaning of an ordinary word of the English language is not a question of law' (*Brutus v Cozens* 1973, at 861). This issue arose in relation to S 5 of the Public Order Act 1936:

> Any person who in any public place [. . .] uses threatening, abusive or insulting words or behaviour with intent to provoke a breach of the peace or whereby a breach of the peace is likely to be occasioned, shall be guilty of an offence.

The context was an anti-Apartheid demonstration which briefly disrupted the Wimbledon tennis tournament during a match in which a South African was playing. The House of Lords ruled that the definition of 'insulting' was not a technical matter of law, and the magistrates had been entitled to apply their own understanding of the term, provided that it was a reasonable one. However, the general scope of the dictum is unclear, as for example the court did make a legally grounded observation about the kind of definition that was relevant (at 858):

> An insult is something which is ad hominem – conduct aimed at or intended at a person's susceptibilities. A strict definition is required here for otherwise all kinds of conduct could lead to conviction of this quite serious offence. It is to be remembered that this is a civil liberty question and the ambit of the section should be confined. The Divisional Court's construction would be correct if section 5 were to read 'behavior which affronts other people, and evidences a disrespect or contempt for *them*'. (emphasis in original)

It was argued against this by the respondent that dictionary definitions of 'insult' show 'the element of giving deliberate offence in a contemptuous manner'. Counsel referenced a wide range of dictionaries, arguing that the definitions showed that 'there is more than just attacking a person's dignity but there is also the element of contempt towards him'. The appellant had by interrupting play been 'contemptuous of those present and was being deliberately offensive to them' (at 859–60).

Lord Reid stated that he could not see the point of law at issue, and then made the statement that the 'meaning of an ordinary word of the English language is not a question of law' (at 861). But this statement has to be taken in its context, including the next sentence which clarifies that the 'proper construction of a statute is a question of law'. What Lord Reid was arguing is that no special meaning of 'insulting' seemed to be at stake in this case, but that argument was grounded in legal considerations which determined the relevance of discussion about the meaning of the word. There was no evidence to show that the word was being used in an unusual sense:

> It is for the tribunal which decides the case to consider, not as law but as fact, whether in the whole circumstances the words of the statute do or do not as a matter of ordinary usage of the English language cover or apply to the facts [. . .] If it is alleged that the tribunal has reached a wrong decision then there can be a question of law but only of a limited character. The question would normally be whether their decision was unreasonable in the sense that no tribunal acquainted with the ordinary use of language could reasonably reach that decision. (at 861)

However, Lord Reid then went further in defence of this position (at 861–2), one which cast doubt on the usefulness of the dictionary:

> When considering the meaning of a word one often goes to a dictionary. There one finds other words set out. And if one wants to pursue the matter and find the meaning of those other words the dictionary will give the meaning of those other words in still further words which often include the word for whose meaning one is searching.

The court could in theory 'act as a dictionary' by directing the tribunal 'to take some word or phrase other than the word in the statute' and asking it to 'consider whether that word or phrase applied to or covered the facts proved'. But the courts had been 'warned time and again not to substitute other words for the words of a statute', and this was good advice, since few words had 'exact synonyms', their 'overtones are almost always different'. Alternatively, the court could 'frame a definition', but this led again to further words in need of explanation. Definitions were sometimes provided in statutes, and these were often problematic, and further: 'the purpose of a definition is to limit or modify the ordinary meaning of a word and the court is not entitled to do that'. In conclusion therefore the question of law was 'whether it was unreasonable to hold that the appellant's behavior was not insulting' and to that question there was only one answer: 'No' (at 861–2).

As the Divisional Court had expressed a view as to the relevant meaning of 'insulting', and pointed in particular to the hostile reaction of the crowd, Lord Reid felt obliged to consider the matter further. The Divisional Court had not offered a full definition, but decided that the relevant meaning was 'behaviour which affronts other people, and evidences a disrespect or contempt for their rights, behaviour which reasonable persons would foresee is likely to cause resentment or protest'. For Lord Reid, this set the limits of permissible speech too narrowly. The legal limits on free speech were 'all limits easily recognisable by the ordinary man', such that '[f]ree speech is not impaired by ruling them out'. There could be no definition of insult, but 'an ordinary sensible man knows an insult when he sees or hears it' (at 862). Lord Reid concluded as follows (at 863):

> Parliament has given no indication that the word is to be given any unusual meaning. Insulting means insulting and nothing else. If I had to decide, which I do not, whether the appellant's conduct insulted the spectators in this case, I would agree with the magistrates. The spectators may have been very angry and justly so. The appellant's conduct was deplorable. Probably it ought to be punishable. But I cannot see how it insulted the spectators.

This judgment is framed in terms of common sense and the ordinary person's view of what a word means. But at a higher level it is framed in terms of discussion of whether an issue of law or fact is at stake. Since the House of Lords decided that it was a matter of fact whether the behaviour fell within the meaning of 'insulting' or not, then there were no grounds to set aside the magistrates' determination, since it was not evidently unreasonable. At a still higher level of abstraction, Lord Reid invoked the policy desire not to curtail freedom of speech except where properly defined exceptions were identified, and in so doing also pointed to his own separation of his personal view and his view as a judge. The dictum arises out of the interpretative politics of the case; its general applicability is thus subject to potential constraints, but it can also be cited as a free-standing maxim if the interpretative politics of a further case demand it. But as a statement of legal principle intended to explain in general how the law deals with statutory language it has little or no value (Elliott 1989; Bennion 1989).

The idea of literal meaning frequently emerges as important in a case where there is a perceived divide between two possible meanings available to, or forced upon, the attention of the reader/interpreter. This may often be a question of the extension of a term from a concrete domain to a more abstract one. A simple example of this arose in the famous case of *Olmstead v United States* (1928), discussed in White (1990: 141ff). In the United States Constitution, the Fourth Amendment states that:

> The right of the people to be secure in their persons, houses, papers, and effects, against unreasonable searches and seizures shall not be violated; and no Warrant shall issue except where is probable cause, supported by Oath or affirmation and particularly describing the place to be searched and the persons or things to be seized.

In this case federal and state officials tapped the telephone of suspected bootleggers. They did so without probable cause or a warrant, which would normally be required to enter and search someone's property. Evidence obtained in this manner was material in gaining a conviction. On appeal the question at issue was whether the wire-tapping had violated the defendant's Fourth Amendment rights. If this right had been violated then the evidence would be excluded and the conviction quashed. The court ruled by a majority that the wire-tap was not a search, with the leading judgment written by Judge Taft. Taft argued that the Amendment required the search to be of 'material things' such as 'the person, the house, his papers or his effects'. The warrant that was required was obliged to specify 'the place to be searched and the persons or things to be seized'. There had been no entry or seizure (at 464):

> It is plainly within the words of the Amendment to say that the unlaw-
> ful rifling by a government agent of a sealed letter is a search and seizure
> of the sender's papers of effects. [. . .] The Amendment does not forbid
> what was done here. There was no searching. There was no seizure. The
> evidence was secured by the use of the sense of hearing and that only.
> There was no entry of the houses or offices of the defendants.

The new technology lay outside the purview of the statute (at 465):

> By the invention of the telephone 50 years ago, and its application for
> the purpose of extending communications, one can talk with another at
> a far distant place. The language of the amendment cannot be extended
> and expanded to include telephone wires, reaching to the whole world
> from the defendant's house or office. The intervening wires are not part
> of his house or office, any more than are the highways along which they
> are stretched.

Justice Taft stressed the location of the interceptors outside the house, and ascribed an intent to communicate into the public domain (at 466):

> The reasonable view is that one who installs in his house a telephone
> instrument with connecting wires intends to project his voice to those
> quite outside, and that the wires beyond his house, and messages while
> passing over them, are not within the protection of the Fourth
> Amendment. Here those who intercepted the projected voices were not
> in the house of either party to the conversation.

A dissenting opinion by Justice Brandeis (1856–1941) still resonates today. Brandeis argued that constitutional interpretation required a broader style of interpretation: one took the language of the statute as expounding general principles, not specific, time-bound prohibitions. Each constitutional provision 'must be capable of wider application than the mischief which gave it birth'. The provisions were not 'ephemeral enactments, designed to meet passing occasions'. As Chief Justice Marshall had said, the provisions of the Constitution were 'designed to approach immortality as nearly as human institutions can approach it' (at 473). Looking into the future, Brandeis evoked the possibility of almost unlimited government scrutiny of the private sphere, including the human mind itself (at 473–4):

> Subtler and more far-reaching means of invading privacy have become available to the government. Discovery and invention have made it possible for the government, by means far more effective than stretching upon the rack, to obtain disclosure in court of what is whispered in the closet. Moreover, 'in the application of a Constitution, our contemplation cannot be only of what has been, but of what may be.' The progress of science in furnishing the government with means of espionage is not likely to stop with wire tapping. Ways may some day be developed by which the government, without removing papers from secret drawers, can reproduce them in court, and by which it will be enabled to expose to a jury the most intimate occurrences of the home. Advances in the psychic and related sciences may bring means of exploring unexpressed beliefs, thoughts and emotions.

Taft's judgment can be understood as a literalist or plain meaning judgment; Justice Brandeis rejected this 'unduly literal' style of construction, and argued that the general spirit of the Constitution of the United States should be taken into account and the central value be placed on the 'right to be let alone', which was 'the most comprehensive of rights and the right most valued by civilized men' (at 478).

Can the lexicographers help us take a view on the correctness of this decision? A late nineteenth-century law dictionary defines a search in the criminal law context as follows (Black 1891: 1069):

> An examination of a man's house or other buildings or premises, or of his person, with a view to the discovery of contraband or illicit or stolen property, or some evidence of guilt to be used in the prosecution of a criminal action for some crime or offense with which he is charged.

The definition in the 1910 edition is unchanged. This definition if applied to the case might be taken as conclusive, since it only mentions physical searches. Alternatively, it might be seen as merely framing the question at issue, namely whether, given that law conventionally defines a search in terms of a physical intervention into the private sphere, the constitutional protection should be extended to an indirect and less tangible trespass/search. In lexicographic terms, a search is generally understood first as a physical search. The *Oxford English Dictionary* gives this basic meaning for the noun: 'The action or an act of searching; examination or scrutiny for the purpose of finding a person or thing'. The contrast between the material and abstract comes through more strongly in the definition of the verb:

1. trans. To go about (a country or place) in order to find, or to ascertain the presence or absence of, some person or thing; to explore in quest of some object.
2. To look through, examine internally (a building, an apartment, a receptacle of any kind) in quest of some object concealed or lost.
3. a. To examine (a person) by handling, removal of garments, and the like, to ascertain whether any article (usually, something stolen or contraband) is concealed in his clothing.
   [. . .]
4. To peruse, look through, examine (writings, records) in order to discover whether certain things are contained there.
5. a. With immaterial object: To investigate, make oneself thoroughly acquainted with; to examine rigorously (one's own heart, thoughts, etc.); to examine, penetrate the secrets of (another's mind or thoughts).

The lexicographer and the court share common ground in understanding the basic meaning of 'search' as a physical search. For the lexicographer, there is an implication of a range of meanings, from the material, physical search to 'the immaterial object'. Meanings (1) to (4) evoke different types of physical search, with the most abstract being (4), the searching of a text or written record. However, the facts of *Olmstead* fall in between, as there is no direct physical search, but the searching is not the abstract kind involved in meaning (5), where the investigation or becoming acquainted is in relation to an immaterial object, contextualised as profound introspection or the penetrating contemplation of the soul of another.

The court did not consult a dictionary in *Olmstead*, and the definition cited above is in the current *OED* edition. The organisation of the dictionary entry reflects the concrete–abstract dichotomy but, like the Constitution, does not directly cover the case at issue. The closest point of connection to the facts of the case would be to apply the entry by analogy. A 'search' includes examining linguistic objects to discover things that are 'contained' within them. Spoken words are linguistic objects which can be recorded and written down. However, Brandeis, in commenting on the possibility of mind-reading technology, did bring in the type (5) meaning, applying a classic 'slippery-slope' argument. If mind-reading by the government without a warrant is forbidden (which it surely would be), then steps along that road should be treated with extreme caution. He places the facts of *Olmstead* in between the physical search and mind-reading; if there is a continuum between physical and mental, and both ends are subject to the need for a warrant, then logically every point between is also subject to the same condition.

This case can be framed as a classic jurisprudential clash of literal versus figurative meaning, but the figurative meaning that is at issue in the case is of a highly specific kind. It can also be understood as one where narrow (strict) as against broad (purposive) construction was preferred. An alternative framing is in terms of a dispute about the priority to be given to the punishment of wrong-doing when set against the protection of freedom and privacy. The problem comes in understanding how these different levels can be linked. In the context of this particular case, the argument for a literal reading is aligned to a strict reading, and these two in turn are aligned with the favouring of punishment over the right to privacy in this case. This set of associations between literal meaning, strict construction and punitive adjudication arises in this case, but its generality is open to question. As Hutchinson remarks (2000: 333), '[c]ontrary to received wisdom, the more expansive or flexible interpretation does not necessarily correlate with the most liberal or progressive outcome'.

Textualism in US jurisprudence

The interpretation of written constitutions as opposed to ordinary statutes is often presumed to involve a more active, imaginative style of construction. However, in *The Tempting of America*, Robert Bork, whose nomination by President Reagan to the Supreme Court was rejected by the United States Senate in 1987, frames this as inviting politics into the domain of legal adjudication. Politics is a constant threat to professional and academic disciplines since it 'invariably tries to dominate another discipline and use it for politics'. When a judge succumbs to this temptation, he or she 'has begun to rule where a legislator should' (Bork 1990: 1). For Bork, either there is autonomy and integrity, or there is a political free-for-all (Bork 1990: 2):

> Either the Constitution and statutes are law, which means that their principles are known and control judges, or they are malleable texts that judges may rewrite to see that particular groups or political causes win.

However, Bork concedes that 'judges to some extent must make law every time they decide a case, but it is minor, interstitial lawmaking' (Bork 1990: 5).

This powerful trend in constitutional interpretation is known as 'textualism', and is often associated with a conservative reaction against the judicial activism of reformist Supreme Courts since 1945. The dominant figure in this trend is Justice Antonin Scalia. From the textualist point of view, these courts, notably the so-called 'Warren court' (named after Earl Warren, chief justice 1953–69), tended to see their job as applying constitutional provisions in broad-brush strokes, furthering a progressive social agenda, and favouring federal jurisdiction in disputes over states-rights. One high point of this liberal policy making was the post-Warren decision in *Roe v Wade* (1973) where the court found that state criminal abortion laws 'violate the Due Process Clause of the Fourteenth Amendment, which protects against state action the right to privacy, including a woman's qualified right to terminate her pregnancy'.

Scalia rejects the mischief rule, or any other creative, flexible or purposive approach. This emerges in his commentary on some much-discussed key cases. In the *Church of the Holy Trinity v United States* (1892), a federal statute (The Alien Contract Labor Act 1885) had made it unlawful for any person to 'in any way assist or encourage the importation or migration of any alien [. . .] into the United States [. . .] under contract or agreement [. . .] made previous to the importation or migration of such alien [. . .] to perform labor or service of any kind in the United States'. The church in question had brought a minister from England. The Supreme Court reversed the decision of the lower court, holding that this had violated the law. It reasoned that it could not have been the intention of Congress to prevent the importation of Christian ministers (at 458–9):

> This is not the substitution of the will of the judge for that of the legislator; for frequently words of general meaning are used in a statute, words broad enough to include an act in question, and yet a consideration of the whole legislation, or of the circumstances surrounding its enactment, or of the absurd results which follow from giving such broad meaning to the words, makes it unreasonable to believe that the legislator intended to include the particular act.

The court drew in its decision on the notion that the United States was a Christian nation. Scalia's comment is straightforward: 'the act was within the letter of the statute and was therefore within the statute: end of case' (Scalia 1997: 20).

An important case in looking at literal meaning is *John Angus Smith v United States* (1993), where in effect two potential literal readings were in competition. Smith offered to trade an automatic weapon (MAC-10) for cocaine and was arrested by an undercover police officer. Title 18 U.S.C. S 924(c)(1) requires specific penalties if the defendant 'during and in relation to [a] drug trafficking crime uses [. . .] a firearm'. The Court of Appeals in *United States v John Angus Smith* (1992) upheld Smith's conviction and sentence as the 'plain language' did not impose a requirement that a firearm be used as a weapon. Trading the firearm was a way of using a firearm as understood by the statute. Case law conflicted on the interpretation of this statute, with the Court of Appeals for the Ninth Circuit holding for example that trading a gun was not 'use of a firearm' (*United States v Phelps* 877 F.2d 28 1989). The Court of Appeals disagreed with the decision in Phelps (at 4):

> We believe the Phelps opinion's stress on a defendant's alleged intentions to use the weapon offensively is incorrect. The plain language of the

statute supplies no such requirement [. . .] and in this circuit, the plain meaning of the statute controls 'unless the language is ambiguous or leads to absurd results, in which case a court may consult the legislative history and discern the true intent of Congress.' [. . .] We see no ambiguity in section 924(c)(1) and disagree with the conclusion that use in relation to a drug trafficking crime somehow excludes use in trade for drugs.

The Appeals court added (at 5) that the appellant's argument was 'particularly puzzling in the light of our position that violations of section 924(c)(1) do not require that firearms be "fired, brandished, or even displayed during the drug trafficking offense"'.

The Supreme Court upheld the decision, on the grounds that any non-technical word or a word not specifically defined in the statute should be construed 'in accord with its ordinary or natural meaning'. The majority quoted definitions from Webster's (2nd edition, 1939) and Black's *Law Dictionary* (6th edition, 1990) in support of its claim that 'to use' had a range of meanings including 'to employ', 'to utilize', 'to derive service from'. The words 'as a weapon' did not appear on the statute (at 229):

Had Congress intended S 924(c)(1) to require proof that the defendant not only used his firearm but used it in a specific manner – as a weapon – it could have so indicated in the statute. However, Congress did not. The fact that the most familiar example of 'us[ing] [. . .] a firearm' is 'use' as a weapon does not mean that the phrase excludes all other ways in which a firearm might be used.

The dissenting opinion was led by Justice Scalia (in a court which divided 6–3). He used the analogy of using a cane as an adornment in the hallway to show that some 'uses' lay outside the normal scope of the verb (at 242):

When someone asks 'Do you use a cane?' he is not inquiring whether you have your grandfather's silver handled walking stick on display in the hall; he wants to know whether you walk with a cane. Similarly, to speak of 'using a firearm' is to speak of using it for its distinctive purpose, i.e., as a weapon. To be sure, 'one can use a firearm in a number of ways' [. . .], including as an article of exchange, just as one can 'use' a cane as a hall decoration – but that is not the ordinary meaning of 'using' the one or the other.

Scalia distinguished between possible use and ordinary use (at 242):

The Court does not appear to grasp the distinction between how a word can be used and how it ordinarily is used. It would, indeed, be 'both reasonable and normal to say that petitioner "used" his MAC-10 in his drug trafficking offense by trading it for cocaine.' It would also be reasonable and normal to say that he 'used' it to scratch his head. When one wishes to describe the action of employing the instrument of a firearm for such unusual purposes, 'use' is assuredly a verb one could select. But that says nothing about whether the ordinary meaning of the phrase 'uses a firearm' embraces such extraordinary employments. It is unquestionably not reasonable and normal, I think, to say simply 'do not use firearms' when one means to prohibit selling or scratching with them.

The principle of 'lenity' requires that where a criminal statute is ambiguous the court should take a narrow construction in favor of the defendant. However, the majority argued (at 239) that the mere possibility of 'articulating a narrower construction did not make the rule of lenity applicable'. The petitioner's use of a weapon fell 'squarely' within common usage and the relevant dictionary definitions. Further, Congress had shown that it positively wanted to include such transactions by its language in S 924(d) which criminalised both 'belligerent and non-belligerent' uses of firearms, including those for 'barter or commerce'(at 223).

The dissent argued that the majority had failed to understand the distinction between how a word can be used and how it is ordinarily used, so that to speak of using a weapon is to speak of using it for 'its distinctive purpose', as opposed to scratching one's head (at 242 fn. 1):

> The ordinary meaning of 'uses a firearm' does not include using it as an article of commerce. I think it perfectly obvious, for example, that the objective falsity requirement would not be satisfied if a witness answered 'no' to a prosecutor's inquiry whether he had ever 'used a firearm', even though he had once sold his grandfather's Enfield rifle to a collector.

Disputing the majority's reading of S 924(d), the dissent argues that (at 247 fn. 4):

> [s]tretching language in order to write a more effective statute than Congress devised is not an exercise we should indulge in. But in any case, the ready ability to use a gun that is at hand as a weapon is perhaps one of the reasons the statute sanctions not only using a firearm, but carrying one. Here, however, the Government chose not to indict under that provision.

For Scalia, this decision was literal-minded nonsense, since the ordinary, contextually available meaning of the word 'uses', combined with the principle of 'lenity', gave a clear right answer in this case. Scalia thus denies a link between textualism and literalism, since a literal reading may in some contexts do violence to ordinary usage. Scalia reasoned in this case like an ordinary language philosopher, teasing out a reasonable meaning by thought-experiments in usage. But this approach also makes Scalia's textualism look somewhat like a very narrow form of the 'mischief rule'.

Brisbin (1997: 330) characterises the differences between the more originalist Bork and the more textualist Scalia as follows:

> First, Scalia has been less confident than Bork that the original meaning is knowable and can be correctly applied by busy judges. He has stated that original intent is captured by the words of the Constitution and has to be respected, but he has regarded further exploration of the meaning of language as difficult and sometimes involving discretionary choices.

Secondly, Scalia recognises the profound effect of precedents on how the Constitution is read, and therefore that 'some words [. . .] lack an original meaning and that some clauses are open-ended and contain an evolutionary element' (Brisbin 1997: 330–1). Further, Scalia recognises that in a democracy law cannot rest on the traditional moral base of the Constitution, whereas Bork has 'harshly derived the moral relativism of contemporary intellectuals and judges' (Brisbin 1997: 331).

Under the influence of Scalia's textualism, the use of dictionaries has become increasingly important in recent Supreme Court jurisprudence (see Garner 2003). Thumma and Kirchmeier (1999) object to the lack of principles and guidelines governing the use of dictionaries. Similarly, Werbach (1994) denies that dictionaries are as 'neutral' or 'reductive' as the court seems to presuppose, and as sources external to the legal process cannot be expected to throw light on the meaning of statutory terms. Dictionaries are fundamentally indeterminate, in that they frequently offer more than one meaning for a word, and cannot capture the full contextual meaning of a word in a statute, since meaning in its fullest sense does not exist outside context.

Dictionaries and linguists

In a 1995 conference held between academic lawyers and linguists one of the questions put to the linguists by the lawyers was 'What have you guys got against dictionaries?' ([Conference Proceedings] 1995: 823). In a case studied by a team of three linguists and a lawyer, the question was whether the Pro-Life Action Network (PLAN) a network of anti-abortion activists engaging in a campaign of violent disruption against abortion clinics, was an 'enterprise' as that word was used in the Racketeer Influenced and Corrupt Organizations Act (RICO, 1988, S 1962c). The specific provision of RICO at issue stated:

It shall be unlawful for any person employed by or associated with any
enterprise engaged in, or the activities of which affect, interstate or
foreign commerce, to conduct or participate, directly or indirectly, in the
conduct of such enterprise's affairs through a pattern of racketeering
activity or through collection of an unlawful debt.

Cunningham et al. (1994: 1563) put the case for the superiority of linguistic
analysis of meaning over traditional lexicography as follows:

Unfortunately, compared to the analysis of a particular textual problem
by a trained linguist, dictionaries are a crude and frequently unreliable
aid to word meaning and usage. In fact, for one of the three cases [con-
cerning the definition of the word 'enterprise'], the leading dictionaries
have definitions that differ exactly as the parties differ over the meaning
of the statutory term, and thus provide no objective way of resolving
that dispute over ordinary language meaning.

The linguist's analysis by contrast 'articulates linguistic distinctions that all
members of the relevant speech community can recognize once they are
brought to conscious attention' (Cunningham et al. 1994: 1563). The courts,
however, have been reluctant to acknowledge the relevance of evidence produced by linguists, whether through corpus methods, formal analysis or social
surveys, where the issue is the interpretation of statutory language (Kaplan
et al. 1995; Harris and Hutton 2007: 187–92). The dictionary definitions
studied by Cunningham et al. seem to have precisely reflected the definitional
dilemma confronted in the case, and it is far from clear what additional linguistic facts of the matter could be brought to bear to reduce that indeterminate applicability to a yes–no certainty.

National Organization for Women v Scheidler (1994) has a complex history
of litigation beginning in 1991 and including three Supreme Court decisions.
It ended with a series of decisions between 2003 and 2007 undoing the original 'racketeering' finding of liability under RICO. The Supreme Court further
ruled that the 'class women's right to seek medical services from the clinics',
'the clinic's doctors rights to perform their jobs', and 'the clinics' rights to
conduct their business' did not constitute 'property' under the Hobbs Act 1951
(see [NOW] 2008; [PLAN] 2008; *National Organization for Women v Scheidler*
1994; *Scheidler v National Organization for Women* 2003, 2006).

Conclusion

From the judge's point of view, the dictionary is literally a handier guide to
meaning than the linguist. Unlike the linguist as expert witness, the dictionary
has no notice of the facts of the case. In this sense the dictionary entry is like

the text of the statute: it is 'closed' prior to the case and can be presented as neutral with respect to it. The dictionary is useful to the judge not because it can provide sociolinguistically accurate guidelines to follow, but because it offers an authority seen as objective and general. The dictionary strips language of its sociological and normative complexity, and is the external authority closest in spirit and form to the statute. Its entries are often divided into sub-sections with distinct meanings, with the help of which the judge can experiment with different framings of the interpretative problem. In this sense – for the judge at least – the linguist's manifold objections to the dictionary are beside the point, as the flaws in the dictionary from the linguist's point of view are precisely what make it a useful tool for the judge.

6 Representation, Reproduction and Intention

T-shirts and triads

On 1 November 2007, police officers from the Organized Crime and Triad Bureau in Hong Kong raided the lifestyle, furniture and design store known as G.O.D. This followed a story in the press (*Sing Pao Daily*, 30 October 2007) highlighting their 'illicit' products. At issue was primarily a T-shirt, though postcards were also seized. The T-shirt bore a logo which the police claimed was a reference to an illegal organised crime (or 'triad') group in Hong Kong, known as the 14K. Eighteen people were arrested under Hong Kong's Societies Ordinance (1949, amended in 1964), including the co-founder of the store, Douglas Yeung. The store specialises in puns, provocative slogans (including playing with the language and imagery of Maoism) and language games, often involving using Chinese (Cantonese) slang in interaction with English. A key marketing slogan adorning G.O.D. products is the English phrase 'Delay No More', a play on a taboo Cantonese expression meaning 'Fuck your mother.' Recently the owners also opened a 'Delay No Mall' shopping centre in a popular shopping district of Hong Kong.

The Hong Kong Special Administrative Region of the People's Republic of China was founded on 1 July 1997, bringing an end to British colonial rule. The colony had been formally established in 1842 following the First Anglo-Chinese war. Hong Kong has retained its common law legal system, status as a financial centre, socio-political system and civic culture. The Societies Ordinance is a colonial era law which requires clubs, organisations and associations to register with the police. The law also criminalises all aspects of triad societies, including the performing of any rituals, the attending of any meeting, and the possession of insignia and membership lists, S 20(2) states:

> Any person who is or acts as a member of a triad society or professes or claims to be a member of a triad society or attends a meeting of a triad society or who pays money or gives any aid to or for the purposes of the triad society or is found in possession of or has the custody or control of any books, accounts, writing, lists of members, seals, banners or insignia

of or relating to any triad society or to any branch of a triad society whether or not such society or branch is established in Hong Kong, shall be guilty of an offence and shall be liable on conviction on indictment.

Thus the arrests involved a potentially very serious criminal charge. The law in Hong Kong criminalises statements whereby someone simply claims membership of a triad society, without requiring the prosecution to prove that the defendant is actually a member. The logic of this is that whether individuals are members of not, they can use triad names and terminology to intimidate and extort 'protection money' or further other criminal aims. On the same day as the G.O.D. arrests, a schoolboy was arrested for claiming triad membership in an internet forum. The boy claimed to police that he had done it 'just for fun', but a police spokesman commented that '[c]laiming to be a member of a triad society is a crime in the physical world as well as in the cyber environment' (Lee and Wu 1997: C3).

The law also aims to prevent the circulation and depiction of triad symbols, and this aim is also promoted by censorship bodies in Hong Kong. Reference to triad symbols and codes is also banned in personalised licence plates. A mark will be refused registration if it is 'likely to be offensive to a reasonable person, or has a connotation offensive to good taste or decency', or if it 'refers to any triad title or nomenclature or otherwise has a triad connotation' (see [HK Government] 2008). For example, the number 426 refers to an office or rank within the hierarchy of the society, a so-called Red Pole 'enforcer'. Significantly, there is no 'reasonable person' test for the triad exclusion, as the 'reasonable person' cannot be presumed to have knowledge of triad culture, and an objection by the police expert is the standard applied. The Hong Kong Film Censorship Guidelines permit 'scenes showing triad ceremonies, rituals, hand signs and paraphernalia including cryptic poems and icons' and 'promotion or endorsement of triad society, triad activities or values', but only in 'Category III' films (i.e. those restricted to viewers aged 18 and over), and the guidelines forbid the 'glorification of the power of triads and membership in a triad society' ([TELA] 2007). None the less, triad gangster films are one of the main genres in Hong Kong cinema: some are alleged to be funded or produced by triads, or by those with triad connections.

The T-shirt in question did not reproduce the name of the triad society in the form in which it conventionally circulates, namely as '14K'. Rather it used formal Chinese characters(拾肆) in an unusual font to represent the numbers. These characters are generally reserved for formal contexts such as banknotes and cheques, where the everyday Chinese characters(十四) are too easily altered. The T-shirt thus read 拾肆 K instead of 14K. '14K' also refers to a standard of the purity of gold, that is, fourteen karat. Ultimately, the Department of Justice decided not to prosecute, and the store was given a warning, though police stressed that wearing the T-shirt could be a criminal offence.

Since the G.O.D. case did not go to trial, it is not clear how the law would have been applied. Hong Kong also has a so-called mini-constitution, the Basic Law (a national law of the People's Republic of China which establishes and regulates Hong Kong's political and legal order), and a Bill of Rights (Cap 383). Article 16 of the Bill of Rights echoes the Basic Law in guaranteeing freedom of expression, including 'in the form of art' or 'through any other media'. However, restrictions may be imposed for 'respects for the rights or reputations of others' (i.e. defamation law) and 'for the protection of national security or of public order (*ordre public*), or of public health or morals'. Opinion in Hong Kong was mixed, with some support for the police in their attack on any attempt to promote or glamorise triad culture, with analogies made with German laws forbidding Nazi insignia (Crawford and Gentle 2007). However, there were accusations that G.O.D. was being targeted because of its involvement in Hong Kong cultural and heritage politics. There was no suggestion that there was any actual connection between G.O.D. and any illegal organisation.

One theoretical issue raised by the case is authority over the meaning and status of a representation. The basis of puns, wordplay and other linguistic games is often a play with accountability. Sexual innuendo can only function if the addressee also has a 'dirty mind', cooperates with, or is trapped into, recognising a subversive or taboo meaning. Thus if someone is offended by the 'Delay No More' slogan, it is because they themselves (or a third party who has 'explained' or pointed to the underlying meaning) have supplied a link from the English slogan to the taboo Cantonese phrase. In that sense, the Cantonese phrase is at an interpretative remove from the overt or public meaning. The author of the slogan could of course be understood to have invited the link (since they also take credit for the wordplay itself) but it retains a quality of deniability, since to complete the link some act of outside agency or interpretative intervention is required. In the case of the 14K, the T-shirt's 'underlying' meaning is retrievable in the same way, though the association with 'gold' adds a further possible dimension of deniability. Since it is the addressee who completes the triad link, the addressee might also, or even alternatively, have made the link to gold jewellery, a meaning which was also claimed for the T-shirt by the store. Just as the author of the statement must balance proximity to the message to be inferred with deniability of the link, so interpreters may be faced with a dilemma arising from a fear that they may impute 'bad faith' without good cause. Litigation over the slogan 'BONG HiTS 4 JESUS' displayed on a banner by US high school students reached the Supreme Court in the First Amendment case *Morse v Frederick* (2007).

One accusation made against the police is that they lacked a sense of humour. This can be translated as a claim that the police failed to recognise the deniable element implicit in the agency given to the addressee, who must accept the invitation to re-read the Chinese characters in a triad context. Instead of a mobile and playful accountability in the assignment of meaning, and the framing as a designer item, the police took the T-shirt as simply a direct reference to a triad name, taking differences in the way the name was written as irrelevant. This was a police-imposed collapse of the distinction between a representation and one of its possible underlying meanings, rather than a 'reasonable interpreter' meaning. This raises the question of how to define a 'proximate' link between any two meanings, and criteria for when the derived or underlying meaning is 'remote' enough to free the author of threshold agency and therefore of criminal responsibility.

The logic behind the official view is that the law requires the police to prevent the circulation of triad symbols, and they should not make exceptions for certain classes of people or commercial undertakings; further, in the wrong context, the T-shirt could arguably be used for intimidation regardless of the humorous gap between the conventional written form and the 'fancy' one. Against this, the view was expressed that the police action would have a 'chilling effect' on artistic freedom, and on the rights of artists to push at or question socially significant boundaries. Ironically, very few of the offending T-shirts had been sold before the raid: they are now a collector's item.

Genuine fakes: the counterfeit artist

One can compare the G.O.D. case instructively with the prosecution of an American artist, J. S. G. ('Stephen') Boggs, in London in 1986. Boggs developed a form of performance art in which he offered banknotes which he drew himself at face value as a form of 'payment' in shops, and then kept the receipt and the change. One form this took was as follows: a dealer would be alerted that the note had been accepted, and the artwork was completed when the dealer bought the note and it was mounted with the receipt and the change, if any (see the artist's website, www.jsgboggs.com). In this way the art form mimicked or parodied the circulation of real currency notes, and offered a commentary on how value is ascribed to representations. Boggs was prosecuted under S 18 of the Forgery and Counterfeiting Act, which makes it a crime to 'reproduce on any substance whatsoever, and whether or not on the correct scale, any British currency note or any part of a British currency note'. The notes were not exact copies and included humorous amendments (including a six pound note), and were drawn on only one side of the paper. A note drawn by Boggs replaced the metaphysical statement 'I promise to pay the bearer on demand the sum of 1 pound' with the deconstructive 'I promise to promise to promise to promise' (Weschler 1999: 14). The notes did, however, have real serial numbers, which seemed to make conviction inevitable, since a serial number is undeniably 'part' of a currency note.

Boggs's exchanges with the arresting officer included the following (Robertson 1999: 269):

Chief Inspector: But you agree that some of the items contain many if not all the detail of Bank of England currencies?

Boggs: A painting of a horse may contain depictions of details created by God, yet you would not place a saddle on that painting.

[. . .]

Chief Inspector: Did you, with your hand, with a pen, pencil or paint-brush, irrespective of the reasons, paint, draw, or colour this item?

Boggs: If you are asleep and you have a dream, are you then responsible for the creation of that dream? I have bled onto this piece of work.

In his arguments for the defence (see Robertson 1999: 262–81; Weschler 1999: 85–116), Geoffrey Robertson made the case that a reproduction was not always a 'reproduction'. He referred to René Magritte's *The Treachery Of Images* (*La trahison des images*, 1928–9), with its famous inscription under the drawing of a pipe, 'Ceci n'est pas une pipe' ('This is not a pipe'). He further argued the point with reference to Andy Warhol's depiction of Campbell soup cans: this was not a reproduction, but an image 'which makes people think about mass-production and common experiences and advertising messages, about being left on the shelf in a supermarket society'. The art critic Robert Hughes made a distinction between reproduction as exact copying and repro-duction as representation (Robertson 1999: 270–1). On this view, a represen-tation is an intervention involving artistic agency between the original and the representation. Unlike mechanical reproduction or copying, it breaks the chain of authorship/ownership between the original and the representation. In this sense Boggs had not 'reproduced' the banknote; rather it was a start-ing point for an autonomous artistic act.

Robertson writes that it was clear that the court, that is the judge, was completely unconvinced by these artistic arguments, and evidently regarded the case as open and shut. However, the trial was before a jury, which very rapidly returned a not-guilty verdict. Unlike the police in the G.O.D. case, the jury apparently took the parodic distance between the original (the Bank of England notes) and the representation (Boggs's drawing) as sufficiently wide, that is, they thought that the Treasury, which had brought the prose-cution after the police had declined to prosecute, lacked a sense of humour. The performative aspect of the art required a deliberate drawing of atten-tion to the gap between Boggs's notes and real money, and in so doing it inevitably had to 'reproduce' or 'represent' that money. The 14K T-shirt might also be said to have pointed to its own inauthenticity as a repre-sentation, by using non-conventional Chinese characters in an unusual font in a designer context. Another way to look at this is to speculate that the jury in the Boggs trial was concerned with a commonsense notion of 'intent', that is, the question of whether Boggs was a counterfeiter or a fraudster, whereas for the professional lawyers this was, under the law, strictly irrelevant.

In such cases, the law denies or collapses the distinction between an image and the reality it is deemed to depict (in these cases the 'true' name of the 14K, the genuine banknote). It denies the autonomy of the representation both in relation to what it represents and as 'art' or 'design', and discounts the playful movement back and forth between the 'real' and the 'image'.

Taboo language and 'images that wound'

On college campuses in the United States 'hate speech' controversies have arisen in relation to litigation over campus speech codes seeking to control public language. These are targeted at hostile use of racial epithets in particular, but cover a wide range of discriminatory language. In the United States context, the existence of a written Constitution with its the First Amendment guaranteeing freedom of speech means that in state universities such codes are liable to challenge in the courts. Problems in the definition of 'speech' are central to the case law explicating the First Amendment to the United States Constitution. This mandates that:

> Congress shall make no law respecting an establishment of religion, or prohibiting the free exercise thereof; or abridging the freedom of speech, or of the press; or the right of the people peaceably to assemble, and to petition the government for a redress of grievances.

The Supreme Court has been called upon several times to determine the constitutionality of state and federal laws which seek to ban the burning of the United States flag, that is, to decide whether the act of burning the national flag fell within the constitutional protection for free speech. In *Texas v Johnson* (1989) the court held that if the act of flag-burning could be seen as 'expressive conduct', then it could qualify for protection under the constitutional provision guaranteeing the right to free speech. In *Community for Creative Non-Violence v Watt* (1983), in which the question arose as to whether sleeping in a public park to protest against homelessness was protected as expressive speech, the Court of Appeals held that it was. But Justice Scalia, dissenting, took the opportunity 'flatly to deny that sleeping is or can ever be speech for First Amendment purposes' (at 622). The Supreme Court upheld the park's regulation against camping, on the grounds that while the sleeping may have been expressive speech, the regulation was a 'reasonable time, place, or manner restriction' on it. MacKinnon has argued that speech is fundamentally a form of social action, so that 'while the doctrinal distinction between speech and action is on one level obvious, on another level it makes little sense'. In terms of social inequality, 'discrimination does not divide into acts on one side and speech on the other' (MacKinnon 1993: 30–1).

In Austin's speech act theory, the conventional force of an utterance, if it is successfully taken up by the addressee, will lead to a certain result: if the minister states 'I now pronounce you man and wife', and all the surrounding circumstances are in order (the 'felicity conditions'), then the couple are in fact married. However, utterances also have other consequences, which may be special or contingent. This is termed 'perlocutionary effect', which is the effect of the utterance in the context, 'such effects being special to the circumstances of the utterance' (Austin 1970: 251). If I address a racially offensive remark to a member of the group conventionally the target of such remarks, then within Austin's framework I perform the illocutionary act of insulting or racially abusing them, and the reasonable observer would concur in holding me morally responsible and at least potentially liable under a speech code. But if I make what I – reasonably (but that is the point at issue) – believe to be a non-insulting remark, but it none the less causes offence, should a strict liability to addressee standard be applied?

This issue arose in 1999 when a senior white employee of the Washington DC city administration resigned after his use of the word 'niggardly' in the workplace caused offence, though he later returned in a different position. The employee had used the term in the context of stating the need for budgetary restraint, using the conventional dictionary meaning 'mean with money', 'stingy', 'ungenerous', and it was not suggested that he had consciously intended to use a racial insult. The question was discussed in the media in terms of linguistic correctness, with commentators arguing that no one should be held accountable for using the term in its correct meaning.

The *Concise Oxford Dictionary* gives the origin of 'niggardly' as a derivation from 'niggard': 'a parsimonious person, grudging giver', and suggests a link to 'niggle': 'spend time, be over-elaborate, on petty details; find fault in petty manner'. It gives a Scandinavian origin or etymology, and does not suggest a link to the meaning 'black'. This appeal to etymology and lexicographical norm clashed with a situated perception that this word was undesirable, since it clearly echoed a taboo form and therefore was capable of giving offence. If we see meaning as lying in the intention of the speaker, then the utterance was likewise to be viewed as harmless in this case, since there was in general no suggestion that the speaker was being consciously racist. The hearers' taking offence, on this view, must then be seen as arising from ignorance of the 'correct' meaning of the word 'niggardly' (see Kennedy 2003: 94–7; Woodlee 1999). A different etymological issue was raised by the 'That's so gay!' case. This phrase was used by a young teenage girl in California as a playground retort to persistent teasing about her Mormon background. The litigation arose out of the disciplining of the student by the school. The girl argued that it was a commonly used phrase which simply meant 'That's so stupid!', and no reference to sexual orientation was intended ([AP] 2007). The argument claimed in effect that the 'sexual orientation' meaning was, in the context, merely part of the word's history.

Harris (1990: 416–19) points out that in relation to taboo language there has often been a 'double prohibition', that is, not only should bad language not be used, but it should not be mentioned or quoted. This arises in newspaper reports of incidents where 'bad language' is used in the public sphere, as in the celebrated Pakistan–England test match in 1987 (Davis 1989). This double prohibition explains the widespread use of substitute forms such as the 'N-word', the 'C-word', the 'F-word', and again illustrates the tenuousness of intention in the ascription of moral as well as legal blame, and the blurred lines in many contexts between 'use' and 'mention'. By 'quoting' a taboo form or mentioning it, we are relying on the addressee not to make the inference that the mention implies an intentional endorsement of its circulation, at the same time as potentially inviting such an inference, as well as exposing ourselves to the possibility of an overhearing unsympathetic to, or ignorant of, our intention to 'quote' rather than to 'use'. An absolutely strict standard of liability would of course make any use in any context an offence, including the recording of forms in dictionaries.

As in the 14K and the 'forged' currency cases, we are faced with a dilemma about proximate inference from a surface meaning (available to a hypothetical reasonable observer) to an underlying form. The hearers perceived that proximate link, or experienced a similarity. It is clear for example that puns can be used to insult, and puns often make use of the fact that there is no conventional connection between two words. For example, an unpopular office manager called Mr Smith might be called 'Mr Shit' behind his back. The insult derives its force from the speaker's 'desecration' or 'corruption' of the name, combined with a vague, contextually generated similarity of sound, not from any generally agreed convention linking 'Smith' and 'shit'. However, in such cases, the intent to insult is presumed. There is no doubt that the word 'niggardly' could similarly be used with the intent to insult, exploiting the deniability of the link to the taboo meaning as a defence. The question then becomes a more complex and nuanced one of balancing the appropriate level of sensitivity to audience, context and social history against the appropriate level of good faith or informal 'dispute resolution' one might presume in the same context.

It is not clear what the intended standard of liability is to be under the 'tort of racial insult' proposed by some critical race scholars (Delgado and Stefancic 1997: 9):

The need for redress for victims also is underscored by the intentionality of racial insults. Their intentionality is obvious: what other purpose could the insult serve? There can be little doubt that the dignitary affront of racial insults, except perhaps those that are overheard, is intentional and therefore most reprehensible. Most people today know that certain

> words are offensive and only calculated to wound. No other use remains
> for words such as 'nigger', 'wop', 'spic', or 'kike'.

This statement argues in effect for a strong presumption, based on a widely
recognised set of socially established meanings, that the use of particular words
is an insult. Another way of expressing this is that the utterer is fixed with 'constructive' intent – that is, intent implied by operation of law – to insult. This
would suggest a shift in the burden of proof, that is, the onus would be on the
utterer to show why the remarks were not intended to be insulting, that for
example the word was being 'mentioned' rather than 'used', itself a problematic
distinction, as we have seen, which can be exploited for deniability. Matsuda
(1989: 2364) proposes the application of the 'recipient's community standard',
which amounts to applying a standard of addressee-assigned meaning. However, Kennedy argues that this neglects the range of literary contexts and
the 'malleability of language', as well as the complexity of social groups and the
'reality of cultural conflict' within them (Kennedy 2003: 126). The argument for
a tort of racial insult is grounded in an assertion that certain forms have only
one meaning, and that meaning should be assigned culpability by law.

This proposal is at the opposite end of the spectrum from the 1960s ideal,
summed up in the comedian Lenny Bruce's strategy of 'subversion through
overuse' (Kennedy 2003: 31, 88). One application of this utopian idea was in
Lee v Ventura County Superior Court (1992). In that case it was held that the
appellant had no constitutionally protected right to change his name legally
to 'Mister Nigger'. The court ruled that Mr Richard Lawrence Lee retained
the common law right to call himself as he wished, and therefore the state's
refusal to approve the name change was not a denial of his First Amendment
right to freedom of speech. Lee's declared intention was to 'steal the stinging
degradation – the thunder, the wrath, the shame and racial slur' from the word
(Kennedy 2003: 88).

The idea of speech as an open space or as constituting a public forum is a
fundamental metaphor (whether accepted or contested) in debates about the
role of law in relation to language. In Britain, under the Racial and Religious
Hatred Act 2006, anyone using 'threatening words or behaviour' or who 'dis-
plays any written material which is threatening' is guilty of a criminal offence,
'if he intends thereby to stir up religious hatred'. 'Religious hatred' means
'hatred against a group of persons defined by reference to religious belief or
lack of religious belief' (Part 3A). A 'body corporate' can also be convicted
under this Act. However, there is a proviso in relation to freedom of speech,
so that the 'discussion, criticism or expressions of antipathy, dislike, ridicule,
insult or abuse of particular religions or the beliefs or practices of their adher-
ents' are not prohibited. For many critics, none the less, this act represents an
erosion of free speech and open debate (Hare 2006).

In effect, the argument for a tort of racial insult is paralleled by the idea that
offensive terms and labels should be kept out of circulation as brand names

by a register of 'no-marks', that is, words or phrase that were legally not available for use. This idea was mooted following the marketing of 'Adolf Hitler' wine and alcoholic products under the names of other political figures such as Karl Marx, Stalin, Mussolini and Che Guevara by an Italian company. While an 'Adolf Hitler' mark could not be registered (with its accompanying Nazi slogan 'Ein Volk, Ein Reich, Ein Führer'), there was no European law directly forbidding use of offensive labels in a commercial context (though it would have been illegal in Germany). Such a register of 'no-marks', like the tort of racial insult, raises difficult questions concerning the boundary between acceptable and unacceptable. The owner of the company commented: 'It is strange that Stalin murdered 15 million people, but there is no fuss about the bottle.' The charge of promoting fascism was ruled non-proven by the Italian courts (Phillips 2004: 327). The tort of racial insult is an attempt to create a register of 'no-words', but the exemption for subcultural or specific community standards would create further problems of definition. The fact that difficult boundary questions arise, or a slippery-slope argument can be deployed, is not in itself a conclusive argument against legislative intervention, since drawing difficult boundaries is the very stuff of law.

A parallel conflict in the framing of representation as action has arisen in the debate over pornography and free speech in the United States. In arguing that women and images of women are not distinct within male sexuality, the feminist legal scholar Catharine MacKinnon rejects the classification of pornography as a free speech issue. Her argument collapses the distinction between sexual abuse and pornography: 'Sex in life is no less mediated than it is in art. Men have sex with their image of a woman' (MacKinnon 1989: 199). Pornography is not a form of expression, it is an act. MacKinnon makes the feminine in effect a category of which men are the authors, and this conclusion is rejected by Cornell (1991). This view of the feminine as a total construct of male-dominated culture forecloses the possibility of an alterity built out of engagement with the feminine (see Clark 2005: 124ff). As Coetzee points out (1996: 71), MacKinnon's understanding of interpretation 'draws into doubt and even collapses the distinction between the reality and the representation', positing a phenomenological fusion of action and representation. Coetzee poses the hypothetical case of a film which though its violent sexual content sought to understand and explore this form of desire ('its own desire to know its desire'), asking whether that would also be delegitimised. In effect, Coetzee is asking whether the opening sequence of MacKinnon's work *Only Words* (which describes violent sexual abuse), would not also be deemed pornographic (MacKinnon 1993: 3).

Commenting on Matsuda and MacKinnon's positions, Judith Butler terms them 'illocutionary', since the hate speech utterance does not merely act in a number of possible ways upon the addressee (a perlocutionary model) but 'reinvokes and reinscribes a structural relation of domination'. Butler argues that this model assumes that hate speech does not merely reflect 'a relation of social dominance', it enacts it and 'constitutes its addressee at the moment of utterance'. The utterance does not 'describe an injury or produce one as a consequence; it is, in the very speaking of such speech, the performance of the injury itself, where the injury is understood as social subordination' (Butler 1997: 18). MacKinnon points out that the fusion of speech and act is also effected by the United States policy on gays in the military, in which the statement 'I am homosexual' is considered 'a homosexual act', and therefore an offence (Butler 1997: 107).

Butler's position reflects a rejection of a politically interventionist determinism, where the interpreter assigns a culpable meaning to a decontextualised sign, and presents the addressee as defined by an utterance of that sign, and in need of the law's protection in the same way as the victim of a physical attack. This illustrates the role played by indeterminacy in the divide between Critical Legal Studies and Critical Race Theory. Drawing on Foucault, Butler sees the attempt to coopt the law in 'purifying language of its traumatic residue' (Butler 1997: 38) as deeply paradoxical. Butler questions the view of communication, arguing that the model assigns 'sovereign power' to hate speech when it is said to deprive someone of their 'rights and liberties' (Butler 1997: 77):

> The power attributed to hate speech is a power of absolute and efficacious agency, performativity and transitivity at once (it does what it says and it does what it says it will do to the one addressed by the speech).

This is ironically the model upon which legal language itself is based; it assigns total definitional power to language (and therefore to anyone who employs that language), and seems to deny the vulnerability of racist structures (Butler 1997: 101). It therefore denies the agency of the addressee to resist (since that becomes the task of law itself), and cuts off the possibility of a 'counter-mobilization', of 'insurrectionary speech' (Butler 1997: 163).

One recurrent question is whether and how state power should be coopted to achieve progressive ends (see Kirby 2006). A further dilemma for a left-progressive position might be that under laws enacted with this deterministic/ strict liability model of communication, 'flag-burning' might also be criminalised. While burning the United States flag is much more plausibly presented as having genuine expressive or political content than racial abuse, the level of offence and hurt caused can also be extremely high, for example to those who associate the national flag with a family member killed in combat. The argument could be plausibly made, applying MacKinnon's theoretical framework, that burning the flag performs as conduct an actual injury to the United States, rather than expressing a political view about some aspect of its socio-political order.

In his dissenting judgment in *Texas v Johnson* (1989), the case in which flag-burning was ruled (by five votes to four) to be constitutionally protected expressive conduct, Chief Justice Rehnquist quoted patriotic songs and evoked the place of the flag in the history of the United States (at 429):

> The American flag, then, throughout more than 200 years of our history, has come to be the visible symbol embodying our Nation. It does not represent the views of any particular political party, and it does not represent any particular political philosophy. The flag is not simply another 'idea' or 'point of view' competing for recognition in the marketplace of ideas. Millions and millions of Americans regard it with an almost mystical reverence regardless of what sort of social, political, or philosophical beliefs they may have.

The flag is a sacred symbol which cannot be separated from the historical identity and constitution of the United States (at 435):

> Surely one of the high purposes of a democratic society is to legislate against conduct that is regarded as evil and profoundly offensive to the majority of people – whether it be murder, embezzlement, pollution, or flag burning.

Justice Stevens, also dissenting, stated that the case had (at 436) 'an intangible dimension' that made rules applying to other symbols inapplicable. In argument before the court, the Dallas assistant district attorney, Kathi Drew, had made clear that the 'motive of the actor' was not relevant (Goldstein 2000: 95). In a parallel to views about 'hate speech', Judge Rehnquist flag denied that flag-burning could articulate a position, it being (at 432) 'the equivalent of an inarticulate grunt or roar that, it seems fair to say, is most likely to be indulged in not to express any particular idea, but to antagonize others'.

In *Johnson*, Justice Scalia voted with the majority, arguing later that the First Amendment 'protects your right to show contempt' (Goldstein 2000: 228), a logic which the court applied rigorously in its opinion in the 'cross-burning' cases *R. A. V. v St. Paul* (1992) and *Virginia v Black et al.* (2003). While the status of cross-burning as conveying a message of bigoted racial hatred was not in doubt, the court declined to hold that this of necessity (i.e. as an illocutionary act) showed an intention to intimidate or threaten, or constituted unprotected 'fighting words', and struck down state laws. In the *St Paul* case, the cross was burned on the property of an African-American family (see Butler 1995).

In the Hong Kong case of *HKSAR v Ng Kung Siu & Another* (1999), Hong Kong's highest court, the Court of Final Appeal, upheld the constitutionality of laws forbidding the desecration of the national flag and the regional flag. In a case which raised delicate issues about the extent of the autonomy of Hong Kong's legal system within the People's Republic of China's legal order (see Chan 1999; Chen 2002), it was common ground to the judgments that this was a specific exception which did not 'interfere with the person's freedom to express the same message by other modes' (at 921). Bokhary PJ, while expressing scepticism about the court's application of *ordre public* (at 929), argued that it was possible to reconcile freedom of expression with the 'natural' wish to protect collective symbols. This was possible because there was a fundamental difference between a symbol or emblem and a statement or specific message. A prohibition on desecration was 'specific' and did not affect 'the substance of expression'; it touched upon the mode of expression 'only to the extent of keeping flags and emblems impartially beyond politics and strife', so that '[n]o idea would be suppressed by the restriction' (at 932).

Against this it could be argued that a restriction on flag desecration is not a limited restriction on freedom of expression (which is not necessarily the same thing as saying that the case was wrongly decided). There is such immense political and ideological investment in the flag as an inviolate symbol: an attack on a 'sacred' symbol is by definition not a trivial act, and therefore its prohibition cannot be seen as a trivial or minimal infringement of freedom of expression. This same issue can arise in trademark law. On occasion courts in the United States have applied an 'alternative means' test to cases where the trademark is used as a means of attacking the trademark proprietor, asking whether the same message could have been communicated in any other way (Rumfelt 2006: 394). By putting a symbol beyond attack, a political-symbolic order is placed beyond criticism on its own most fundamental terms, i.e. in terms of the emotive, narrative and coercive power of collective symbols.

Conclusion: who is to blame?

The denial of an interest in intent, and the assertion of the fusion of image and reality (or original and representation), is common ground to many deterministic 'strong readings' which seek to apply the sanction of law to statements, representations and symbols. MacKinnon's model of pornography, the Forgery and Counterfeiting Act, and the Societies Ordinance are not concerned with, nor interested in reconstructing, the intent behind the representation. The question of why the image was produced, and what it was meant to mean, is not of forensic relevance. A similar issue has been diagnosed in respect of Restoration theatrical productions, where there was anxiety that if the correct utterances were spoken voluntarily before witnesses (i.e. on stage), then the actors might actually be lawfully married (O'Connell 1999). Similarly, in defamation law there is no 'jester's licence' for comedians and satirists (Munro 2007). This represents a 'strict liability' model of communication, or, failing that, one in which the burden of proof shifts to the speaker, and in which the objective degree of proximity (or actual fusion) in the relationship between the representation and the forbidden reality is the overriding criterion. In legal terms, authors are responsible for meanings which they do not control.

Questions of intention and interpretation have been at the heart of debates in literary theory. One longstanding view in literary theory is that meanings are to be sought in a careful scrutiny of the language of the text, and that no interpretative status need be accorded to the intentions of the author (Wimsatt and Beardsly 1946). This view in literary theory is associated with a broad set of tendencies known as New Criticism: literary texts 'are verbal structures made out of public language which is governed by the conventions of a language community' (Raval 1980: 262). For some theorists, agency has been attributable to language itself, with the idea that 'language thinks for us' or 'thinks us' variously attributed to literary critics and philosophers: 'language is not the work of human beings: language speaks. Humans speak only insofar as they co-respond to language' (Heidegger [1927] 1998: 57). In literary theory, the idea that the author controls or creates the meaning of a text in some privileged way has come under sustained intellectual attack (Barthes 1977). These theoretical shifts have empowered the reader and theories of reception, including Fish's idea of 'interpretative communities' (Fish 1980), where it is through the agency of readers or the public reception of the text in a particular community of readers that meaning is established.

Deconstruction as a technique of reading also denies any special status to the author: it concentrates on 'conceptual and figural implications rather than on authorial intentions' (Culler 1982: 110). One way to understand deconstruction is that it recognises that readings are always imposed, and that texts do not provide for their own interpretation. But since some form of reading is none the less offered, deconstruction represents a relative empowerment of the reader-critic, a partial freeing of the reader from the surface structures and orderings of the text. This partially liberated reader-critic then imposes a paradoxical controlled disorder on a text. As a style of reading, deconstruction disrupts the text at the very level at which it takes itself for granted. But this disruptive interventionism makes any idea of 'application' to law problematic (Culler 1988: 139), since law is generally seen as imposing order on disorder, rather than a form of controlled disorder on apparent order.

Butler takes this empowerment of the reader and positions it in the hate speech situation itself. Indeterminacy creates a space for resisting appropriation though language and its labels and categories, so that the addressee of hate speech is not passively constituted by the language of racial abuse. This allows for a re-reading of Louis Althusser's 'primal' street scene, in which the police officer, by calling out 'Hey you there!', positions passers-by as subjects of the law (Althusser 1971). Since the intention of the author is not determinative, a deconstructive reading ascribes the possibility of agency and a resistant reading-against-the-grain to the addressee. By contrast, proponents of a tort of racial abuse seek to coopt law to disempower and punish the author/utterer of abusive language.

Foucault seems to occupy a third position, beginning as he does with an account of authorship in the context of public censorship in pre-modern Europe. Foucault argues that literary or political authors became legally recognised primarily as a means of punishing transgressive thinking. One possible role for the 'author-function' is as a site of punishment, and discourse became at this historical juncture 'a possession caught in a circuit of property values' (Foucault 1977: 124). In effect the author has to be invented as an agent in order to assign responsibility. Foucault makes a market point: it is efficient within an economy of control to assign ownership responsibility to speakers and authors, so long as the power to determine meaning, or at least a certain category of meaning, is assigned to the censor.

Deconstruction, by its marginalisation of the author/utterer, undoes the text as historical construct or fiction, opening it up to a multiplicity of readings. But it is crucially reliant on the relative empowerment of the reader-critic-addressee, an element missing from Foucault's vision in which the author, or 'author function', is 'a variable and complex function of discourse'. The logic of Foucault's position can be applied to the jurisprudential principle that the people are the authors of law. The preamble to the Constitution of the United States reads as follows:

We the people of the United States, in order to form a more perfect union, establish justice, insure domestic tranquility, provide for the common defense, promote the general welfare, and secure the blessings of liberty to ourselves and our posterity, do ordain and establish this Constitution for the United States of America.

On this theory of the constitution, the makers of law act in the name of the people, who are its ultimate owners and authors. In a wider sense of authorship, the law attributes ownership of acts to the actor, and assigns responsibility on that basis, subject to the relevant set of legal rules. Law is language in action backed by the coercive power of the state, and this coercion is in general justified by a vague but powerful appeal to the foundations of law in popular will or consent and the democratic frame within which law operates. To meet concern about law's coercive power, Habermas attempts to show how the addressees of law are also ultimately its authors, even if law operates in a medium which escapes their control (Habermas 1996: 454). If the addressee is also the author, then an underlying symmetry is revealed which is obscured by surface power relations. If we accept Foucault's commentary on the nature of authorship, then the ascription of moral ownership and authorship of law to the people represents under certain conditions the assertion of a right to punish transgression under the law. But in Foucault's objectivist framing, there is no transparency or mutuality to the social contract that underwrites the coercive language of the law. Law's normative disciplining of society operates as an autonomous discourse, so that just as 'language speaks us', 'law makes us'.

In deconstruction the marginalisation of the author, by the very logic of deconstruction itself, returns to haunt the liberated critic-reader. If the addressee can be empowered to some extent, then how can we deny that possibility to the author? Intellectual property law must confront issues as diverse as rights to indigenous knowledge, McDonald's ownership of its trademarks, and the place of parody and satire in intellectual property law. Law is the shadow co-author of the language of advertising (as governed by consumer rights legislation) and of the terms of every contract. This implies a diverse set of cultural concepts and practices of authorship, alongside the recognition that texts are always co- or multi-authored, and that one of those authors is the law itself.

Further, the ascription of intention is fundamental to the everyday normativity and reflexivity of language, and without a concept of intention there is no way to make sense of the recognition that a remark, literary work or artwork is also at the mercy of the relevant 'interpretative market place' (a network of friends, a literary scene, etc.). This does not preclude the author from asserting moral authority over the meaning, or seeking to institutionalise control over reception, but depending on the context, this may be countered by other forms of informal, institutional, intellectual or legal authority. Foucault's radical rejection of the idea of an autonomous agentive subject seems to render the accountability of authors and speakers to law besides the point, since that accountability masks a deeper sense in which the subject is constituted by law in order to be held accountable to it.

7 Idols of the Market

Das Wort is preisgegeben; es hat uns gewohnt
Das Wort is zur Ware geworden.

The word has been abandoned; it used to dwell among us;
The word has become commodity.

Hugo Ball (1886–1927)

Introduction: signs in circulation

Modern theorists of language have tended to see language as constituting the primary social bond in modern nation states, so that a shared language expresses the common conceptual world and shared values of a community or nation. Political entities are seen as communicational spaces, defined by a common linguistic order. For economically oriented theorists, states are primarily markets, with language and information just one of many parallel and interacting media of exchange. In legal terms, states are legal jurisdictions, and law, rather than economics or language, is the all-pervasive medium within which social spaces are defined and social interactions take place. The liberal ideal in relation to the language culture of a particular polity would be that words and formulations, and therefore associated ideas, should circulate as freely as possible. In metaphorical terms, a language should be an open-access space or 'commons', where no single participant or group of participants has a monopoly and there is no central planning agency or centralised oversight. Linguistic change should arise from the uncoordinated, conscious or unconscious acts of individuals, and markets of exchange should work constantly to produce variants and innovations as well as a corrective mechanism to prevent fragmentation and disorder. The market itself determines an overall balance between the centrifugal effects of acts of individualistic agency and the common centripetal interest in preserving a degree of uniformity across the speech community.

Liberal and libertarian understandings of free speech strongly emphasise the overall positive value to the community of language users of minimal interference in the circulation of words and ideas. John Stuart Mill (1806–73) spoke of 'the peculiar evil of silencing the expression of an opinion' (Mill [1869] 1999: 59). This parallels liberal economic theories which likewise argue for the greater efficiency of market mechanisms in allocating resources (Hayek 1946). Richard Posner describes these liberal views of language as follows (Posner 1983: 44–5):

> Language is like the free market. No legislature or bureaucracy pre-scribes the forms of speech, the structure of the language, or the vocabu-lary that individuals use. Like a free market, a language is an immensely complicated yet private and decentralized institution.

Writers like George Orwell in *1984*, who imagined a state creating a language (Newspeak) which would make it impossible even to think dissenting thoughts, believe that 'to control language is to control thought, communica-tion, and ultimately action' (Posner 1983: 44):

> On this view, traditional language, as distinct from Newspeak or other invented languages, is a social institution with an enormous stabilizing influence because it embodies and perpetuates habits of thought, modes of reasoning, and traditional values that act as a bulwark against pre-cipitate change and absolute government.

Posner appears to regard the market place of language as an inherently con-servative and stabilising force, since change is fundamentally incremental in nature. Thus he compares language to custom or customary law in 'primitive' societies, that is, societies which do not have written legal codes or indepen-dent judicial bodies. A characteristic of 'primitive law' is that it 'resembles lan-guage in being a complex, slowly changing, highly decentralized system of exact rules' (Posner 1983: 178).

Alongside the market metaphor we can find competing, often overlapping, biological and ecological metaphors. The ecological metaphor is often used to suggest that language or languages have a natural and desirable state. This may be suggested by the use of metaphors of disease, corruption or commodification as damaging the transparency and communality of lan-guage. There is, however, a familiar tension in the idea of the language of a community as an open-access space, or as either an ecological system itself or part of a wider ecological system. Historically, interventionist voices include that of Jonathan Swift (1667–1745). For Swift (1712), centralised control through an academy was required to remove the language from the control of the vanities of fashion, and fix it as a pure and transparent medium of exchange. This is the paradox of the market or eco-system that requires regu-lation or protection to fulfil its function as a medium of exchange which trans-parently reflects conceptual values, or as a healthy or naturally evolving medium, or as part of natural human diversity.

Two landmark American cases can be briefly mentioned here. In *Abrams v United States* (1919), a case concerning the limits of free speech in criticising the government and advocating its overthrow, Oliver Wendell Holmes, dissenting, argued that the Constitution itself recognised the provisional nature of received wisdom, and used the liberal economic metaphor to express this (at 630):

> But when men have realized that time has upset many fighting faiths, they may come to believe even more than they believe the very foundations of their own conduct that the ultimate good desired is better reached by free trade in ideas – that the best test of truth is the power of the thought to get itself accepted in the competition of the market, and that truth is the only ground upon which their wishes safely can be carried out.

In *First National Bank v Bellotti* (1978) the question at issue was that of determining the status of a company as a speaker and whether a company's speech was protected by the First Amendment. The case concerned the status of a Massachusetts statute forbidding a corporation or 'body corporate' to spend funds to influence voters and the political process. Corporations are at law entities with qualities of personhood known as 'legal personality', a legal fiction with uncertain boundaries and a history of intense academic and judicial scrutiny (Schane 2006: 57ff). By five to four the court ruled that the law could not prohibit 'corporate expenditures' designed to influence the political process, even in relation to issues without 'material connection with the corporate business'.

At issue was a dispute about whether a corporation's free speech rights went beyond constitutional protection for the free flow of commercial information and should be granted a level of protection comparable to that enjoyed by an individual or 'natural person'. Dissenting, Justice Rehnquist argued that the corporation was a creature of the law, and the law did not automatically endow a company with all the liberties of a natural person (at 823). The special legal privileges attaching to incorporation meant that there was a need for caution (at 825–6):

> A State grants to a business corporation the blessings of potentially perpetual life and limited liability to enhance its efficiency as an economic entity. It might reasonably be concluded that those properties, so beneficial in the economic sphere, pose special dangers in the political sphere.

In effect, Rehnquist argued that in order to secure the free circulation of ideas from inordinate control by large corporations, it was necessary to curb their free speech (at 828):

The free flow of information is in no way diminished by the Commonwealth's decision to permit the operation of business corporations with limited rights of political expression. All natural persons, who owe their existence to a higher sovereign than the Commonwealth, remain as free as before to engage in political activity.

Underlying the judgments in this case were two conflicting views about how to maintain a neutral 'market place of ideas'. One view was that corporations as persons had as much right as any other person to participate freely in public debates, and this would benefit the free exchange and competition of ideas. The opposing view was that companies, unlike natural persons, are potentially immortal; they have very substantial funds available and if left unchecked may be able to obtain an unbreakable grip on the market place of speech.

For many scholars, the idea of a neutral market place is itself a myth which masks entrenched socio-ideological interests: 'we must pierce the myth of the neutral market-place of ideas and expose the flawed market model assumptions of objective truth and the power of rationality' (Ingber 1984: 90). On this view, all public and private spaces are defined economically and ideologically and represent sites of contestation and conflict. Ideas of autonomy and neutrality, including affirmations of the autonomy of law and of language, merely operate to obscure this underlying reality.

Trademark law

A trademark is a distinctive sign which associates a product or service with the business that produces it. The law regards trademarks primarily as a sign indicating the commercial origin of the product (the 'badge of origin' function) and seeks to protect the 'referential link' between the sign, the product and the business and thereby prevent 'referential confusion' (Tiersma 1999: 121). The UK Trade Marks Act (1994, Part 1, S 1) defines a trademark as 'any sign capable of being represented graphically which is capable of distinguishing goods or services of one undertaking from those of other undertakings'. A right in a trademark is a property right, and since these, in contrast to copyright, are not time-bound (though they may be lost through lack of use), that right is potentially perpetual. Trademarks play a central role in defining corporate personality through image-manipulation or 'branding'. This combination of a potentially immortal being and a personality constituted in part out of perpetual intellectual property rights is immensely powerful.

Trademark law is in effect a form of legally operational notice of linguistic change or innovation, and the law relies on both formal registration and the recognition of the courts that social practices may give rise to a legal right. There is implicit within the deep structure of the law an ideal of what a trademark should be, namely an invented word which is more than an idiosyncratic respelling of a common word, which has no recognisable meaning, and no associations with any attribute of the product. In the famous case of *Perfection: Joseph Crosfield and Sons' Application* (1909) counsel for the registrar stated that a trademark 'ought to have a perfect denotation as denoting the origin of the goods; it ought to have no connotation at all', though he recognised that this principle had been somewhat relaxed by Parliament in successive acts (at 134). As a corollary of this (*Reddaway v Banham* 1896, at 210):

> Where the trade mark is a word or device never in use before, and meaningless, except as indicating by whom the goods in connection with which it is used were made, there could be no conceivable legitimate use of it by another person. His only object in employing it in connection with goods of his manufacture must be to deceive.

It is an ideal of the trademark, because any use of the trademark to indicate a product must arise purely as a result of marketing or through the experience of the product in the market place by consumers, and therefore there has been no 'annexation' or 'trespass' on the ordinary meanings of ordinary words. The trading house has the absolute moral right to exploit a resource which it alone has created, and to prevent others from taking advantage of this.

Underlying this is a theory which suggests that a language is a stock of words and phrases with associated meanings, and that these represent the common resource of all users of the language. This language can be used in a competitive way to create goodwill for a product and its trademark, but a specific referential link between a word or phrase, a product and a producer will only be protected if it has been fairly earned. All the credit for meaning attributed to an otherwise 'meaningless' word must logically accrue to the company which has created that meaning in the form of a referential link to a product. Close to this ideal is the use of a word 'inappropriate for the goods concerned', such as 'North Pole' for bananas (see *British Sugar v James Robertson* 1996). Since there is no pre-existing conceptual link between the place-name and the fruit, then credit for any such link which has been established in relation to a product must accrue to the activities of the trader in the market place, and therefore there has been no 'freeloading' on the semantic resources of the language itself. At the other end of the spectrum is the use of a generic word as a trademark, such as sugar being sold under the trademark 'Sugar'. This is unacceptable, since the trademark would not work as a 'badge of origin' to distinguish one producer/trader from another. Giving the example of 'Soap' for soap, Jacob J. reasoned that it could not be registered since the applicant 'will be unable to prove the mark has become a trade mark in practice'. He called this a factual not a legal prohibition (at 305). This suggests that it would be in principle possible in law for a company to seek to coopt a generic term as a trademark, since evidence that the generic term had acquired an overpowering meaning as a trademark would satisfy the legal requirement of distinctiveness. In *Reckitt & Colman v Borden* (1990), at 505, Lord Oliver of Aylmerton confirmed that:

> even a purely descriptive term consisting of perfectly ordinary English words may, by a course of dealing over many years, become so associated with a particular trader that it acquires a secondary meaning such that it may properly be said to be descriptive of that trader's goods and of his goods alone, as in *Reddaway v Banham* [1896] A.C. 199.

In the latter case, the House of Lords had protected the use of the term 'Camel-hair' in relation to belting, since its use by another trader was such as to lead consumers to confuse products of one origin from those of another. This case has been described as 'clearly the exception rather than the rule' (Torremans 2005: 462).

Judges have generally recognised the common ownership of the English language by its speakers. From *Crosfield* comes the most famous statement about an underlying moral principle of ownership (Cozens-Hardy MR, at 141):

> Wealthy traders are habitually eager to enclose parts of the great common of the English language and to exclude the general public of the present day and of the future from access to the enclosure.

A similar statement from Lord Herschell is found in *Eastman Photographic Materials Co. v Comptroller-General of Patents, Designs, and Trade-Marks* (1898, at 580):

> The vocabulary of the English language is common property: it belongs alike to all; and no one ought to be permitted to prevent the other members of the community from using for purposes of description a word which has reference to the character or quality of goods.

This is distinct from the case where a word is invented (at 580):

> But with regard to words which are truly invented words – words newly coined – which have never theretofore been used, the case is, as it seems to me, altogether different; and the reasons which required the insertion of the condition are altogether wanting. If a man has really invented a word to serve as his trade-mark, what harm is done, what wrong is inflicted, if others be prevented from employing it, and its use is limited in relation to any class or classes of goods to the inventor?

Davis (1996: 261) links this judicial protection of a common property to Locke's notion of language as fundamentally a shared good for which all were responsible (Locke [1690] 2001: 424):

> For words, especially of languages already framed, being no man's
> private possession, but the common measure of commerce and commu-
> nication, it is not for any one at pleasure to change the stamp they are
> current in, nor alter the ideas they are affixed to; or at least, when there
> is a necessity to do so, he is bound to give notice of it.

Cozens-Hardy argued that 'it would be wrong to allow a monopoly in the use
of such a word, which, moreover, may in course of time become false and misleading' (at 143). However, Fletcher Moulton LJ took the 1905 Trade Marks
Act as having abandoned 'the policy of absolute exclusion of all the members
of specified classes of words and substituting therefore a judicial examination
of the merits of each individual case' (145). There was no relation of mutual
exclusion between distinctive and descriptive qualities, 'no natural or necessary incompatibility between distinctiveness and descriptiveness in the case of
words used as trade marks'. There was no absolute exclusion of 'an ordinary
laudatory term' (at 149), but the word 'Perfection' was on the facts on the
wrong side of the line:

> The use of inordinate laudation of his goods by a trader is too deeply
> rooted and too ineradicable not to be well known to all the public, and
> I do not believe that any person buying soap would suppose that it was
> perfection merely because the maker calls it so. But to my mind this tells
> against the applicants. It shews that the word is one that probably, and I
> might almost say naturally, would be used by others in the description
> of their soap.

Farwell LJ stated that it was his opinion that usage ('user') alone could not
ground a claim to a proprietary right: 'no amount of user could possibly withdraw the word "perfection" from its primary and proper meaning in the soap
trade and make it mean "Crosfield's" instead of perfect' (at 151). The second
and third judgment fall short of making any general moral statements about
the ownership of language, and instead focus on the question of 'user', suggesting an extremely high practical or evidential barrier rather than an insur-
mountable moral boundary.

One further aspect of this should be emphasised. While social practices and
social meanings ascribed to trademarks in their circulation may lead to legal
protection, the same process of circulation may also lead to loss of distinctiveness and therefore of legal protection. While it might be thought that a
commercial undertaking has an unlimited interest in promoting the circulation of its trademarks, this is far from being the case. While, broadly speaking, the more established and recognisable the trademark, the stronger legal
protection it attracts, this is only true if the referential link is preserved to the
associated products and services. A trademark which circulates in contexts
where it is no longer serving as a strict 'badge of origin' may lose its legal

protection and become a generic term. Thus in *Bayer Co. v United Drug Co.* (1921), the invented word or 'artificial trade mark', Aspirin, was deemed to have lost its legally enforced monopoly: 'There is no invention in the word, qua word, which [the producer] can protect' and among consumers 'the name has gone into the public domain'. Another way of understanding this is that a trademark name, by virtue of its association with a type of product rather than a particular producer of the product, becomes a descriptive label, that is, it joins the mainstream of the English language and thus can no longer serve to distinguish one producer from another. The greater the success of the product associated with the trademark, and the greater the market recognition of the trademark, the greater the vigilance required to protect it.

In his study of trademark law from the point of view of linguistics, Shuy (2002: 2) rightly characterises trademark law as a form of 'language planning' involving 'the right to monopolise the use of language' and direct state intervention through the courts in the public sphere. For Shuy, trademark law raises directly the question of who is entitled to the ownership of language and the right of one segment of the speech community 'to change the rest of that community's use of language' (Shuy 2002: 2). In effect, Shuy looks at trademark law through the lens of a popularist understanding of language ownership. He is thus somewhat hostile to the law's activities in this area, notwithstanding his comment that trademark law seems to represent 'a genuine effort to bring order to a potentially chaotic business practice' (Shuy 2002: 3). Noting that language planners have a variety of socio-political goals (pluralism, assimilation, purism, promotion of co-official languages, promotion of access to information), he concludes that the language planning involved in trademark law 'can only claim one of the goals listed above: the attempt to create a purism which tries to eliminate what it considers to be the deviant varieties of the language, a goal that is consistent with law's innate need to be prescriptive' (Shuy 2002: 3).

It is worth examining Shuy's views in some detail, since they represent a sustained commentary upon the tensions and difficulties associated with the question of authority over language, and are based on Shuy's direct involvement as an expert in language in a number of contentious trademark cases. His remarks also offer a window on a set of ideological assumptions made by many linguists about language, which are rarely made so explicit. Framing the book's treatment of individual cases, there is a discussion of the question of ownership of language and the relationship of language to social power. Shuy links trademark law to sociolinguistic inequalities, accusing law in effect of employing legal prohibitions to reinforce its control over language and over the hierarchy of value associated with 'high' and 'low' language varieties. Shuy evokes 'a long tradition of prescriptivism and authoritarianism in language use', and associates trademark law with the 'suppression of optional variation at all levels of language', as well as a desire to prevent language change, and the stigmatisation of those who use non-standard forms of language as

'deviant, stupid, ignorant or immoral'. Those who hold mastery of 'high' varieties use their privileged position to act as 'gatekeepers' under a regime of
'legitimized discrimination' (Shuy 2002: 6). Shuy associates trademark law
with elitism, prescriptivism and purism. Purism combines with the authoritarianism of prescriptivism and the coercive power of law to eliminate linguistic variants and to impose illegitimate control over ordinary users of the
language.

Shuy's viewpoint could be understood either in ecological terms, whereby
trademark law is seen as an attack on natural variation and diversity, or in
market terms, where trademark law creates excessive, state-sanctioned private
rights (i.e. monopolies) out of communal property (the words and phrases of
a language) and even out of private property such as personal names (Shuy
2002: 2):

> So a restaurant owner named McDonald is prevented from naming his
> business after himself. Even a hotel company is prohibited from using
> the patronymic prefix Mc- in the name of its proposed hotel chain,
> McSleep, since McDonald's was determined to have the sole legal right
> to that prefix.

Further, trademarks that have developed generic meanings and usages,
whether these have led to the loss of legal protection or not, are not
recorded accurately in contemporary dictionaries. The words 'kleenex', 'band-
aid' and 'xerox' are frequently defined with reference to their function as trademarks, so that the 'threat of law' has been used 'to quash the obligation of
lexicography to report the actual usage by the public' (Shuy 2002: 55). Thus
language planning and policy 'violates natural language usage', and the
authority of law is seen to 'override the authority of the public' (Shuy
2002: 55).

A further target for Shuy is the legal provisions that allow a primarily
descriptive label to be granted legal recognition none the less. For example, a
geographical term, such as the name of a city, would in general be viewed as
non-distinctive for a product, since it is a badge of regional rather than commercial origin, and could not serve in theory to distinguish a particular
product from other similar products produced in the same locale. However,
the courts will recognise that such signs can acquire a distinctive character
through use. As seen above, this may also apply to descriptive words that
ascribe positive qualities to the product. This is sometimes referred to as a 'secondary meaning', and this 'meaning', argues Shuy, can be simply purchased,
since the greater the resources of the company, the more likely it is to be able
to create this secondary meaning: 'Secondary meaning is achieved through the
massive expenditures on advertising and marketing, and secondary meaning
often trumps everything else in trademark cases' (Shuy 2002: 103). Shuy
argues as follows (2002: 196):

Perhaps the power of money could be reconsidered in pursuing decisions based on 'secondary meaning', which is not really 'meaning' at all
but, rather, an economic condition that is used to interpret other economic conditions. It is a stretch to consider 'secondary meaning' as
meaning in the linguistic sense. As the term currently applies, the
law appears to be using 'secondary meaning' as a euphemism for 'previous financial investment'. If it's money that matters here, why not openly
say so?

Underlying Shuy's position is a moral theory of ownership, one in which ownership of language naturally falls to the people who speak it, and any interference with the natural processes of language change by the artificial power
of money is rejected (Shuy 2002: 199):

> Trademark law appears to want to freeze the natural and healthy phe-
> nomenon of language change, instead prescribing fixed meanings that
> allow for no variability. This may make sense to the field of law, but it
> runs counter to human creative and intellectual behavior.

What Shuy objects to is the assumption of authority over language by the law
as the 'high segment of society' in this respect, which relegates others (including linguists) to the 'low' segment in 'matters of policy and use' (Shuy 2002:
5). This commodification is achieved in the context of trademark cases, where
law, not linguistics, is placed at the top of the hierarchy, 'buttressed by the
power of coercion that linguistics does not share' (Shuy 2002: 192). This leads
to a dilemma for linguists involved in trademark cases who must be 'true to
their ideology that the people who speak a language are the real owners of it',
while working in a team with attorneys 'whose ideology is that law owns language' (Shuy 2002: 194).

It is not explained by Shuy why training in academic linguistics should
commit someone to this ideological position. This is not to say that Shuy's
position is not widely shared, both within linguistics and without, nor that
many of the concerns he raises are unjustified. In reference to the question of
whether 'Google' should be capitalised or not when used as verb, a web commentator, Adam Messinger, asserts that efforts by companies to control trademark use are 'a sign of the creeping trademark fascism that corporations
are trying to impose upon the natural evolution of the English language'
(Messinger 2007). A discussion of EMI's (Entrepreneur Media) legal actions
against the use by other companies of the term 'entrepreneur' contains the
rhetorical question: 'Should one company be allowed to take an important
word like "Entrepreneur" away from the American people?' ([Iventure] 2007).
Lexicographers, whether they deal with proper names or not, have a well-
recognised problem in relation to trademark terms (Stein 1958). Higgins
(1997: 383) quotes this statement from *Merriam-Webster's* third edition:

The inclusion of any word in this dictionary is not [. . .] an expression of the publisher's opinion on whether or not it is subject to proprietary rights. Indeed, no definition in this dictionary is to be regarded as affecting the validity of any trademark.

Obviously a generic usage recorded in a dictionary is good *prima facie* evidence that a trademark has become non-distinctive, but it is hard to see what legal liability a dictionary could face, so long as it can document that it is reflecting accurately contemporary usage. But Higgins reports that in later editions *Merriam-Webster's* followed strictly the conventions of the United States Trademark Association, and omitted generic meanings, though other dictionaries differ in their submission to the priority of trademark use (Higgins 1997: 383ff).

Shuy's points about power and ownership are taken up in a review of his work by a trademark lawyer (Westerhaus 2003). In response to Shuy's comment that: 'Unintentionally perhaps, law may give the impression that it is king over language and that fields that feed it must humbly submit to law's ownership of words and expressions' (Shuy 2002: 193), Westerhaus responds as follows (Westerhaus 2003: 295):

The fact of the matter is that law, as a construct, does, absolutely and inevitably, consider itself king over language (as well as pretty much everything else, arrogant though that may be). It considers itself the overarching, overlying framework within which every element of society operates.

However, the sovereignty of law is not absolute, even in the area of trademark law (Westerhaus 2003: 295):

But if law is indeed king over language, it is important to remember that sometimes its subjects revolt. In the case of trademark law, in particular, it is true, for example, that sometimes marks become generic, and thus lose trademark protection, through the very use that created trademark rights in them in the first place.

Westerhaus also chides Shuy for neglecting the primary, underlying rationale for trademark law, namely the 'protection of the consumer' (Westerhaus 2003: 295). By commodifying the relationship between the trademark, the product and the producer, the law offers consumers a guarantee that the products they buy are 'genuine'.

Shuy's position is that the linguist is the natural representative of the people when it comes to language, and that law has usurped the rights of linguists, and denied them proper audience within its intuitional structures. One way to understand this is as a dispute about academic authority and the right to represent the point of view of the 'ordinary consumer'. Shuy makes the emphatic statement that (Shuy 2002: 1):

> Linguistics is based on the truth about the way language works. Such knowledge is especially important in trademark cases, since trademark disputes are largely about language.

Shuy explains this in relation to meaning as follows. One issue that arose in a case for which Shuy was consultant was whether 'Healthy Selections' and 'Healthy Choice' were so similar that consumers would be likely to confuse them, and they would 'cease to operate to distinguish between two products' (Shuy 2002: 70). A subsidiary question than arose as to whether these two trademarks had the same meaning. The linguist for the opposing side argued that the two names had the same 'significance meaning'. Although there were differences in pronunciation, morphology and word choice between the two product names, consumers would merely retain the 'gist' of the meaning. In addressing this point, Shuy took this as a claim that the two words were operating as synonyms, and then set out the relevant conditions. To be synonymous the pair of terms had to have 'identical meaning', be 'synonymous in all contexts', and 'identical in all dimensions of meaning' (Shuy 2002: 77). Shuy then adduced evidence of the different use patterns of 'choice' and 'selections'; for example, in sentences such as 'they don't give you much choice in the matter', 'choice' cannot be replaced by 'selection'. His conclusion was that there was a more intimate connection between 'choice' and the person choosing 'as an animated agent' than in the case of 'selections', which 'exist outside the meaning of the beneficiary and are made by someone else', and also that choice was generally made *between* two items, whereas a selection was *among* several (Shuy 2002: 79). However, the judge ruled that the two trademarks names meant essentially the same thing, though this was not conclusive to the outcome of the case.

Intellectual property laws 'mediate a politics of contested meaning that may be traced in the creation and appropriation of symbolic forms and their unanticipated reappropriations in the agendas of others' (Coombe 1998: 8). Shuy's definition of synonymy is an artefact of linguistic theory, and has no direct relevance for the contested perception of similarity. This may suggest that 'the pronouncements of professional linguists about language are not likely to be of much use to the practice of trademark law' (Davis 1996: 261). By analysing language out of context, the linguist is effectively removing this time and perception element: 'The linguist examines the message to determine all the reasonable possibilities that language offers the reader or listener about what the text could have meant and how it could have been understood' (Shuy 2002: 107). The judgments of linguists as to what are identical or similar linguistic forms (e.g. in arguments about confusion of trademarks) are of no relevance unless they can claim to mimic the perceptions of ordinary consumers going about their business, such as a thirsty customer choosing a beer (*Thomas Montgomery v Thompson and Others* 1891) or a harried shopper selecting a brand of toilet paper in a rush (*Kimberley-Clark v Fort Sterling Limited* (1997).

In the latter case, the question of relevant expertise was central to the discussion, and the judge accepted that it was a 'matter for the court alone' to 'assess the likely impact of the marks or get-up in issue and decide for itself whether they will cause relevant confusion'. This matter was 'not to be handed to experts, no matter how proficient', although what the court was trying to do was 'decide how members of the relevant public will react to the defendant's use of marks or get-up in the real world'. While the court proceedings involved the packaging in question being 'examined and dissected in minute detail by many of the witnesses and both sides' counsel', what was relevant was 'what would happen in the environment where the defendant's products are being sold', one in which a 'combination of point of purchase decision making and rapid selection means that misleading packaging is particularly likely to influence consumer purchasing choices' (at 884).

In Britain, under the influence of the European Court of Justice, there is a trend towards taking distinctiveness as established by the market ('acquired distinctiveness'), rather than distinctiveness as established by linguistic analysis out of context, but the lines are not always clearly drawn. In *British Sugar v James Robertson* (1996) the word 'treat' was rejected as a mark, as was 'doublemint' in *Office for Harmonisation in the Internal Market (OHIM) v Wm Wrigley* (2004). However, in the 'Baby-dry' case (*Procter & Gamble v Office for Harmonisation in the Internal Market (OHIM)* 2002), in spite of the apparent descriptive nature of this in relation to nappies, the court took the distinctive word order or word combination as lifting the trademark out of the prohibition. Nestlé has since 1978 owned a trademarked slogan associated with the Kit Kat chocolate bar, 'HAVE A BREAK . . . HAVE A KIT KAT'. It 1995 it sought to register 'HAVE A BREAK' as a stand-alone slogan, an application which was opposed by Mars UK on the grounds that it did not have the required 'distinctive character'. The Trade Marks Registry refused registration, and this was upheld in the High Court. The Court of Appeal declined to overrule the High Court, and it referred the question to the European Court of Justice for an opinion. It was ruled that part of a slogan could become distinctive by use ('acquired distinctiveness') if associated by consumers with the trade origin of the product, and the mark was registered in 2006 (*Société des Produits Nestlé SA v Mars UK Ltd* 2005).

One important area of uncertainty in trademark law is the question of use in a 'trademark sense'. In the Scottish case of *Bravado Merchandising Services Ltd v Mainstream Publishing* (1996), in which the owner of the trademark 'Wet Wet Wet' (the name of a pop band) had sought to restrain use of the trademark (which had been registered for books) in a book title, *A Sweet Little Mystery – Wet Wet Wet – The Inside Story*, Lord McCluskey offered this extremely broad interpretation (at 602):

The repeated reference to 'Wet' has nothing to do with moisture or political timidity. On the contrary, the use of 'Wet Wet Wet' is avowedly and obviously a use of the name which the group has registered. Accordingly, even if the use is appropriate to indicate the subject matter of the book on whose cover it appears, that use does not thereby cease to be use in a trade mark sense.

Commenting on the 'Wet Wet Wet' case, Jacob J said in *British Sugar* that: 'It would be fantastic if the new trade mark legislation had the effect of enabling a quasi-censorship of books about people or companies just because those people or companies had registered their names as trade marks for books' (at 293).

Trademark law is best understood simply as one arena in which meanings are debated and given normative values. In this sense it is in principle no different from any other social context. Norms backed by law have state power behind them, but high-profile trademarks also create targets for political attack by activists. One area in which this arises is in internet domain names and search engines. While the law recognises certain legal rights of trademark holders in relation to the registration of domain names, any web search using a well-known trademark may well reveal the use of that trademark against the company. Examples include: 'Just do it! Boycott Nike!', as well as the adoption and discussion of the trademarked slogan in a wide range of contexts, not necessarily used in a way hostile to the trademark holder. One particular target is McDonald's, as their massive investment in the 'Mc-' prefix has led to a very powerful link between it, the product and the producer. The 'Mc-' as a badge of origin offers a resource for attributing negative meanings both to the company and also to the wider socio-political and corporate culture for which it is held to stand. On-line dictionaries include these meanings, and there is an entire lexicon of 'Mc-' vocabulary items from McAss to McZit. The general term used for the 'non-exclusive appropriation of content' is known as 'glomming on'. An example would be the non-authorised use of characters and plot-lines from famous works such as *Harry Potter* to create unauthorised adaptations (Balkin 2004: 7).

Noami Klein (1999), analysing the rise of a small number of extremely powerful global brands, notes that as the companies which own these brands become more powerful, they gradually divest themselves of much of the materiality that goes with the production of goods and services. In the new global knowledge economy, brand-name multinationals (Klein 1999: 195)

are in the process of transcending the need to identify with their earthbound products. They dream instead about their brands' deep inner meanings – the way they capture the spirit of individuality, wilderness, or community.

Klein quotes the president of a branding agency as saying that '[p]roducts are made in the factory, but brands are made in the mind', so that after establishing the 'soul' of the product, 'the corporations, the superbrand companies have gone on to rid themselves of their cumbersome bodies', in particular the factories and production processes, with their employees, that produce the objects on which the logos are stamped. The brand becomes a free-floating sign, which is not anchored to any defined process of manufacture or even product type. Another CEO is quoted as follows: 'Machines wear out. Cars rust. People die. But what lives on are the brands.' The company's resources are primarily directed at sustaining and feeding the brand identity, by sponsorships, packaging, advertising, and creating synergies between the company, distribution and retail networks. The massive investment in the brand comes at the cost of the conditions under which these products are produced under licence, since the company can 'source' its products in the country offering the lowest wages and the most compliant workforce, without directly having any employees there. In a postmodern inversion, 'image is everything', and 'there is no value in making things anymore' (Klein 1999: 196–7).

The massive domination of brand over product creates its own phobias, for if the company's value is almost entirely found in its brand identity, then that identity must be protected at all costs. The corporate personality of the brand-name multinational is characterised by a drive to world domination and universality, but its dark side is fear that it will lose control of its own images, and the smiling corporate welcome hides a deep fear that the vast edifice has been erected on a mere pattern of semiotic circulation. That circulation must be monitored, to prevent the brand becoming generic, or otherwise circulating out of control, but there is a vulnerability to market fads and trends. Hip marketing concepts like 'brand hijack' seek to harness this lack of control to create a form of paradoxical anti-marketing, thereby maintaining an 'edgy' image: 'Let go of the fallacy that your brand belongs to you. It belongs to the market' (Wipperfürth 2005: 31). But for powerful mega-brands this is not possible, and control is therefore the key. McDonald's website (www.mcdonalds.com/terms.html) asserts its control over its own material: 'Material from www.mcdonalds.com [. . .] may not be copied or distributed, or republished, uploaded, posted, or transmitted in any way, without the prior written consent of McDonald's.' McDonald's also annexes all 'remarks, suggestions, ideas, graphics, or other information communicated to McDonald's through this site', which will 'forever be the property of McDonald's'. The annexation is not total, since, even though '[w]ithout limitation, McDonald's will have exclusive ownership of all present and future existing rights to the Submission of every kind and nature everywhere', legal liability remains with the sender 'for whatever material you submit, and you, not McDonald's have full responsibility for the message, including its legality, reliability, appropriateness, originality, and copyright'. A large number of trademarks are listed, including 'Always Quality. Always Fun', 'Black History Makers of Tomorrow', 'Have

You Had Your Break Today?', 'McScholar of the Year', 'World Children's Day' and 'You Deserve a Break Today'.

It is in the United States that the sense seems strongest that aggressive companies are commodifying increasingly large amounts of linguistic territory and protecting that territory with fierce legal bulldogs. This reflects a wider sense of the commodification or privatisation of public spaces, and the uncertain legal status of quasi-public spaces such as shopping malls in relation to the exercise of rights of free speech. In the landmark case of *Pruneyard Shopping Center v Robins* (1980), the Supreme Court held that activists collecting signatures in a private mall were exercising their 'state-protected rights of expression and petition'. This meant that individual states could enact laws protecting freedom of space in such spaces (provided they did not violate Fifth Amendment property rights), but there was no federally protected right as such, since a shopping mall, unlike a company town, does not fulfil a function normally exercised by the state. This remains a contentious area (Fuchs 2005/6).

The United States Trademark Dilution Revision Act (2006) offers protection to owners of 'famous marks' from 'dilution by blurring or dilution by tarnishment', regardless of 'actual or likely confusion, of competition, or actual economic injury' (S 2). The revision was primarily aimed at clarifying that no actual harm had to be shown, merely the 'likelihood' of harm (Hofrichter 2006/7: 1928). The Act protects certain uses, including the use of the name to refer to a product ('a nominative or descriptive fair use'), and also protects acts of 'identifying and parodying, criticizing, or commenting upon the famous mark owner or the goods and service of the famous mark owner', and 'any non-commercial use' (S 3). On its face, this should not impede freedom of speech by commodifying linguistic territory or preventing free discussion.

One problem is that for a large corporation the act of threatening legal action comes with minimal transaction costs, whereas for a small company or publication under threat these costs may be prohibitive. There is a widely shared sense that companies are colonising and commodifying public spaces, one reflected by Shuy's and Klein's books. There is no doubt that many large corporations in the United States seek to use intellectual property law to silence critics and extend their control over the public domain (Balkin 2003, quoted in Rumfelt 2006: 391):

> Trademark, like copyright, has now become a general-purpose device for private parties to use when they want the state to suppress speech they do not like. And they are trying to suppress the speech of others not merely to protect their legitimate economic interests but because of aesthetic and political disagreements.

In the US case of *Ford Motor v 2600* (2001), the court ruled that the domain name 'fuckgeneralmotors.com', which automatically directed users to the Ford official website, was 'noncommercial':

This court does not believe that Congress intended the FTDA to be used by trademark holders as a tool for eliminating Internet links that, in the trademark holder's subjective view, somehow disparage its trademark. Trademark law does not permit Plaintiff to enjoin persons from linking to its homepage simply because it does not like the domain name or other content of the linking web page.

In 2003, Fox News sought to use trademark law to attack Al Franken's satirical publication, *Lies (And the Lying Liars Who Tell Them): A Fair and Balanced Look at the Right* (2003). 'Fair and balanced' is a slogan employed by Fox News, an avowedly right-wing cable channel owned by Rupert Murdoch's News Corporation. In dismissing the application for a preliminary injunction as 'wholly without merit, both factually and legally', Judge Chin noted that it was 'highly unlikely' that 'fair and balanced' could be a valid trademark: 'I can't accept that that phrase can be plucked out of the marketplace of ideas and slogans.' In any case, the First Amendment protected the strong public interest in free expression. Chin concluded (*Fox News Network, LLC, v Penguin Group (USA), Inc., and Alan S. Franken*, 2003):

Of course, it is ironic that a media company that should be seeking to protect the First Amendment is seeking to undermine it by claiming a monopoly on the phrase 'fair and balanced.'

The full transcript is available at Franken (2008).

Opponents of large multinational brands look for the narrow definition of trademarks and high thresholds for registration. Richardson (2004: 192) argues that this reflects a naive view of language politics, and the desire that 'the language commons should remain in their pristine natural state'. For Richardson, this view is out of touch with the strong presence of brand names and slogans within popular culture: trademarks are embedded in the linguistic experience of the whole population (Richardson 2004: 196):

Like them or not, trade marks tell stories. Their expressiveness is the basis of commercial activity, the trader-author the conduit of meaning, and the market-audience the monitor and arbiter of taste. And the combination of a vivid visual characterisation and aural sound-bite effect makes them easy to remember (and difficult to forget) across the entire base of the population.

Richardson sees 'commercial norms' as providing a better form of control than 'restrictive registration', and points to the light legal regulation of domain names as preferable to the 'complex and laborious' systems set up for trademarks (Richardson 2004: 197, 198). Viewing trademarks as freely circulating linguistic signs with their own socially acquired meanings, Richardson rejects the 'badge of origin' and 'language commons' paradigm as superseded by sociolinguistic reality, within which trademarks are 'a language of their own' (Richardson 2004: 211, emphasis removed). Trademarks are a creative form of language which deserves the protection afforded other forms of creative originality (Richardson 2004: 213):

> The utilitarian justification for copyright protection, lying in providing incentives for artistic and cultural development for the broader social benefit, can be extended to these new cultural items. For these trade marks, at least, infringement can be rationally extended to encompass uses that will likely blurr or tarnish their expressive associations, reducing them to 'the commonplace' or rendering them socially 'unacceptable'.

This implies protection from various forms of 'dilution' in the public sphere. Carty by contrast regards this as an ill-defined concept which is threatening to extend the law beyond its traditional boundaries (Carty 1996: 491–3), and highlights doubts about whether exclusive control should be given to celebrity images and brands which are the co-creation of the public sphere, historical memory and popular culture (Carty 2004: 249–51). Authorship can also include 'the practice of state recognition of intellectual investment' in works covered by intellectual property law (Coombe 2003: 1171).

Conclusion: trademarks and the commodification of the public sphere

For many commentators the dominant presence of trademarks in popular discourse is simply a reflection of the highly commodified nature of the public sphere, in particular in the United States, in which the boundaries between news, entertainment and advertising are not always clear. For such critics the law often appears to be the only potential counterweight to such powerful forces, so that even radical critics of law are reluctant give up on it. Brion (1987: 95–7), rejecting William Kowinski's pessimistic vision in *The Malling of America* (1985) of 'the mall as fortress in a futuristic feudal world', foresees a potential for ordinary people (called by Brion 'everyperson') to seek to transform the mall, a process in which 'the judiciary will be open to the possibility of ratifying what they do'. If the state progressively privatises its traditional functions, and politics itself resembles a branch of advertising, then law may be the last remaining autonomous domain of the secular state.

The record of the courts is a mixed one, with crucial ambiguities arising in the definition of 'non-commercial use' and 'use in a trademark sense', and in the notion of trademark 'dilution'. Traditionally, trademark law was understood as a means of protecting the integrity of the market for consumers as much as producers, and the right attached to a trademark was a right to prevent confusion and protect 'goodwill', rather than absolute 'ownership' of a sign. But the concept of dilution 'exists outside of this traditional framework' (Hofrichter 2006/7: 1931). This creates a degree of uncertainty around the use of a trademark to criticise and parody the trademark proprietor, one which can be exploited by sending threatening 'cease and desist' letters. The liberal plea might be for governments and courts to offer a robust defence of open debate, satire and parody, and to apply a narrow definition of 'commercial use' or 'use in a trademark sense'. The US judge Alex Kozinski, in a published article, put this as follows (Kozinksi 1993: 973):

> Trademarks are often selected for their effervescent qualities, and then injected into the stream of communication with the pressure of a firehose by means of mass media campaigns. Where trademarks come to carry so much communicative freight, allowing the trademark holder to restrict their use implicates our collective interest in free and open communication.

The author or originator 'must understand that the mark or symbol or image is no longer entirely its own, and that in some sense it also belongs to all those other minds who have received and integrated it' (Kozinski 1993: 975).

A Marxist view might dismiss the liberal faith in the courts and look to the ultimate triumph of global brands as a necessary stage on the road to the end of capitalism and the 'withering away of the state'. The development of trademark law seems to confirm the association between capitalism and the loss of connection between things and their representations. In Kozinski's words, they have become 'unplugged' from their origin (Kozinski 1993). Modern trademark theorists no longer regard trademarks as referential marks which serve primarily to designate a producer; they are potent, autonomous, if contested signs. Marxism, for all its materialist philosophical roots, is essentially a celebration of the dynamism and abstract energy of capitalism. It was capitalism that broke down the feudal order, disrupted and subverted its fixed hierarchies, and set loose the commodity. Capitalism is motion. It liberates the magic power of mobile symbols and sets in circulation increasingly abstract forms of value which are beyond human understanding and control. The brand names themselves are now hyper-fetishised commodities.

As globalisation pulls more and more domains and regions into the centripetal forces of capitalist circulation with their increasingly abstract forms of financial instruments, the ability of any power centre to control events diminishes. The more 'value' is concentrated in commercially promoted signs and abstract, high-speed exchange systems in financial markets, the more difficult the political control of that value, and the greater the gap between the materiality of basic human existence and the 'hallucinations' of the market. Following this logic, the Marxist utopian vision of the 'withering away of the state' is more likely to be achieved by hyper-capitalism than direct political revolution. Luhmann's pessimistic view of the blindness of modern systems to their environment can be set alongside Marxist-postmodernist optimism that capitalism and its global mega-brands will ultimately deconstruct themselves. This view assumes that modern markets and brand images are not just quantitatively different from their predecessors, in that they circulate faster across a wider variety of domains, but also represent a qualitatively different historical stage, a postmodern inversion of classical capitalist values expressed in hyper-fetishisation. The dystopian prospect within this frame is total alienation, as the self with its needs and desires is integrated into a seamlessly commodified semiotic order (Baudrillard [1973] 1981; Kellner 2003). For political liberals, however, the rule of law and the critique of law will remain key elements in the defence of the integrity of the public sphere.

Part III

Key Issues

Insider Judges and Outsider Critics

In an essay entitled 'How judges fool themselves' (1988), Robert Bensen draws on the work of anthropologist Marvin Harris (1987) in examining judges' self-understandings. Harris argued that Hindu farmers' narrative of the legitimacy of the prohibition of slaughter of domestic cows was from the outsider's viewpoint in conflict with their practice of underfeeding male calves. These calves had little value in the economic system in that region (Kerala, India), and in practice the underfeeding meant that most died. Applying this anthropologically uncomfortable dichotomy to judges, Bensen points to the contradiction between an internal and an external view. From within, judges feel themselves highly constrained by the legal materials (the body of texts they are called upon to apply) and the conventions of legal reasoning, and see most cases as having obvious and unproblematic answers. The external view identifies this as a professional mystification, drawing on 'priestly and later quasi-scientific traditions of interpretation'.

This theory of adjudication relies on the nature of language as 'a referential labeling system corresponding to things or ideas that existed "out there" in the world or the mind', allowing transparent access to the intent of the lawmaker (Bensen 1988: 33). Bensen argues that with the rise of twentieth-century modernism, this paradigm for understanding language and representation has crumbled, though 'the profession still veils itself in mystifying exegetical practices and is still a power elite' (Bensen 1988: 33). From the outside perspective, it is evident that the legal materials are 'indeterminate', and the perception that most cases are 'easy' is the product of a contingent alignment of factors in the internal culture and group norms of law, which for judges are preferably, but not necessarily, also aligned with public opinion. The adjudicative behaviour of judges is marked by 'self-deception', in which they mistake their social position and mystique for objective authority. They lack training in 'language analysis or interpretation theory', except for what is acquired within the profession, and like 'tribal shamans and Western psychiatrists' they believe in their own methods 'despite lack of empirical evidence' (Bensen 1988: 54–5). Bensen argues for a number of reforms, including accountability of law to public debate, the use of lay judges and lay practitioners ('since legal training

is largely irrelevant and antithetical to what actually takes place in the interpretation of law'), and the promotion of alternative methods of dispute
resolution. Bensen's solution to the insider-outsider problem is in effect to
abolish law (though he does not take his arguments explicitly to this conclusion), since the features that make law a distinct and autonomous culture, its
beliefs about language and textual interpretation, and its pre-modern
mystification of the authority of the priest-caste are, from the external
observer's point of view, at odds with the reality of how law actually works.
Instead of judges in black robes reading the runes or tarot cards of law, law
should be become transparent to the political forces and conflicts with which
society is confronted, and become 'candidly accountable to public debate'
(Bensen 1988: 55).

The idea that judges are the prisoners of the illusion of law raises a set of
further issues. Bensen does not accuse the judges of 'bad faith', of conscious
manipulation of law for political ends, though he would probably not deny
that these also exist within the system. Let us presume that judges are sincere
in drawing boundaries in social space, labelling an action legal or illegal, or
deciding whether an exchange is valid or invalid given the text of a contract.
Judges have a genuine sense that they are constrained by the legal materials,
and work to apply objective legal principles to facts to achieve just outcomes,
rather than merely working backwards 'from just outcomes that accord with
their chosen themes – their reality' (Brion 1988: 75). What would be the effect
of persuading judges that the lines or distinctions they are drawing are the
product of illusions and therefore that the lines themselves must also be illusory? If the anthropologist for example had persuaded the Kerala farmer that
he was in fact simply killing his male calves, the economic framework might
have constrained the farmer to continue as before, but he would now be bur-
dened by the awareness of violating his religious convictions for the sake of
economic survival. But the farmer might also reject the outsider's view as
invalid or irrelevant, on the grounds that 'I am a good Hindu and this is what
we do and this is how we attach meaning to these actions.'

Law has its own taboos, including the fundamental prohibition that binds
judges to respect the boundary between the domain of the law-maker and that
of the interpreter, and the demand that judges show fidelity to the law rather
than to their private morality or politics. Law also has taboos against conflicts
of interest, which again an external sceptic might regard as largely mythical,
given the class (gender, race) origins or class interests of judges as a collectiv-
ity. The judge who was persuaded that adjudication was a distorted form of
politics, and that there were no independent legal principles and texts with
stable meanings to be consulted, might also continue adjudicating in bad faith,
producing judgments that mimic conventional legal reasoning. But like the
farmer, the judge might simply respond (in quasi-Wittgensteinian fashion) in
this way: 'I am a good judge and this is what we do as judges and this is how
we attach meaning to these actions and these texts.'

The sharp dichotomy between the insider and the outsider viewpoint is itself a creation of the outsider's frame of reference and the assumptions that underlie it. The Kerala farmer who makes a fundamental cultural distinction between underfeeding and slaughtering is, like the judge (as Bensen's insider), drawing on cultural practice, beliefs and group norms to maintain a conceptual boundary between two practices. The outside observer takes as determinative the similar consequences (not identical, since not all the male calves die) of the two practices, and also diagnoses a materially necessary cultural blindness to the similarity. The conclusion is that the farmers are in fact killing their male calves, in violation of Hindu cultural norms. Ironically, the anthropological observer is in an analogous position to the judge as outsider-observer of social life. The anthropologist takes the everyday narratives and categories of social life and imposes a rational and normative reading on them, and assumes both a shared and stable frame of reference between the observer's position and that of the farmer, and a hierarchy of observation and judgment.

A second anthropological observer might dispute the validity of the rational objectivist frame within which the cultural 'contradiction' emerges. The 'reflexive' or 'postmodern turn' in Western anthropology produced a disciplinary crisis precisely over the status of the outsider's intellectual framework and the nature of the anthropological 'gaze'. While the judge in Western societies is not a traditional object of anthropological scrutiny, the same paradoxes of reflexivity arise, once we begin to regard law as a culture and judges as its shamans. The distinction drawn by the farmer might be understood to rely on a culturally salient distinction between a partial omission (male calves are only allowed to suckle briefly) and a positive act (slaughter). A third (legally trained) observer might point to the complexities of the assignment of 'duty of care' in common law systems, and thus to the great problems of understanding these issues cross-culturally. In general, common law systems do not assign liability for a failure to act to prevent an accident, unless it is established that the 'non-actor' owed a duty of care to the victim. These systems are thus generally reluctant to penalise non-actions ('omissions'), even if the consequence is the same as an illegal action (murder), that is, avoidable death: 'In theory, it is possible to watch a child drowning in a puddle without attracting legal liability' (Harpwood 2005: 108).

Bensen's external viewpoint relies on an objectivist framework itself, for example 'empirical evidence' and the rational analysis which allows the outsider to diagnose the self-deception of the insider, who is presented as what in sociological theory is termed a 'judgmental dope' (Heritage 1984: 117–18). If the authority of law is demystified, then the question arises as to where adjudicative authority is to be found. A lay judge is still a judge, and, unless law is abolished, law is inevitably text-based. Bensen from one point of view offers a Protestant call for transparency, which suggests that authority can rest on a shared system of meaning and interpretation available to all, and a form of socio-political accountability. At present, according to Bensen, socio-political issues are refracted and distorted by their representation within the culture of law, before being resolved by political actors hiding behind the veil of the law's rituals. Within law, 'language and legal meaning are cultural artifacts, produced in time and space through specific social institutions' (Bensen 1988: 38), but this would apply to any institution, as each 'form of life', even a 'lay legal system', would create its own meanings as cultural artefacts. Either there is a possibility of objective language, and it is the culture of law that distorts it, or the idea is a myth, and abolishing legal culture will not create a transparent system of representation.

Western legal systems assign judges a high degree of personal authority over court proceedings, and as the face of the legal system, its personification at the point where law intersects with society, the judge operates as a direct agent impacting decisively on individual lives. This has led politically critical studies of legal discourse to emphasise how the rules of evidence, and judges' control of them, restrict the ability of ordinary participants to narrate their own stories in their own words. The legal process 'manages the voices of ordinary people', and constrains their narratives: 'Perhaps the most common complaints of litigants at all levels of the legal process are that they did not get a proper opportunity to tell their story and that the judge did not get to hear the real facts of the case' (Conley and O'Barr 1990: 19, 172). This is often understood as the claim that 'law gives voice only to the powerful' (Conley and O'Barr 1990: 172). Philips argues that judges, by their differing styles of discourse, and in their management of the courtroom, reflect a range of political ideologies of which judges are not aware in any systematic sense: 'the clearest ideological stance that judges take is that they are not ideological' (Philips 1998: xiv). The links between written law and court procedure, while they are explicit to the judge as legal insider, are opaque to non-lawyers (Philips 1998: 119): 'The hiddenness stems in part from the hiddenness of the written law itself. The defendant usually does not see the written law, does not know what it is, and does not know how to find it.' Further, judges are not just practising a profession but practising politics and exercising power. And law is neither a coherent nor a truly separate form of thought in American society (Philips 1998: 123). Thus a study in 'anthropological linguistics' ends in a general critique of the autonomy and internal coherence of law, even though anthropology as a discipline is defined by its sensitivity and orientation towards insider characterisations.

Conley and O'Barr (1990: ix) distinguish between litigants who offer accounts of their problems in rule-oriented terms, in which they focus on the general rules and neutral principles of law, and present their case in these terms to the court, and litigants who display a 'relational orientation', and who seek redress for their own specific problems and for the wrongs that have been done to them by appealing to an idea of law as expressing social interdependence. The first group's understanding of law coincides largely with the legal insiders' view, thus facilitating their interaction with the legal system.

The relationally oriented litigants discussed by Conley and O'Barr are, from a less sympathetic view, in essence egocentric narrators: their demand is that law should address and rectify wrongs that have been done to them, as identified and characterised by them.

At a more general level, this opposition is between a view of law as faceless rule (where the very facelessness of the rule is what makes it just) and law as the doing of justice to individuals, where what is just is customised to the individual circumstances and morality of the case. It is perhaps misleading to assimilate the relationally oriented litigants described by Conley and O'Barr to ideals of community and social interdependence. Adjudication can by definition never wholly assimilate the subjective narratives of its litigants, and this is as true of everyday 'vernacular' justice, the process by which social actors informally assign blame, as it is of formal legal systems. The criticisms of judges for being self-deceiving or ideological fail to confront the wider question, namely that any institutionalisation of adjudication will involve a concentration of authority over language and a social hierarchy under which the adjudicator is in a superior position.

Judges are often criticised as wrongly empowered readers, in that they usurp the authority of the author of statutory texts (the legislature) or of the language of the text, and impose their own ideological meanings, and for their assumption of priest-like autonomy and mystification. A British judge, Lord Devlin, writing in the aftermath of the courts' involvement in the enforcement of the socially divisive Industrial Relations Act 1971, denied, however, that judges were merely neutral and detached arbitrators: 'British judges have never practiced such detachment. The reason may lie in their origin as servants of the Crown or perhaps in the fact that for a long time the law they administered was what they had made themselves' (cited in Griffith 1997: 293). Judges had an independent and autonomous role, which endowed them with 'high powers', the wise deployment of which 'had enabled the judiciary to use its reputation for impartiality and independence for the public good'. However, these powers should only be used in support of 'consensus law':

> If judges are to do more than decide what the law means, if they are also to speak for it, their voice must be the voice of the community; it must never be taken for the voice of the government or the voice of the majority. (cited in Griffith 1997: 293)

While Griffith criticises Lord Devlin's distinction between consensus and nonconsensus law, he stresses that Lord Devlin correctly denies the neutrality of the judiciary in criminal law and at all points where judges have to act in setting limits to government powers and individual rights, or decide to intervene in the public interest (Griffith 1997: 295). Lord Devlin also argues in effect for an independent source of sovereignty, which means that judges speak for law as the voice of the community.

Bensen compares judges not only to shamans and Western psychiatrists, but also to artists producing a collage', assembling materials into a work which they then 'display for the public in the form of a written opinion' (1988: 34). If the judge is an artist, then the legal theorist is the critic, but one who assumes authority over the interpretation of the work. Critics of judges as 'ideological' and self-deceiving assume interpretative authority over judges and reject judges' insider self-narratives. The origin and grounds of this inter-pretative authority are, it might be argued, no less mysterious than the author-ity of law. The power of the critic of law appears to derive from a combination of intellectual framework (Marxism, in the case of Philips) and a self-authorised assumption of agency, whereby the critic speaks for ordinary people, ordinary discourse and ordinary language. This involves not only an assumption of political authority over law and judges, but also interpretative authority, in that meanings which are opaque to judges are transparent to the outside critic. It is unclear why, in the chain of authors and critics, one criti-cal stance should be elevated above all the others.

In passing a statute, the legislature offers an implicit or explicit critique of the previous law, including judge-made law, as well as a response to whatever public commentaries have been offered on the previous state of the law, and may draw on specific or general empowerment from the electoral process. Once the law is passed, judges become its readers and law is primarily addressed to judges, even if all those who are subject to law are deemed to have notice of it. Judges are not only readers of law but its critics, and, in the legal philosopher Ronald Dworkin's famous image of law as a 'chain novel', also its authors. Dworkin views judges as 'creative interpreters' who do not seek to reconstruct the intention of the author or artist, but rather are forward-looking, and '*essentially* concerned with purposes rather than mere causes' (Dworkin 1986: 51, emphasis in original). Artistic interpretation and the inter-pretation of social practice, unlike ordinary conversational interpretation and scientific interpretation, are creative but constrained: 'For the history or shape of a practice or object constrains the available interpretations of it' (Dworkin 1986: 52). Creative interpretation 'aims to impose purpose over the text or data or tradition being interpreted', and can be compared to a 'literary critic teasing out the various dimensions of value in a complex play or poem' (1986: 228). However, 'judges are authors as well as critics' 'and judges write the next instalment of the novel by maximising what Dworkin sees as 'the dimension of fit' in terms of formal or structural characteristics, as well as 'his more sub-stantial aesthetic judgments', and these together relate to judgments about textual coherence and integrity. Dworkin's author, is constrained by fidelity to the novel as it has been written so far, but is an author, not a mere reader or passive critic (Dworkin 1986: 254):

> Judges who accept the interpretative ideal of integrity decide hard cases
> by trying to find, in some coherent set of principles about people's rights

and duties, the best constructive interpretation of the political structure and legal doctrine of their community.

However, like other commentators on judges and interpretation, Dworkin's theory is at least in part at odds with how the insider judges themselves understand their role. Judges as critics can on occasion suggest that the legislator has lost the plot entirely. In the English case of *Dyson v Qualtex* (2006), Jacob LJ made the following comments on S 213 of the UK Unregistered Design Act 1988 (at 14):

> It has the merit of being short. It has no other. [. . .] It is not just a question of drafting (though words and phrases such as 'commonplace', 'dependent', 'aspect of shape or configuration of part of an article' and 'design field in question' are full of uncertainty in themselves and pose near impossible factual questions). The problem is deeper: neither the language used nor the context of the legislation give any clear idea what was intended. [. . .] The absence of any clear policy, as to where the line of compromise was intended to run, means that brightline rules cannot be deduced.

'Brightline rules' is a term for statutory rules and precedents that create clear demarcations, and allow judges to apply them relatively unproblematically to a range of factual situations in what is felt to be a consistent and predictable fashion. Here the judge is frankly dismissive of the previous author's contribution to the chain of law, as the privileged reader who must 'make the text work' in the context of commercial practice. Further, the judge presents the interpretative activity as one of discerning the intention behind the legislation, and this seemingly contradicts Dworkin's account.

But Dworkin is not offering (at this point at least) a description of insider accounts of interpretative practice, and has anticipated this problem. If the goal of interpretation is taken as finding the author's intention, then this must be 'a *consequence* of having applied the methods of constructive interpretation' (Dworkin 1986: 54, emphasis in original). This seems to reduce the distinction to naught: what Dworkin is saying is that, whatever the judge says or thinks, the judge is involved in creative construction. We can of course dismiss Jacob LJ, this judge-critic-author, as having no more authority than any other reader, as looking and failing to find an intention that is merely a construct of his judicial training. The use of 'intentional language', the ascription of intention to a will located in an autonomous self, has been attacked in postmodern and other intellectual frameworks as relying on a fiction. Judges on this view live in a world of conceptual phantoms and ghosts. Yet it is hard to see how an insider reading can be dismissed as 'ideological' or 'self-deceptive' merely on the basis of generic outsider claims.

Legal theorists operate both as critics of the law and critics of judges and what they say about the law. The only reason to bestow some special privilege on the legal theorist as critic is that they stand outside the legal process itself, and that is indeed Bensen's position. But this viewpoint relies crucially on the assumption of methodological objectivity by the outsider, that is, paradoxically on one of the fundamental foundations of rule of law 'ideology' itself. As we have seen above, it is not only external critics that claim to speak on behalf of the community; judges sometimes also make this claim, and it is not clear what kind of adjudicator we require to evaluate their respective positions.

At stake here is the extent to which adjudicators (and interpreters of all kinds) can be said to have insight into the principles, assumptions and social and psychological forces that determine their decisions. On the basis of an empirical-statistical study, Farber suggests that the decisions of theory-conscious judges cannot be neatly mapped onto their theoretical positions, but that theories of statutory interpretation are none the less important and worth studying (Farber 2000). For Jackson, there is a radical divide between 'decision-making' and 'justification', and law falsely presents these as identical (Jackson 1988: 194). While functionalists believe that 'man is the master of his language', rather than its servant', theories of semiotics tend to deny that choices made within a system reflect conscious intent, and that 'the subject is spoken by language' (Eco 1984: 45, cited in Jackson [1985] 1997: 27). Fish argues that we cannot stand to the side of our own ways of thinking to reach an objective self-critique (Fish 1989: 437). Total scepticism about insider insight, however, ends up by undermining any claim to outsider insight. Arguably, a better anthropological framing for the judge would be as 'bricoleur'. Claude Lévi-Strauss ([1962] 1966) limited this image to the 'primitive' thinker, who is the 'amateur craftsman who turns the broken clock into a pipe rack, the broken table into an umbrella stand, the umbrella stand into a lamp and anything into something else' (Douglas 1987: 66). In contrast to Lévi-Strauss, Douglas sees this style of thought as universal, arguing that the 'notion of bric-a-brac describes well the recurrent analogies and styles of thought that characterize any civilization' (Douglas 1987: 66).

B Hard Cases and Ideal Interpreters

Debate over so-called 'hard cases' is fundamental to legal theory and its discussion of language. For H. L. A. Hart, most cases were decided within the core meaning of legal rules. Rules had a certain core, but the language of rules was surrounded by a 'penumbra of uncertainty'. This was referred to by Hart, following Waismann (1965), as the 'open-texture' of language and legal rules, and in relying on an idea of a stable linguistic meaning Hart's model parallels the linguist's distinction between a stable 'core' meaning and marginal variations which are a feature of language in context (see Figure 1).

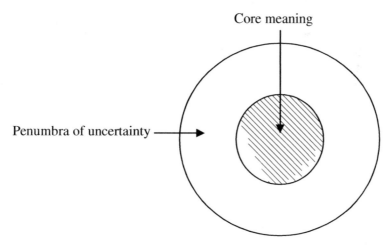

Figure 1 Hart's model of linguistic meaning

'Hard cases' were those where law in effect ran out, and the judge had to resort to extra-legal means to resolve the dispute. Judges had to use their discretion and balance possibly conflicting policy considerations. In 'plain cases' they could apply the plain language of the relevant legal textual authority (Hart [1961] 1994: 126):

Even when verbally formulated general rules are used, uncertainties as to the form of behaviour required by them may break out in particular concrete cases. Particular fact-situations do not await us already marked off from each other, and labelled as instances of the general rule, the application of which is in question; nor can the rule itself step forward to claim its own instances. In all fields of experience, not only that of rules, there is a limit, inherent in the nature of language, to the guidance which general language can provide. There will indeed be plain cases constantly recurring in similar contexts to which general expressions are clearly applicable ('If anything is a vehicle a motor-car is one') but there will also be cases where it is not clear whether they apply or not. ('Does "vehicle" used here include bicycles, airplanes, roller skates?')

There was no set of interpretative techniques that could fully solve these problems (Hart [1961] 1994: 126):

Canons of 'interpretation' cannot eliminate, through they can diminish, these uncertainties; for these canons are themselves general rules for the use of language, and make use of general terms which themselves require interpretation. They cannot, any more than other rules, provide for their own interpretation. The plain case, where the general terms seem to need no interpretation and where the recognition of instances seems unproblematic or 'automatic', are only the familiar ones, constantly recurring in similar contexts, where there is a general agreement in judgments as to the applicability of the classifying terms.

There was a core of certainty surrounded by a 'penumbra' of uncertainty attaching to every rule: 'Nothing can eliminate this duality of a core of certainty and a penumbra of doubt when we are engaged in bringing particular situations under general rules' (Hart [1961] 1994: 123). Hart's model can be interpreted schematically as in Table 1.

Dworkin rejected this way of understanding hard cases, and sought to defend an 'integrity' view whereby decisions in hard cases fall within law. According to what he terms the 'rights thesis', 'judicial decisions in hard cases are characteristically generated by principle not policy' and 'by confirming or denying concrete rights' (Dworkin 1975: 1074, 1078). The precise target of Dworkin's argument is Hart's view that in hard cases judges 'legislate interstitially' (Dworkin 1975: 1080), that is, that judges become a kind of second-class or 'deputy legislator' (Dworkin 1975: 1058) operating in the 'interstices', the narrow gaps that the hard case has revealed.

Dworkin sought to defend the autonomy of law by showing that the boundaries of law legitimately extend to include decisions in hard cases, that is, that judges are not obliged by hard cases to engage in what are in effect constitutionally *ultra vires* acts, acts which exceed the powers allotted to them under the law:

Table 1 Rule: 'No vehicles in the park'

Easy cases	Hard cases
Buses, commercial lorries, fuel tankers, military vehicles, private cars, motorcycles	(From easier to harder?): bicycle, skateboard, child's bicycle, roller-skates, . . ., statue of a tank (as a war-memorial; see Fuller 1958)
Core meaning of the word 'vehicle'	'Penumbra of uncertainty' in relation to scope of word 'vehicle'
Autonomous, 'internal', decision process	Resort to 'external aids': reconstruction of legislative intent; use of dictionaries
Decision is determinate, based primarily on the plain meaning of the rule; judge applies the rule objectively; decision is derived formalistically (mechanically, . . .)	Decision involves policy, politics, sociological context; judge must balance competing criteria
Objective decision making	Subjective decision making
Legal certainty; predictability of outcome	Absence of legal certainty; arbitrary 'justice'?
Judges apply the law	Judges make law

'Once an autonomous institution is established, such that participants have institutional rights under distinct rules belong to that institution, then hard cases may arise that must, in the nature of the case, be supposed to have an answer' (Dworkin 1975: 1081). The question then arises as to how a judge identifies the intention or purpose of the statute in question, and the principles that underlie it. Dworkin's answer is in terms of an ideal judge whom he terms 'Hercules'.

Dworkin's omniscient judge Hercules in some ways occupies an analogous position to Chomsky's 'ideal speaker-hearer' (Chomsky 1965). Just as Chomsky's ideal speaker-hearer knows the language perfectly, so Dworkin's Hercules is 'a lawyer of superhuman skill, learning, patience and acumen'. Hercules is a judge in an American jurisdiction who accepts 'the main uncontroversial constitutive and regulative rules of law' (Dworkin 1975: 1083). Hercules does not operate in hard cases to supplement what the legislature has done, nor does he attempt 'to determine what it would have done if it had been aware of the problem presented by the case'; nor does Hercules go beyond the wording of the statute, since the statutory language which was enacted provides a limit which 'enables the process to operate without absurdity'. This 'permits Hercules to say that the legislature pushed some policy to the limits of the language it used, without also supposing that it pushed that policy to some indeterminate further point' (Dworkin 1975: 1087).

Unlike a legislator, the judge will feel the 'gravitational force' of previous decisions, and seek to discern a rule that is 'immanent in the law as a whole'

or available through the law's 'internal logic' (Dworkin 1975: 1090). In taking
such decisions, Hercules 'must construct a scheme of abstract and concrete
principles that provides a coherent justification for all common law precedents, and so far as these are to be justified on principle, constitutional and
statutory principles as well' (Dworkin 1975: 1094). This must include the
ability to discard some part of the institutional history as mistaken (1975:
1097, 1099ff). The rights thesis offers both a description and explanation of
the 'institutional structure of adjudication', and a 'political justification' for
that structure (1975: 1101).

It is important in this context not to lose sight of what is at stake here for our
understanding of the role of language within law. For Dworkin, it does not make
sense, except in highly exceptional circumstances, to say that the language of the
statute runs out. Dworkin, however, imagines a second judge, Herbert (a somewhat mischievous reference to H. L. A. Hart, whose first name was Herbert),
who takes this view (Dworkin 1975: 1103). For Dworkin, legal interpretation
and adjudication are not clearly distinguished, though he does acknowledge that
the language of the statute places an outer boundary on the range of possible
interpretations, whereas for Hart/Herbert the process in hard cases is in two distinct stages, one which is interpretative of the language of the statute, and the
subsequent step which is not. Dworkin in this sense is defending not only the
integrity of law but also the integrity of legal language as part of law.

It is not possible here to follow all the many lines of this debate, the threads
of which are taken up by Dworkin in his *Law's Empire* (1986). There Dworkin
adds a further fictional judge to his cast of characters, namely Hermes, 'who
is almost as clever as Hercules and just as patient, who also accepts law as
integrity but accepts the speaker's meaning theory of legislation'. This means
that Hermes believes that 'legislation is communication', and that 'he must
apply statutes by discovering the communicative will of the legislators' when
they passed the statute (Dworkin 1986: 317). One line of objections to
Dworkin's concept of a super-hero judge has attacked this idealisation for
eliminating factors that are essential for applying it in an explanatory way
(Kim 2007: 383): 'We do not know whether Hercules has colleagues, whether
he votes as part of a multi-member court, or whether he has inferior courts he
supervises or superior courts to which he must answer.'

Chomsky's ideal-speaker concept has similarly been the target of sustained
criticism. Just as Dworkin's judge can look through the surface forms of law
to discern the deep structure of rules, principles and their interrelationships,
so Chomsky's ideal speaker-hearer has perfect knowledge both of language
and of the particular language, since the speech community is perfectly homo-
geneous. Linguistic knowledge, in one of Chomsky's formulations, consists of
tacit knowledge of 'principles and parameters', and these are entirely distinct
from the contingent factors that render language in social action problematic, unsystematic, fragmented, contested and so on. Just as Dworkin's judge
can distinguish a mistake from a true principle of law, Chomsky's ideal

speaker-hearer, in acquiring mastery of a language, can distinguish between so-called 'performance errors' such as slips of the tongue and utterances that reflect correctly the underlying system. Both these ideal constructs serve to illuminate a particular vision of the object of study.

An alternative way to conceive of an ideal system of law is not to invent a judge that has a total and unmediated grasp of the entirety of law, but to imagine a legal code that would have no need of such a judge, or perhaps any judges at all. This was the utopian vision that can be glimpsed below Bentham's utilitarian dream of law without lawyers. Bentham was deeply hostile to the common law and argued that legal rules should be codified into a 'simple, readily understandable code that would largely dispense with the need for lawyers' (Posner 2001: 58). A system of specialised mediation was inimical to justice. The density of legal language and the dispersed and elusive location of legal principles meant that this class of mediators was in a position to maximise their profit unchecked through their control of the linguistic transactions of law. Bentham's cost–benefit (pain–pleasure) analysis of legal language was in this sense a further development of the secularised Protestant argument for linguistic transparency.

Bentham's thinking did have an impact on debates over the merits of codification, but contrary to his intentions, it remained largely theoretical. Often the ideal of law is contrasted with the reality of actual law, as here was evoked by the American jurist Benjamin Cardozo (1870–1938) (Cardozo 1921: 143):

> No doubt the ideal system, if it were attainable, would be a code at once so flexible and so minute, as to supply in advance for every conceivable situation the just and fitting rule. But life is too complex to bring the attainment of this ideal within the compass of human powers.

The ideal legal code would permit a mechanical jurisprudence to operate, since it would be a system in which each factual situation was provided for in all its particularity in the code. No act of an interpreter to apply the law would be necessary, as the correct legal characterisations of a situation would appear on the face of the law. Since law cannot be a code of this kind, we must rely on judges to grapple with the uncertain fit between the law, language and the world. The adjudicator or judge is a necessary evil given the inherent limitations of language. In cases where there were gaps in the law, or in the evolution of law through decided cases, there was inevitably a retrospective element to rule-making (Cardozo 1921: 145):

> In each system, hardship must at times result from postponement of the rule of action till a time when action is complete. It is one of the consequences of the limitations of the human intellect and of the denial to legislators of infinite prevision.

Cardozo somewhat unconvincingly argues that this retrospectivity normally involved no hardship, as in general such cases concerned 'something that would have happened anyhow' (Cardozo 1921: 145–6).

Cardozo's comments are those of a practising judge who experienced at first hand the pressures of adjudication that accompanied the development of tort law in the United States. They reflect a sense of the law's deficiencies when set against an ideal system 'so certain and rigid that it could be applied to any conceivable situation with mathematical precision and accuracy' (Goble 1933: 229). In discussing Cardozo's ideal legal code, Solan brings in Chomsky's understanding of grammar to offer a partial solution for a judge facing two conflicting precedents (Solan 1993: 15):

> The core of our linguistic knowledge, the part that linguists call a 'generative grammar', is, however, indeed the type of 'code' for which Cardozo yearns. Therefore, to the extent that a judge can decide a case by resort to this special human power, he can avoid the difficulties of having to rely, for example, on one set of precedents when he and the parties know full well that a different body of precedents could have been invoked to justify the opposite result.

The judge as ideal speaker-hearer can at least minimise the area of legal uncertainty. Even if law runs out, language does not.

This discussion gives us a number of possible positions. Hart suggests that law and language run out together, and that legal interpretation is tied to the core meaning of words and expressions. Once the core meaning of those expressions fails to offer a solution to the legal problem, the judge must look beyond law and the legal language to make a moral, political or economic decision. Dworkin likewise sees law and the language of statute as coinciding in extent, but he denies that law-language ever runs out, as there is a 'right answer' immanent in the totality of the legal materials. Another way of seeing Dworkin's position is that whether language runs out or not, and whether case law precedent runs out or not, there is a legally valid solution available to Hercules. It makes no sense for Dworkin to say that language runs out, as he does not distinguish between the core and the penumbra meaning of statutory language. But he does see language as posing a limit to interpretation, so that it would be illegitimate for law to go beyond language. That is indeed his objection to Hart's model, namely that it in effect makes judges into second-class legislators who are obliged by the limits of law-language to enter non-legal territory. By contrast, Solan suggests that law may run out, but that language does not, as language is an ideal code or 'special power' which unlike law is equipped in advance to characterise every situation. The 'nightmare' of mechanical jurisprudence is also the linguist's 'dream', so that the 'language machine' (Roy Harris 1987) serves also as a 'judicial machine'.

C The Judge as Tennis Umpire

In thinking about the relation of legal language to reality, and the question of lines between concepts, we can consider the case in property law of 'lease' versus 'licence' as a characterisation of a form of occupancy right. This might be understood as a question of definition, that is, if we define these two words clearly, then we can then use the definitions as criterial in determining whether a given factual situation involves a licence or a lease. On this view, definitions set limits between adjoining areas of conceptual space, like a map showing the border between countries. Neither the terms themselves, nor the social situation, are on this view indeterminate, and we can use linguistic definition as a lens to disclose clearly the underlying social categories. Hard or marginal cases would not undermine that determinacy, since any boundary drawn will inevitably have a smaller or larger zone of uncertainty, just as in tennis there are cases where it is difficult to determine whether the ball landed on the line so as to be counted in, or outside. The fact that there are sometimes disputes as to whether the ball was in or out does not mean that the whole process is indeterminate – on the contrary, these difficult cases arise against a large majority of cases where the ball is generally clearly determined to be in or out. Those determinations are shared as public perceptions by players, spectators (including television viewers) and officials. The aim of the system is to reduce as far as possible the zone of uncertainty by – in the case of tennis – better training of umpires and use of new technology and – in law – sharpening and clarifying the criteria.

A simple diagram can represent these decisions as follows:

IN	?	OUT
LEASE	?	LICENCE

In tennis, the lines are laid down in advance of the game. The lines of the court are marked out according to the measurements laid down in the rules. The space of the court is already marked out into zones with specific and shared meanings in the context of the game. These are stipulated in the rules of tennis. All involved share a common understanding of the significance of those lines, and the role which they play in winning and losing. There is no disjunction between the semiotic layout of the court (the nets, lines, etc.), the labels used by umpires and line-judges, and the intentions of the players. What form of indeterminacy if any can we find in this aspect of the rules of tennis and where is that indeterminacy located?

Even given the small number of disputed calls, it would be possible to argue that tennis is fundamentally indeterminate, since the result of a match can potentially hinge on a single call. But that indeterminacy is arguably found not in the rules of tennis, nor in the intentions of the players, but in the physical-temporal-psychological situation, that is, the nexus between speed and location of the ball, the surface it is striking, the material of the ball, and human vision which must operate in 'real time' and is notoriously subject to contextual influences, stress, bias, etc. Arbitration is only required in cases where the ball has landed in the small zone of uncertainty. In professional tennis 'Hawk-Eye' technology is now available which tracks the path of the ball. Players are allotted a limited number of appeals against calls, and there is ongoing debate about the technology and the role it should play. The better the Hawk-Eye system functions, the less indeterminacy there should be in the arbitration process.

If the analogy holds, then in law, the line between lease and licence is marked out and 'visible' in conceptual or social space in the same way as the line of the court is visible in tennis. But to what extent does it hold? The distinction between lease and licence is understood metaphorically as a division in space: 'the definitional knife-edge separating lease from licence' (Gray and Gray 2005: 496); 'Since medieval times the criterion of exclusive possession had tended to mark off the boundary between the lease and the licence' (Gray and Gray 2005: 499). The courts have insisted that the inner reality of the agreement, not the labels used by the parties, define whether occupation is under a tenancy or a licence. This is particularly true in the residential context where the two parties are not of equal power (compare the case of two commercial concerns bargaining with the benefit of professional legal advice). Thus an agreement which uses the word 'licence' may be determined to involve a lease (*Street v Mountford* 1985), and one which uses the word 'lease' may be determined to involve a licence (*Clore v Theatrical Properties Ltd and Westby & Co* 1936).

The court therefore looks beyond the labels agreed and assigned by the participants themselves to affix a legally and normatively 'true' label on the situation, one which may be deemed to reflect the 'real intention' of the parties: Bingham LJ in *Antoniades v Villiers* (1990, at 444B): 'A cat does not become a dog because the parties have agreed to call it a dog'. Lord Templeman in *Street v Mountford* (1985, at 819E–F) stated that the parties to an agreement 'cannot turn a tenancy into a licence merely by calling it one'. Thus, '[t]he manufacture of a five-pronged implement for manual digging results in a fork even if the manufacturer, unfamiliar with the English language, insists that he intended to make and has made a spade'. This 'rectification of names' is possible because the court has the power in the context to determine the correct legal label to attach to a particular situation, and the power to impute a specific intention to create a certain kind of legal relationship to the parties, looking at the formal agreements they may have drawn up, but also at the totality of their behaviour and mutual dealings. A court can confidently declare certain labelling practices to be a 'sham' and apply the correct labels so as to reflect the true legal nature of the relationship or situation. But the reality to which the court is referring is not found independently of the legal process; rather reality is put together from different kinds of 'pre-digested' evidence, as well as from intentions imputed by law to social actors. Within the court's field of vision are simultaneously present a large number of previously decided cases, each with its own specific facts, the legal status of which has been determined by the operations of law.

Judicial sceptics suggest in effect that the judge is like a tennis umpire who draws the line on the tennis court, while simultaneously adjudicating as to whether the ball was in or out. Worse, the umpire claims, or, worse still, even actually believes, that the line was there clearly visible to everyone all along. This is the force of Cornell's observation that '[i]t is interpretation that gives us the rule, not the other way round' (Cornell 1992: 12). One response to this view is that there cannot be a 'judicial Hawk-Eye' to give objective justice. Law could not be essentially other than it is; law, like money and language, is animated by faith in a 'form of life'; and any form of life can be shown from an external, sceptical point of view to be an illusion. But this position seems equally unsatisfactory, as it returns the authority of law and the judge to the realm of the pre-modern, putting it beyond reformist critique and moral-political judgment. The argument might more profitably move on to a consideration of how and whether the internal reflexivity of law (its scrutiny of its own concepts and their relationship to the social world) can none the less be integrated into a wider process of socio-political and moral reflection on law. One view is that the internal coherence and autonomy of law is functional in its very distance from the moral and cultural wars of society and its shifts in political power, allowing law to flourish in 'an environment of complexity, diversity and disagreement' (Waldron 2000: 53). Radical critics of law, however, seek constantly to break down the conceptual autonomy of law and translate its fictional legal categories into socio-political ones.

D The Golden Mean?

We can think of approaches to legal interpretation as lying on a spectrum from formalism/textualism at one end to a wide variety of indeterminacy theorists at the other. Between textualism and indeterminacy can be found many attempts to define a degree of relative legal-linguistic certainty or stability, for example by distinguishing between indeterminacy and 'underdeterminacy'. Graff (1982: 406) accepts that there is no 'semantic immanence', that is, meanings do not inhere within texts, but denies that 'our practical ability to make sense of texts and utterances is somehow endangered or impaired'. A case which is 'underdetermined' is one where the outcome in a given legal case is 'constrained by the law, but not determined by it' (Solum 1996: 489). Winter seeks to ground reasoning in the underlying nature of human cognition (Winter 2001: 163):

> A cognitive account denies neither that there is indeterminacy in legal reasoning nor that social, political, and policy considerations play an important role in legal decisionmaking. What a cognitive account does claim is that it is possible to explicate the kinds, degrees, and reasons for the relative indeterminacy that one experiences in working with legal materials.

For Winter, the 'rationalist model' of legal reasoning is itself a source of indeterminacy, since there is a divide between the surface, rational reasoning of law and the underlying, actual processes of human cognition and the human imagination.

A further attempt to find a middle way between textual formalism and indeterminacy, as neither 'wholly discretionary' nor 'wholly mechanical', is found in Fiss (1982). Fiss associates indeterminacy and deconstruction with nihilism. The new nihilists 'have turned their back on adjudication and have begun a romance with politics' (Fiss 1982: 74). Against this politicisation, he sets an ideal of objective interpretation, so that interpretation is constrained by disciplining rules and by the existence of an interpretative community which recognises standards and 'a set of norms that transcend the particular vantage point of the person offering the interpretation' (Fiss 1982: 744). This does not exclude 'the creative role of the reader', nor the possibility of disagreement (Fiss 1982: 744–5). In a response to Fiss, Fish focuses on the idea that '[v]iewing adjudication as interpretation helps to stop the slide towards nihilism' and 'makes law possible', suggesting that what makes interpretation possible is not an underlying theory of adjudication which must underwrite, constrain or inform adjudication, but the existence of a 'field of practice', into which judges have been initiated through professional training and socialisation to become 'competent members' of the adjudicative community (Fish 1984: 1347). Fish can be understood as making a Wittgensteinian point, that we should not look for rules which exist outside social practices or 'forms of life':

> If the rules are to function as Fiss would have them function – to 'constrain the interpreter' – they themselves must be available or 'readable' independently of interpretation; that is, they must directly declare their own significance to any observer, no matter what his perspective.

An alternative way to see this is that Fish proposes an ethnomethodological account of adjudication, namely that it represents a 'situated practice' in which 'competent members' display 'accountability', and where any attempt to state the formal rules that govern that practice cannot exhaustively capture their reflexively available quality.

One discussion that mediates in an interesting way between textualism and indeterminacy is by Schauer (1985). Schauer argues that the focus on unrepresentative hard cases in legal theory and arguments from 'weird cases' and 'antilinguistic' results (i.e. where the language of the legal text is ignored or overridden) distorts our understanding of the role of language in law (Schauer 1985: 426):

> Once we look at easy as well as hard cases, however, once we look at law both outside and within the courthouse, it becomes clear that antilinguistic results occupy but a miniscule fraction of the instances in which the language is applied. By recognizing that following language is a law-applying and law-interpreting act, we can sensibly reject the claim that law is not importantly a function of the power of language.

For Schauer, language is a reliable channel for law to exercise its authority over behaviour. Language is not totally precise because it is 'necessarily limited by the lack of omniscience of human beings, and thus any use of language is bounded by the limitations of human foresight' (Schauer 1985: 422). Scepticism about language derives from 'unrealistic standards of what language is supposed to do', and if these are not met, 'then it is easy to fall into the abyss of nihilistic thinking' (Schauer 1985: 425). For Schauer, the focus within legal theory on 'the distorting metaphor of the core and the fringe' (1985: 427) has been misleading, linguistically articulated rules should be understood as generally excluding wrong answers, and the language of statute has established 'linguistic frames' or reference points: 'Even though the language itself does not tell us what goes within the frame, it does tell us when we have gone outside it' (Schauer 1985: 429). However, highly specific language sets up a relatively small frame, and those clauses with more general language 'are those with a substantially larger frame, giving a much wider range of permissible alternatives. This, however, is a continuum and not a dichotomy' (Schauer 1985: 430–1).

Schauer goes on to distinguish interpretation in art criticism from that in law or literature, in that the pre-existing case law interpreting a statute may affect the frame by either narrowing or extending it. The judge confronts not the original linguistic frame, but the adjustments to it made by previous decisions which have authority within the interpretative culture of law. In general, these pre-existing interpretations narrow rather than extend the frame: 'Interpretations continuously change the options available to subsequent interpreters, thus occasionally making quite precise clauses more open ended in practice but more often making even the most open ended clauses substantially less so' (Schauer 1985: 435). Thus Schauer argues that, while there is no single correct theory of the interpretation of a clause of the constitution, there are many interpretations that are correctly excluded, either by the linguistic frame itself, or by modifications to that frame produced by previous judgments.

In an epilogue to the article, Schauer notes resignedly that he will be characterised as a textualist or a literalist. He then makes a slightly different point, arguing that the idea of literal meaning, while it is correctly described as a myth ('the myth of linguistic certainty, commonly referred to as literalism'), none the less offers a real constraint on what judges do (Schauer 1985: 439–40):

> The text of the Constitution is not, by itself, going to provide answers to hard constitutional questions, and anyone with any sense knows that. The myth of literalism, however, remains the conscience on the judicial shoulder, constantly reminding judges (and hopefully the constitutional theorist) that they are expounding a written Constitution, and that interpretations inconsistent with the written text require an enormous amount of explanation and justification, if indeed they are even legitimate. [. . .]. The myth of literalism, or the myth of textualism, guides and channels the thinking process of the interpreter, just as the language serves the same function. That neither the myth nor the language is perfectly effective is not a comment on the inefficacy of either myths or language; it is a comment only on the human condition, of which both language and uncertainty are essential features. It is not so much the

quality of language itself that constrains and shapes interpretation but the belief on the part of judges that they are responsible to such meanings that is fundamental to adjudication.

Schauer ends by approaching the position of the indeterminacy theorists, since he suggests that literalism and textualism are founded on myths, albeit necessary myths. It is because judges believe in the myth that they are truly constrained, even if the lines they see are in some sense not really there. This implies that law is governed by necessary fictions, and that adjudication requires a degree of willed blindness to their fictional nature.

E Reflexivity and Garfinkel's Dystopia of Reasons

It has been argued that modern societies are especially reflexive, in that self-inquiry, historical debate, the density of regulation and reform are also themselves the subject of inquiry, historical debate, regulation and reform. Modern public culture reflects the mobile, unsettled quality of this reflexive modernity, a process in which modernity is understood to be engaged in modernizing itself (Beck et al. 2003: 1):

> When modernization reaches a certain stage it radicalizes itself. It begins to transform, for a second time, not only the key institutions but also the very principles of society. But this time the principles and institutions being transformed are those of modern society.

Diagnostics of this process include the increasingly blurred boundary between law and regulation, between public and commercial modes of governance, the proliferation of institutional codes of practice and quasi-legal forms, and the restless scrutiny of public forms of authority, including professional expertise, accompanied by the appearance of new forms of expertise, information technologies, media configurations and patterns of semiotic circulation. The experience of law as an ever-advancing social force has been termed 'juridification', one meaning of which is that non-legal forms of social control 'acquire legalistic characteristics' (Hunt and Wickham 1994: 48). Part of this process is the advance of the 'audit culture'. This is characterised by an increasing 'proceduralisation' in which rules for how decisions are to be reached are as important as rules governing behaviour, by a demand for explicitness, transparency and accountability, by a demand for reasons, and by a mistrust of settled institutional practice.

Law shares with art and literature the possibility of intense reflexivity. Reflexivity in postmodernism can be understood as a self-conscious and playful attempt to throw off the weight of accumulated narratives and 'heavy' historical awareness. Linguistics tends to separate the language system (the system of rules understood in the abstract) from language use, and both of these from values ascribed to language within ideology. For linguists, reflexivity is thus a position outside language, not part of language proper, and can thus be separated conceptually from it. This separation is methodologically necessary, since otherwise linguistics could not proceed with its systems analysis. But if we take law as our illustrative example, it is quite impossible to effect this separation: language use in the many domains of law is constitutive of, and understood against, legal and non-legal language norms and prescriptive thinking, both consensual and contested. Law contains or enacts a whole range of beliefs and norms about what language is, how it can or should be used, its limitations as a system of communication, and procedures for identifying the meaning or interpretation of a word, phrase or text, as well as detailed prescriptive rules about how language is to be used in certain contexts in order to effect particular legal meanings.

Observing the law deal with language, interpretation and meaning can be compared to watching a social exchange in slow motion. As with the replaying of a key sporting event, we can observe the process many times from a number of different angles or points of view, but this does not guarantee that all observers will agree on what they are seeing. The law is a highly reflexive and self-conscious institution, and that reflexivity means that a question about the meaning and interpretation of a particular word or expression also becomes a methodological inquiry into how to proceed. Legal reflexivity is employed in the search for a determinative outcome and a definitive, prescriptive reading of a text or label for a situation.

In the English case of *R v Derby Justices, ex p DPP* (1999), the court had to determine whether, when a defendant had assaulted a woman by hitting her head against a glass door, this constituted 'use of a weapon'. It was held that '[i]t would be an abuse of language to describe banging a victim's head against part of a building's structure as using a weapon' (see Bennion 2002: 1014). Bennion, seeking a rationale for the decision, comments: 'Would the answer have been different if the assailant had moved the door against the victim's head instead of moving her head against the door?' Here law moves into the foreground an aspect of the taken-for-granted background, and an ordinary, unproblematic expression, 'use of a weapon', suddenly becomes alien and obscure. This heightened reflexive scrutiny of language involves asking a question which in a surreal manner seems to push past the boundaries of ordinary language. But this is no postmodern game: the context is of course an extremely serious one. The court decided the issue by recontextualising the problem in ordinary usage, but an ordinary usage which is deemed to have (or is assigned) its own normative power of classification, one which should not be 'abused'. A critic of law might foreground other features of this scenario, perhaps the apparent arbitrariness of the appeal to ordinary usage, diagnosing this as an instance where a rule is created out of the case. That rule might be: the weapon must be moved against the victim, rather than vice versa; or, the weapon must be of such a size that it could be held and moved. A psychoanalytical reading might identify an uncanny displacement of 'abuse' from the victim of the assault onto language itself.

A further example of a case where the normativity of ordinary language appeared to run out was *Mandla v Dowell Lee* (1983). A clash between school rules with regard to hairstyle and the wearing of caps, on the one hand, and the Sikh custom of not cutting the hair and of wearing a turban, on the other, led to the House of Lords having to determine whether Sikhs were a racial group within the meaning of the UK Race Relations Act 1976. 'Racial group' was defined to mean 'a group of persons defined by reference to colour, race, nationality, or ethnic or national origins'. The House of Lords reversed the Court of Appeal's determination that Sikhs were not a race, and therefore were not protected against discrimination by the Race Relations Act. In effect the court had to invent a test for race, against a textual background which did not offer a procedure for answering the question, and this led to a jumble of criteria and authorities, including the dictionary (see discussion in Love 1998). One could also see the court here as occupying the problematic space of adjudication, where the background or latent contested normativity of language categories is dramatically foregrounded with a demand for a binary yes–no decision: either Sikhs are a race or they are not. While any concept ('tree', 'table', 'building') can become problematic in this way, the additional dimension to this case was the dimension that, unlike trees and tables, Sikhs themselves had subjective views about the matter at issue. The logic of the case, and the architecture of rights law, predisposes such groups to accept or coopt (or, depending on one's point of view, be coopted by) the categories which law recognises as capable or worthy of protection (see Renteln 2004 for discussion of cultural difference and the law).

This form of alienation of taken-for-granted labels and categories is pervasive in the social life of language, and is not confined to law. It is a constant feature of political rhetoric, for example. To give a well-known example, when the British prime minister Margaret Thatcher famously declared in 1987 that there was 'no such thing' as society (see www.margaretthatcher.org), she could be understood as making a statement about the (proper) meaning or understanding of the word 'society', namely that there is no society apart from or independent of the individuals and families that make it up: 'There are individual men and women and there are families and no government can do anything except through people and people look to themselves first.' There were, in Thatcher's view, too many people who felt they had entitlements without any corresponding obligations, and who failed to understand the mutuality principle which she saw as the basis of social morality. It is often a key part of a debate that linguistic usage is challenged, and Thatcher's denial that there was such a word as 'society', and/or her use of the word and implicit definition attached to it, were the subject of widespread criticism. But it would be odd to denounce this statement for being linguistically prescriptive, since political debate is about attaching normative meaning to words. This does not prevent allegations about abuse of language being routinely traded, but those allegations arise within the political argument *as part of* the political argument in its widest sense.

Further examples of extreme reflexivity and the alienation of taken-for-granted labels can be found in art and literature. This can be illustrated by Michael Craig-Martin's work entitled 'Oak Tree', which consists of a glass of water (currently displayed in Tate Britain in London). In an interview discussing this work, the artist played ironically with the authority of the artist's intentional acts in relation to the artwork and with the power of labels: 'What I've done is to change a glass of water into a full-grown oak tree without altering the accidents of the glass of water. [. . .] I've changed the physical substance of the glass of water into that of an oak tree' ([Craig-Martin] 1972). This work points to the uneasy set of ontological assumptions that lurk behind our labelling practices, and plays on the manner in which visitors to galleries look from the label to the artwork, and from the artwork to the label, in trying to work out what the artwork 'means' or 'depicts'. It also provokes but disarms the response that the artwork is simply a glass of water labelled 'Oak Tree'. The potential for this reflexive alienation or contestation of labels exists in all forms of discourse. Depending on the context, contested labelling can be explosive (e.g. racial insults), but it is not always a threat to social order.

It would be possible to imagine a dystopia where all interactions were conducted in a highly reflexive and contested fashion and where participants questioned the apparently stable meaning attached to words and phrases in common circulation. In August 1925, the philosopher Wittgenstein visited the newly married J. M. Keynes and Lydia Lopokova. When Lopokova remarked to Wittgenstein, 'What a beautiful tree', he responded fiercely: 'What do you mean?' When Joan Bevan observed to Wittgenstein that he was lucky to have been able to visit the United States, he replied crossly, 'What do you mean by lucky?' (Edmonds and Eidinow 2001: 153). A series of sociological interventions in this spirit were designed by Harold Garfinkel. Arguing that the taken-for-granted, commonsense world of daily interaction, the 'natural facts of life', are understood by members of a society as 'moral facts of life', Garfinkel instructed his students to 'engage an acquaintance or a friend in an ordinary conversation' and then to 'insist that the person clarify the sense of his commonplace remarks' (Garfinkel 1967: 35–7, 42).

One of the resulting dialogues is reproduced as follows, where 'S' stands for 'subject', and 'E' stands for 'experimenter':

On Friday night my husband and I were watching television. My husband remarked that he was tired. I asked, How are you tired? Physically, mentally, or just bored? (S) I don't know, I guess physically mainly. (E) Do you mean that your muscles ache or your bones? (S) I guess so. Don't be so technical. (*After more watching*) (S) All these old movies have the same kind of old iron bed-stead in them. (E) What do you mean? Do you mean all old movies, or some of them, or just the ones you have seen?

Predictably, the exchange ends with the subject losing his temper: '(S) You know what I mean! Drop dead!' In one of the dialogues the subject is referred to straightforwardly as 'the victim'. This dystopian world evoked in Garfinkel's staged demonstrations (an example of what is known in sociology as a 'breaching experiment') is one where any commonplace characterisation is subject to the kind of sceptical challenge characteristic of the discourse of professional philosophers and certain moments of legal uncertainty with language.

One loose legal equivalent might be a dystopian society where daily interaction was so saturated with law that any characterisation by a speaker of the character or behaviour of another person was instantly subject to legal proceedings to determine whether that person had been defamed. In practice, defamation law distinguishes between more permanent media such as writing (libel) and speech (slander), and restricts actions for slander to certain classes of statement, or to where actual damage can be shown: 'If all vituperation and ridicule were actionable per se, litigation, and much of it petty, would engulf society' (*Fey v King* 1922, at 155).

Law, like the commonplace, daily world of interaction evoked by Garfinkel, has its own shared, taken-for-granted practices. Law can be understood as a 'culture' with its own rules and understandings, which may be alienating or incomprehensible to an outsider, including many aspects of its specialised use of language. Part of that culture involves techniques and procedures for assigning meaning to words. The 'ordinary language' philosopher J. L. Austin saw law as of necessity doing violence to the niceties and nuanced distinctions of ordinary language (Austin 1956: 12):

> In the law a constant stream of actual cases, more novel and more tortuous than the mere imagination could contrive, are brought up for decision – that is, formulae for docketing them must somehow be found. Hence it is necessary first to be careful with, but also to be brutal with, to torture, to fake and to override, ordinary language: we cannot here evade or forget the whole affair.

This suggests a contrast between the non-contentious, harmonious, ordinary usage, which is adequate for everyday purposes, and the tortured language of the law, as language is twisted and stretched to meet the extraordinary demands of the contentious legal process. Wittgenstein, evoking a situation where a sceptical inquirer insists on a further explanation for each explanatory statement, affirmed that '[e]xplanations come to an end somewhere' (Wittgenstein [1953] 1978: 3).

The problem for law is that it often has to seek answers beyond the point at which the end has apparently been reached in terms of the resources available to determine meaning. One way to understand the process of the law assigning meaning is that it is frequently caught internally in the same kind of dialogue as S and E above. It subjects language to the same relentlessly sceptical questioning (Austin's 'torture') used by E, but it must also reach a reasoned decision about the meaning to be assigned in a particular legal context, and cannot, like S, simply terminate the inquiry. Law is frequently in need of techniques or procedures to close off or limit the sceptical interrogation, to 'refamiliarise' language which has become 'strange' or 'alien' under the scrutiny of law. One simple example of this is the use by judges of dictionaries to orient them in their understanding of the meaning of commonplace words.

Garfinkel sought to reveal the taken-for-granted, consensual world against which daily interaction takes place, and show how the rupture of that order led swiftly to moral condemnation. However, it would be misleading to divide behaviour into the two discrete domains of the consensual and the contentious. One reason for the strong emotions aroused by interventions into public discourse labelled 'politically correct' is that they challenge what some speakers regard as aspects of the taken-for-granted, consensual labelling of the social world, and create uncertainty about aspects of what had been for them previously routine linguistic behaviour. A simple example would be linguistic usage in relation to labels like 'girl' and 'lady', and 'Miss', 'Mrs' and 'Ms'. Such interventions also raise questions about authority over usage, since the rejection of customary usage involves a prescriptive determination of the 'right way' to speak.

Drawing distinctions or analytical boundaries, combined with the ability to question both the boundary and the reasons, is a form of reflexivity. It is a particular feature of reflexive intellectual activity that it questions everyday, taken-for-granted distinctions, and undercuts or problematises them, without seeking necessarily (or being able to) displace them. Law is frequently obliged to undertake parallel inquiries into aspects of the taken-for-granted world, but then is required to reach a determinate decision ('yes–no'). Judges are sometimes required to take a determinate position, justified within the conventions of legal reasoning, under circumstances where a contentious philosophical or definitional issue arises, or where a set of contentious moral and political issues is compacted into a single case.

The judge's role in arbitrating over linguistic meaning can be understood as playing simultaneously three theoretically distinct roles: (1) that of interpretative insider as an ordinary speaker of the language; (2) that of member of the interpretative community of law; (3) that of 'anthropological stranger', alienated from language, who has to ask what expressions like 'use a weapon' mean. A dictionary definition may offer a therapeutic aid, because as a generalisation or idealisation, it maximises the taken-for-granted and minimises the element which is 'under scrutiny'. Another way of putting this is that the resort to the dictionary is an attempt to escape from, or minimise, contextual reflexivity, or to withdraw from Garfinkel's dystopia in situations where the unfolding of the case has led to maximal foregrounding in the framing of language. If we begin from a point of view where 'language is always contextually embedded and [. . .] this contextualization is always open to change' (Toolan 1996: 13), then the context in which no context is evoked is a special and paradoxical 'zero context', one where a word or a phrase is reified into a stable object of the gaze.

F The Single Meaning Rule and Defamation Law

In English laws against obscene libel and blasphemy, 'the essence of obscene libel is a tendency on the part of a "published" article to deprave and corrupt, and blasphemous libel is committed by any scurrilous vilification of the Christian religion including its principal iconic figures' (Kearns 2007: 667). The intention of the author is at best marginal to establishing the offence, and the law applies its own set of procedures to assign meaning to the published words. This amounts to strict liability (an exception to the general rule that criminal law requires proof of *mens rea* or 'guilty mind'), even though 'the often complex cultural nature of the objects' to which the law is applied 'suggests close analysis of the originator's intentions regarding the creation and publication of the article in question' (Kearns 2007: 670). In defamation law, the question posed is whether the words used would 'tend to lower the plaintiff in the estimation of right-thinking members of society generally' (*Sim v Stretch* 1936, at 1240), or in terms of the 'ordinary bystander' test (Mitchell 2005: 35). The defendant is strictly liable according to this standard (i.e. it is not a defence to show that the defendant took reasonable care in the circumstances): 'Liability for libel does not depend on the intention of the defamer, but on the fact of the defamation' (Lord Russell, in *Cassidy v Daily Mirror Newspapers Ltd* 1929, at 354). In *Cassidy* there was strict liability for the defamation, regardless of the surrounding facts and motives (at 355):

> When all is said and done, the defendants have published to the world the statement that Mr. Corrigan was, on February 21, 1928, an unmarried man. That statement was in fact false, and has been found by the jury to be defamatory of the plaintiff [his wife], and to have caused her damage. There is ample evidence to support the findings, unless we can say that the published matter was incapable of being defamatory of the plaintiff. This I am not prepared to do.

In *Hulton & Co v Jones* (1910), a humorous newspaper story which referred in unflattering terms to a fictional character, a churchwarden named Artemus Jones who lived in Peckham, London, was deemed by the House of Lords defamatory of a real-life barrister with the same name, even though the barrister did not live in Peckham and there was no suggestion that the newspaper intended to refer to him (see Rogers 2006: 536).

In some cases, in addition to statements which are capable of being defamatory 'on their face' (i.e. in respect of their natural and ordinary meaning), the law recognises there may be a potentially defamatory meaning below the surface meaning, namely 'innuendo meaning'. This arises in cases where the words themselves are not defamatory, but they invite an obvious and publicly available inference which yields a defamatory meaning (known as 'false innuendo'). Alternatively, there may be knowledge known only to a subsection of the community which renders an otherwise harmless statement defamatory ('true innuendo'). In such cases, the legal fiction of the 'ordinary reader' or addressee is modified (Durant 1996).

In defamation law a yes–no answer is required, and this reflected in what is known as the 'single meaning rule'. This is recognised by lawyers as an essentially artificial construct whereby a statement is fixed with a single meaning. In libel law, there is clearly a strong tension with the real sociological context within which, for example, people read newspapers, or absorb and circulate opinions from the media. There may be a contradiction between the defamatory impression conveyed by the headline and photographs, which are obviously more salient, and the contradictory or clarifying text beneath (*Charleston v News Group Newspapers* 1995). This relationship is known as one between the 'bane' and 'antidote' (Rogers 2006: 524). A reader rapidly perusing the paper may come away with a different impression from a careful, close reader.

Law inevitably involves a series of slow-motion replays when it ascribes meaning to acts or texts. As a construct, the law may attempt to reconstruct a particular 'real-time' form of attention. In a libel action the words complained of 'are no longer being skimmed over on page 5 of the morning paper', but rather the 'proverbial magnifying glass' is put over the words 'through which a judge, lawyers and jury laboriously attempt to ascertain their "actual meaning"' (Harkness 1998: 653–4). In *Slim v Daily Telegraph Ltd* (1968), Lord Diplock commented that a letter which would have taken a newspaper reader 60 seconds to read was subject to minute linguistic examination by three judges and four counsel (at 172):

> If this protracted exercise in logical positivism has resulted in our reaching a conclusion as to the meaning of either letter different from the first impression which we formed on reading it, the conclusion reached is unlikely to reflect the impression of the plaintiffs' character or conduct which was actually formed by those who read the letters in their morning newspaper in 1964.

Mitchell (2005: 39) frames the single meaning question as follows. Whilst linguists might recognise 'the potential for some words to carry multiple meanings to different hearers', the law fixes a standard which it declares to be that of how a reasonable person would understand the words. Mitchell refers to Lord Diplock's words in *Slim v Daily Telegraph Ltd* (1968) for the legal view (at 172):

> Everyone outside a court of law recognises that words are imprecise instruments for communicating the thoughts of one man to another. The same words may be understood by one man in a different meaning from that in which they are understood by another and both meanings may be different from that which the author of the words intended to convey.

The judge noted that 'the whole training of a lawyer' went against the idea that 'the same word should bear different meanings to different men'. For the lawyer, words were 'the tools of his trade', used 'to define legal rights and duties'. They could not 'achieve that purpose unless there can be attributed to them a single meaning as to the "right" meaning'. The fact that, where words are published to the millions of readers of a newspaper, different readers will have understood different meanings is not relevant:

> What does matter is what the adjudicator at the trial thinks is the one and only meaning that the readers as reasonable men should have collectively understood the words to bear. That is 'the natural and ordinary meaning' of words in an action for libel.

For some commentators, these kinds of statements are evidence that 'judges do not make good linguists' (Solan 1993: 59–63).

On the logic of Lord Diplock's remarks, the academic linguist has little to contribute in establishing this 'legally generated fiction' (Harkness 1998: 655), and must be content to stand outside the legal process pointing to its artificiality. Harkness, however, introduces the distinction between 'denotative' and 'connotative' meaning. Denotative meaning is the core of settled, shared, 'neutral' meaning, for example the intersection between two words such as 'clever' and 'cunning'. Connotations are meanings that 'colour' or supply an emotional or judgmental quality in addition to that neutral meaning. Harkness argues that what is at stake in defamation is the attribution of connotative meaning, but connotations are volatile (e.g. the word 'communist'). The denotative–connotative distinction might seem to suffer from a similar problem to that of the legal fiction, namely that it fixes an arbitrary and determinate boundary between two kinds of meaning. If we think of the contextual, ideological and user-variable meanings attached to labels like 'homosexual', 'homo', 'queer', 'gay' etc., it is unclear whether the linguist's distinction gets us much further than the lawyer's fictions in determining whether a remark ascribing one of these adjectives to someone is defamatory (Fogle 1993; Harkness 1998: 676–7; Knight 2006).

Harkness concludes that the distinction between the ordinary meaning and the legal innuendo meaning is redundant, given that all statements may have different meanings for different audiences. Illustrating the gap between the socially oriented linguist and the law, he argues that the question should be not a yes–no one, but one of degree (Harkness 1998: 662). The concept of the 'objective right-thinking person' is 'nothing short of a heresy in natural language interpretation'; it pays no attention to the fundamental maxim in 'pragmatic language theory', namely 'the thoughts of a subjective audience' (Harkness 1998: 667, 668). As long as these notions remain, 'the law of defamation will be fundamentally flawed in its approach to natural language interpretation' (Harkness 1998: 684). Tiersma (1987: 349) argues that 'community standards often vary widely according to time, geography, and social status'. This amounts to a general rejection of the fiction of the 'single meaning' as understood by a 'reasonable reader', and opens up law to empirical sociological and sociolinguistic research.

An interesting case where a linguist did undertake such research into an innuendo meaning is found in Durant (1996). At issue was the phrase 'economical with the truth', which gained a degree of notoriety following its use in 1986 by the British Cabinet secretary Sir Robert Armstrong in legal proceedings in Australia in relation to Peter Wright's 'spy memoir', *Spycatcher*, which the British government was seeking to suppress. The government had written to the publisher William Armstrong to request a copy of the book, when in fact it already had obtained one. The following exchange took place between Malcolm Turnbull and Robert Armstrong:

> Mr. Turnbull: So that letter contains a lie, does it not?
> Sir Robert: It contains a misleading impression in that respect.
> Mr Turnball: Which you knew to be misleading at the time you made it?
> Sir Robert: Of course.
> Mr. Turnbull: So it contains a lie?
> Sir Robert: It is a misleading impression in that respect, it does not contain a lie, I don't think.
> Mr. Turnbull: And what is the difference between a misleading impression and a lie?
> Sir Robert: You are as good at English as I am.
> Mr Turnbull: I am just trying to understand.
> Sir Robert: A lie is a straight untruth.
> Mr Turnbull: What is a misleading impression – a sort of bent untruth?
> Sir Robert: As one person said, it is perhaps being economical with the truth.

The question in the case with which Durant was concerned (which did not go to trial) was whether this phrase was capable of having defamatory meaning when used to describe a well-known businessman. Based on questionnaire and corpus research, Durant's conclusion was that the phrase either involved a suggestion of deliberate deception or was a euphemism for lying, seen widely as the rough linguistic equivalent of the cynical 'professional foul' in soccer. While that meaning could be overridden in some contexts, these were extremely rare.

In compiling this kind of evidence, the linguist is in a different role from the theoretical linguist as expert on linguistic meaning. In effect Durant was producing and interpreting a market survey of how the phrase was understood, similar in nature to the kind of surveys that are accepted as evidence in trademark disputes, and there seems no reason why courts should not accept this kind of survey, just as they accept market research on the public perception of trademarks. Durant, however, stresses the difficulties involved in an academic linguist's communicating with lawyers and judges. An investigation such as that carried out by Durant is only even potentially admissible because of the strict liability to public meanings involved in defamation law; it would be an entirely different matter to subject statutory language to the same procedure. If the court had accepted the survey evidence as persuasive, the conclusion would have been that the playful or humorous invitation to the reader to complete the quasi-deniable link between the surface meaning and the inferred meaning did not break the causal assignment of responsibility to the author/publisher of the statement: liability would have been assigned to the author, not to any joint effort of the author and reader.

Part IV

Conclusion

The Semiotics of Law, Language and Money

A philosopher once wrote:

> There is no more striking symbol of the completely dynamic character of the world than that of language. The meaning of language lies in the fact that it will be addressed to someone. When language stands still, it is no longer language according to its specific value and significance. The effect that it occasionally exerts in a state of repose arises out of an anticipation of its further motion. Language is nothing but the vehicle for a movement in which everything else that is not in motion is completely extinguished.

In actuality, the philosopher, Georg Simmel (1858–1918) wrote 'money' where this quotation has 'language'. The second sentence should read: 'The meaning of money lies in the fact that it will be given away.' This is an extract from the closing pages of *The Philosophy of Money* ([1907] 1990: 510–11). The extract continues: 'It is, as it were, an *actus purus*; it lives in continuous self-alienation from any given point and thus forms the counterpart and direct negation of all being in itself.' The use of the term '*actus purus*' (the state of being where there is no gap between actuality and potential, i.e. the perfect nature of God) reflects in part Simmel's understanding of confidence in money as analogous to religious faith ([1907] 1990: 179). Money is characterised by a paradoxical fixity and motion (Simmel [1907] 1990: 510–11):

> As a tangible item money is the most ephemeral thing in the economic-practical world; yet in its content it is the most stable, since it stands as a point of indifference and balance between all other phenomena in the world. The ideal purpose of money, as well as of the law, is to be the measure of all things without being measured itself, a purpose that can be realized only by an endless development.

To this one could add that, in addition to law and money, the 'ideal purpose of language' has also been understood to be 'the measure of all things'.

What is of interest here is the idea of systems of signs (law, language, money) as being required as stable or 'still' points of reference for other systems, and yet themselves in motion. Seen through Simmel's model, plain meaning or textualist theories of legal interpretation are self-conscious ways of framing the interpretative task in advance in terms of foreground fixity and background motion or 'system noise'. These approaches thus carve out an interpretative space where the intent of the author or utterer is either not relevant or assumed to be exhaustively represented by the very words themselves. The axis of time is also not relevant, in that the gaze of the interpreter does not move backwards to the context of utterance, nor forward to the consequences of assigning a particular meaning in the factual circumstances at hand. The meanings of the words are foregrounded as stable, reliable entities, contrasted with a shifting, inchoate background 'noise' of different ways of contextualising the task (politics, morality, public opinion, and so on). The decontextualised meaning represents the ideal of language as a stable point of reference against a complex contextual background which is 'in motion'. This is the imaginary 'zero context' in which the autonomy of the sign as having an inherent meaning is grasped.

Relegated to the 'background' are investigations that go beyond the text to look for historical evidence of authorial or legislative intent (for example in the mountains of textual evidence from debates in the legislature that might be brought to bear to determine this), styles of interpretation which privilege the reader/addressee (the semi-autonomous common law judge who co-writes the law), the socio-political context of enactment, the socio-political context of interpretation/adjudication, the individualised effect of the judgment on the parties themselves, the sociological impact of the decision itself, the judgment seen as an act of legal reasoning, and the potential effect of the decision within the architecture of law. To this we could add the group dynamics of a panel of judges; the interactions between the legal system, counsel and the court (referred to sarcastically by Bentham as 'the old established firm, Judge and Co'; 1821: 52); and whatever unknowable mix of careerism, laziness, idealism, compassion, vanity, empathy, insight and moral intuition goes into legal adjudication. A 'hard case' as experienced by a textualist judge is one where the foregrounding of the plain language brings into relief, rather than aligning, conflicting elements of the interpretative background.

However, Simmel suggests that the sign which stands completely still is no sign at all, and that signs can only have meaning when they are in motion. To act as a point of reference for other systems, the reference point itself must be put into motion, or, in semiotic terms, be contextualised. When signs circulate 'they are vehicles for a movement' in which every attribute of the sign that is not in motion 'is completely extinguished'. This motion without residue suggests the sign as evoked by the indeterminacy theorist: in order to capture the meaning of the sign, we must impose a meaning upon it, slow down its movement or bring it to a standstill by an act of coercive reading. Determinate readings of signs are acts of power or authority. Speaking of the American mania for law and its reasons ('jurismania'), Campos (1998: 69) writes: 'We can now better appreciate why law becomes presence to us through its absence. For it is in just those situations where law is going to fail to give us answers that we will be most insistent that it do so.' Much the same can be said of language. At the very moment when we most require the Adamic language, or its modern equivalent, a shared system of collective and stable meanings, to tell us whether a chicken coop with iron wheels pulled behind a tractor is a 'vehicle' or not (Endicott 2002; *Garner v Burr* 1951), it fails us. More accurately, it becomes evident that language cannot serve on demand as a set of predetermined labels, any more than law can be relied on to provide remedies for contentious social problems. These 'hard' definitional cases suggest that the stability of plain language in easy cases is merely a perceptual illusion generated by an indeterminate, motion-filled background.

A theory of interpretation predetermines what is relevant to the task at hand, that is, it lays down a frame within which the insider interpreter is to look for answers in carrying out the task, or an explanatory frame for the outside critic in evaluating interpretative acts. The linguist as a commentator on the meanings of ordinary words is caught by this movement between ideal fixity and real motion. If there is a core meaning to every instance which is defined with reference to an underlying abstract system, then the linguist should be able to communicate that meaning to the court. But if it is the core meaning itself which is at issue, then the linguist must choose between the available meanings. In the *Scheidler v National Organization for Women* case, this involved two meanings of 'enterprise', roughly speaking 'organised human activity' versus 'economic activity, business'. But on what basis can this movement or oscillation be determined, that is, brought to an end? In *Southern Pacific Company v Jensen* (1917), Justice Holmes stated in a much-quoted remark that the common law was 'not a brooding omnipresence in the sky, but the articulate voice of some sovereign or quasi sovereign that can be identified' (at 222). Holmes's point in the context of the case (which concerned jurisdictional boundaries and workers' compensation) was that 'judges do and must legislate, but they can do so only interstitially' (at 244). Chafee (1947: 42) responds that 'it is easy to retort that this brooding omnipresence is no more mythical than Holmes' sovereign whom nobody has yet seen'. In one English case, the term 'old friend' was ruled too vague to be defined (*Brown v Gould* 1972); however, in another, the judge embarked confidently on a definition of 'friend' (*Re Barlow's Wills Trusts* 1979, at 282). Language is not a brooding omnipresence in the sky either.

By looking at law closely we gain a slow-motion, hyper-reflexive, hyper-ritualised image of non-legal language. When the language of law is in the foreground, to continue Simmel's analogy between fixity and motion, the background made up of 'ordinary' language moves and circulates at much higher speed. Here the contrast is not between absolute fixity and absolute movement, but between two relative speeds, one slower and one faster. Fixity is the foreground feature of textual interpretation, since the foregrounded element is a section of discourse, a word or a textual fragment requirement. In law a yes–no answer must be found. To find that answer it may be necessary to put the word or phrase in motion, within the multiple contextualisations and recontextualisations, but this of course raises the danger that no single meaning can be retrieved. Goodrich employs this metaphor of speed in his critique of law as 'rapid reading' and 'a rush to judgment, a determination to determine', qualities which make the jurist a 'bad reader' (Goodrich 2005: 192). An ideal 'slow reader' is one who is 'calm, patient, attentive, unhurried', someone 'who reads to learn'; slow reading is 'genealogical, ambulatory, anarchic' (Goodrich 2005: 193–7). For Goodrich, the law rushes to closure, shutting down this movement as it speeds to a conclusion. The contrast between fixity and motion is at the heart of the systems theoretical understanding of system (order) in relation to environment (disorder).

That law is the ritualised and formalised projection of non-legal discourse can be explained from a different point of view. The recognition that language is a form of behaviour has a profound consequence for the understanding of human memory and language. If each utterance changes the state of the social world, then that world is constituted by a past which is dense with utterances. The speaker faces that past, moving backwards into the future, surveying a vast landscape of acts, events and utterances. This landscape is not flat, but shaped by a normative sense of what happened, what failed to happen, what was said, what should have been said, and what should not have been said. These utterances are weakly organised by context, are narrativised, recontextualised, forgotten, associated with individuals, misremembered, misattributed, private and collective (commercial slogans, punch-lines, jokes, jingles, and so on). Linguistic memory is constantly in motion, utterances are recalled and recontextualised, or simply buried under unbounded layers of accumulated experienced utterances and their contexts. Just as the search engine Google is in a sense bigger than the internet (since it reputedly holds a record of all Google searches), so linguistic memory is bigger than language. More accurately, what we call language is an emergent property of individual and shared linguistic memory. (From the point of view of the synchronic linguistic system as imagined by the linguist, this memory-language is 'chaotic' or 'environmental noise' or a huge mountain of linguistic 'wreckage'.)

If a book has millions of pages, an alphabetic index may be of little use. This leads to the conclusion that in relation to the worldwide web and 'cyberspace', what is fundamental not only to memory, but to the creation of a normative order in the present, is the search engine, and other means of tracking, evaluating and organising the massive corpus of information, searches and materials. This is not merely a commercial tool, but also a political and social form, which can reflexively reflect and create different orders of knowledge. This is another way of understanding the role of brand names: they organise memory and reduce 'search costs' for the consumer (Griffiths 2003: 25). Brands and slogans organise and narrativise public spaces and media. Memory is the power to create narrative order out of the past, and is not distinct from the perception of reality in the present.

Law can likewise be understood as an ordered and highly reflexive form of shared memory. The individual lawyer develops an individual history of textual and interactional history in law, and this is formed in dialogue with the wider and deeper textual history of law as a collective enterprise – what we might term 'legal memory'. Legal memory is the foundation of law, since law faces the past as it moves into the future, and lawyers work constantly to create and maintain coherence on many levels, constantly monitoring the integrity and vitality of legal concepts and doctrines. As in the discourse of nationalism (Anderson 1983), the achievement of this coherence requires systemic forgetting as well as remembering (so-called 'structural amnesia'; Douglas 1987: 70) and belief in an ideal, transhistorical 'imagined coherence' of law and its texts. From the point of view of autonomous legal history, the external, social history of law is 'chaos' or 'environmental noise', and is assimilated only with difficulty into the internal history of legal concepts. But even a systems theory of law, as we have seen, must include the dimension of time. The systems view of language as existing outside time is a further step up the ladder towards the Platonic heaven of pure and motionless concepts.

Concepts of fixity and motion, and the related notions of interpretative foreground and background, are useful in thinking about issues in legal interpretation. They offer a way of framing a wide range of issues, and thinking across different models of legal interpretation. For example, in common law jurisdictions citizens arrested or taken into custody are given a warning on arrest or before questioning. The Supreme Court ruled in *Miranda v Arizona* (1966) that suspects were entitled to be informed of their constitutional rights before questioning. Here is the text of a minimal 'Miranda warning' (www.usconstitution.net/miranda.html):

> You have the right to remain silent. Anything you say can and will be used against you in a court of law. You have the right to speak to an attorney, and to have an attorney present during any questioning. If you cannot afford a lawyer, one will be provided for you at government expense.

This warning, or the 'caution' used in Britain (Jason-Lloyd 2005), is in effect a warning that a process of de- and re-contextualisation will take place. An utterance made in the context of the arrest ('It's all my fault!') is 'written down', or 'reduced to writing', and is then potentially recontextualised in the written documents of the legal process, and 'read out' by the police officer in the trial.

If we take the original utterance as A, and the form in which it is represented in the notebook as B, and the utterance read out by the police officer as C, then there is a legally constructed identity between these, so that the defendant can be asked in relation to the police officer's evidence: 'Did you say A?' This of course is a further recontextualisation, D. The original, A, has presumptively the same meaning as B, C and D, so that the meaning assigned to C is assigned to A. The police officer, in reducing to writing and later reading out the utterance, is not presumed to have intervened in a substantive way so as to break the chain of attribution. As in the cases discussed above (Chapter 6), there is an externally imposed collapse to identity of an original and its representation so that A, B, C and D are deemed to be 'the same', and the responsible author of the remarks is identified as the defendant, rather than as a co-author with the police officer and the legal process. It may be possible to argue about what was meant by A, adducing contextual factors, but there is no doubt about where the moral-legal responsibility is assigned. Clearly this processs of multiple recontextualisation involves movement, yet at a particular juncture different attempts will be made to fix its meaning. The process of foregrounding the utterance to determine its meaning is a further recontextualisation. Hence the paradox that Simmel points to about a system (language) which provides fixed points of reference yet must be put into motion in order to function. Deconstructive readings are paradoxical strong readings in which motion is privileged over fixity across all generalised contexts (the 'archecontext'). They determine in advance that no value can be assigned, but they need to fix a frame of non-movement within which this motion can be perceived.

In the case of trademark law, the motion is in the foreground, since the commercial sign is understood as circulating in the market, a shared product of interaction between the creator-author, the consumer, media and the public sphere. Of course law may be required to reduce this movement to a fixed yes–no determination if the case requires it, but there is no immediate assumption that all consumers perceive the trademark alike, or that there is uniformity of reception or meaning. As in defamation law, the 'single meaning' is a recognised, heuristic fiction. A survey as evidence of consumer perception in trademark confusion is unlikely to give a simple yes–no answer, but the vast whirl of the social circulation of signs is reduced to a set of preferences within the framing of the questionnaire. In the same way, an electoral process reduces the massive 'noise' of social opinion to a manageable set of results that determine political control.

This constant shifting of point of view, and changes of frame between different foregrounds and backgrounds, accounts for the widespread use of the word 'fiction' and 'myth' in legal theory and the study of language. Indeed, one way of understanding the relationship between legal language and ordinary language is to see that the latter is a fiction created by focusing on the former. If we foreground the density, syntactic complexity and lexical exoticness of law, an entity we describe as 'ordinary language' appears as the uniform, undifferentiated background. Similarly, to speak of literary language is to imagine a colour-filled foreground against a grey, mundane background.

When we talk of the autonomy of law, we are recognising its relative imperviousness to direct control by certain social forces, but this requires us to perform an initial conceptual separation between law and society. The autonomy of language is similarly only perceptible if we separate language as system from the totality of human behaviour. Language is none the less frequently conceptualised as a semiotic system which is stable, fixed and still, an ideal reference point. Without such a system, the argument goes, communication would be impossible. But this system can only be activated to serve as a fixed, reference point by putting it in motion, at which point the system of fixed, shared meanings becomes 'present to us through its absence'.

The imaginary 'zero context' that writing provides is fundamental to our understanding of language as an autonomous system. The idea that words have inherent meanings or that texts have an autonomous meaning 'inside' them is, in Simmel's terms, part of the faith or trust that maintains signs in circulation. But from another point of view, this is all merely an illusion. Harpham (2002: 237) concludes his study of modernity's 'fetishization of language' with the statement that in the study of language 'the object under analysis fades under examination like the Cheshire Cat, leaving only a gentle mocking smile'. For Harpham, language is a fictional entity which different ideologies and theories construct in their own image. Richards (1968: 103) defined a word first as 'an individual occurrence with a date and a place', but noted that when we talk of a word we normally mean something 'more recondite' (Richards 1968: 104):

> We are thinking with a fiction that represents many such acts of speech; and a word becomes something that a million people use on the same day, and that successive generations go on using through hundreds of years. If we ask how this fiction is constructed, we at once have half the abstruser problems of semasiology [semiotics] on our hands.

The identification of plain meaning, language or authorial intention as fictional depends on their being foregrounded and interrogated, against a background where other related concepts are taken-for-granted.

Crucially, the idea of social practices as constituted by fictions raises the questions of agency, insight and control over meaning that haunt the law and legal theory. The term 'system' is translatable as a complex fictional model. Wittgenstein's concept of 'forms of life' can be read as 'self-sustaining fictions that constitute social practice', but where 'fiction' is not to be contrasted strongly with a domain of given 'fact'. Law recognises that many of its methods involve so-called 'legal fictions'. If lawyers start to believe that valid contracts actually involve 'a meeting of minds' (*consensus ad idem*) as a psychological or social fact, then there are legal theorists who wish to remind them that the world does not come already labelled in 'legal categories' (White 1987: 1971) and that legal categories do not descend to earth from a Platonic heaven of pure ideas (Jhering [1884] 1985; Cohen 1935), but are imposed on it by legal analysis. Legal concepts, such as the standardised 'reasonable person' and the ideal of 'freedom of contract', are acknowledged at some level as fictional within the reflexivity of law. The idea of meanings inhering within texts, of texts as expressing 'intentions', rules such as the default literal meaning rule, or the 'single meaning' rule in defamation, are parallel fictions about language within law. Often these partially or contextually acknowledged fictions are none the less the target of criticism for the role they play in maintaining what is seen as the deeper fiction of the coherence and autonomy of law, as once the processes of law are set in motion, the fictional nature of many of its elements falls from view. Alternatively, the whole process is seen as fictional, so that the act of an interpreter in picking out particular concepts as fictitious loses its analytical bite, and the fictional domain of law is understood as an oppressive hallucination, or contrasted with an alternative 'real' domain, such as economics, social policy analysis or politics.

The ability to frame any general concept as 'fictional', 'mythical' or a 'construct' is a fundamental feature of 'reflexive modernity' (Beck et al. 2003). Within what has been termed the 'social imaginary' (Castoriadis 1987), it is paradoxically only through 'the mediation of the imaginary that we are able to conceive of the real in the first place' (Gaonkar 2002: 7). This may appear to leave us wandering through Luhmann's maze of contingently connected autonomous systems, but the advantage of radical systems theory approaches is that they should more or less automatically provoke a realist reaction. The mutual interactions of law, language and money offer a fascinating challenge for legal theorists, linguists and semioticians to adapt and create cross-disciplinary models which do justice to debates about meaning, interpretation, the circulation of signs, and the nature of the public sphere. Central to any such undertaking must be a self-aware discussion of methodological fictions, systems theories and the 'realist dilemmas' they create.

Appendices: Discussion Materials and Exercises

A The Hogsville files

The basic facts

Below are four fictitious cases from an invented jurisdiction with many of the features of the 'Anglo-American' common law system. The city of Hogsville has passed a law (The Swine Prohibition Law) which under S 1(1)(a) forbids the 'bringing or maintaining of any pig, hog or swine, either domestic or wild, of whatever species, form or kind' within the city's boundary. This law was passed during a period when swine fever was raging and there were fears that the disease could pass from pigs to humans. There was also an influential minority of wealthy retired residents who had always felt that the image of the city suffered because of the public visibility of pigs, and the city council was planning to develop the region as a new technology hub. After the passing of the law, a number of legal actions have been launched. The reader is invited to consider what the outcome of these cases should be.

(1) Perky Co Ltd, a company that breeds guinea pigs for sale as pets, has been prosecuted for violating the Swine Prohibition Law. Perky also sought a declaration that their planned breeding of genetically modified peccaries would be lawful.

(2) A resident, Ms Bertrand, who was obliged to slaughter her pet pigs, since they could no longer live in her back garden, decided in protest at the law to erect a very large plastic statue of a pig on the roof of her house, with flashing lights for the eyes. There is no planning law that forbids this structure, but the city council decided to prosecute Ms Bertrand under the Swine Prohibition Law with the aim of obliging her to remove the plastic pig.

(3) An international agricultural company, AgrarMega, has been using the trademark 'The Laughing Porker' for its pork products produced locally. A trademark is defined as a sign which indicates the commercial origin of a product or service. AgrarMega has shut its pig-farming operation, though it is lobbying for repeal of the Swine Prohibition Law, and its trademark was widely known and used on products made elsewhere. Ms Porter has opened a

vegetarian restaurant which she has named 'The Laughing Porter', and the agricultural company is suing her for infringing their trademark under the Trademark Protection Law. S 2 protects famous trademark holders against 'dilution by blurring' or 'dilution by tarnishing', even where 'no actual or potential confusion' or 'economic injury' can be shown. However, S 4(d) protects 'fair use' in connection with 'identifying and parodying, criticizing or commentating' on the trademark holder or its good and services.

(4) Ms Porter, a student at the University of Hogsville, which as a publicly funded institution is subject to a national law guaranteeing free speech, has been picketing the student refectory with a large sign in red declaring 'MEAT-EATING IS MASS MURDER'. Ms Porter was suspended from her studies under a campus speech code that forbids speech that 'denigrates or shows hostility or aversion' to other groups, and is appealing against the decision to the courts for judicial review on the grounds that her right to free speech has been violated.

Discussion

(1a) The legal action under S 1 against Perky Co Ltd involves a dispute over whether guinea pig are 'pigs', or more precisely, whether the animals being bred by the company fell under, or were captured by, the wording of the law which covers any 'pig, hog or swine, either domestic or wild, of whatever species, form or kind'. Both parties to the dispute accepted that Perky was involved in 'maintaining' the animals in question. Perky argued that guinea pigs are, in scientific classifications of animals, not the same *genus* as the common pig. Further, the word 'pig' in 'guinea pig' did not make a guinea pig a *pig*, any more than a hot-dog is a kind of *dog*. The prosecution argued that the law is not written by scientists for scientists, and the language used is ordinary usage directed at the public. Further, the law contains language of maximal scope, which shows that it was intended to have as inclusive coverage as the word 'pig' would allow, including 'of whatever species', which would bring the guinea pigs clearly within the scope of the law.

The defence called scientific expert evidence about the zoological classifications involved, and the expert witness testified that guinea pigs were not pigs but 'rodents', belonging to the family Caviidae, and the genus Cavia, and were also known as cavies. It was also the case that peccaries were not a kind of pig, though there were many superficial resemblances. Thus these were not kinds or species of pig. The defence introduced scientific evidence that guinea pigs were not susceptible to swine disease, in arguing that the law was passed as a public health measure.

The prosecution introduced testimony from an academic linguist to the effect that ordinary understandings of categories were influenced by labels, so that the general language user might well believe, or at least have a vague sense, that a guinea pig was a kind of pig, or that the two kinds of animals were somehow related. The linguist argued that if a cleaning contractor was asked to remove all the insects from a house, then that instruction would reasonably apply also to spiders, even though in entomological terms a spider was not an insect, since, in the ordinary categories of language users, spiders were a kind of insect. When presented with definitions from a household dictionary that distinguished between pigs and guinea pigs by citing zoological terms, the linguist replied that dictionaries mixed up different kinds of information, and did not reflect only the meanings attached to words by ordinary language users. A scientific expert testified that peccaries might be susceptible to swine fever. Evidence was adduced by the defence from discussions leading up the enactment of the law, where the sponsor remarked in debate that 'guinea pigs' were not intended to be covered; however, the sponsor had been forced to step down before the enactment on corruption charges, and the prosecution argued that this statement should not carry more weight than the final wording of the law as enacted.

(2a) In respect of the plastic pig, the prosecution argued once again that the very wide and inclusive wording of S 1 should be understood to include any kind of pig without exception, especially given the strong wording of the prohibition of pigs of any 'form or kind'. A plastic pig was none the less a pig, and its substantial size meant that it also was required to be 'maintained'. In addition, the law had been passed with the intent of changing the image of the city, with a view to attracting technology companies to invest. This had been made clear in comments by the sponsor of the law, who spoke of a new way forward for Hogsville as a technology centre in the twenty-first century. The defence, however, argued that this statement should not carry more weight than the final wording of the law as enacted, and that the primary purpose of the law was to protect the public from swine fever: no plastic pig could spread disease. In addition, the defence dismissed the prosecution's reading of the statute as 'blind literalism', noting that this would also forbid children from owning soft toys in the likeness of pigs. Further, it was evident that Ms Bertrand's rights to privacy, in the arrangement of the decoration of her own home, and to free speech and protest on a matter of key civic interest were threatened. Against this, the prosecution argued that the pig was in a public place, as it was visible from the street, and even at night, the pig with its flashing lights had become a tourist attraction. There were no privacy issues at stake. Secondly, a plastic pig could not be a form of speech, as it had no intellectual or expressive content.

(3a) AgarMega argued that there was a clear similarity between the name of the restaurant ('The Laughing Porter') and their trademark ('The Laughing Porker'), with only one letter or sound distinguishing them. This infringement was all the more serious as Ms Porter was also in the food business. It might prevent the company setting up a chain of restaurants called 'The Laughing Porker', and this was a serious constraint on its exclusive right recognised by law to use of its own trademark. A survey had shown that a random sample of 85 percent of adults recognised the trademark, and this established it as 'famous' for the purposes of the law. Further, the usage by Ms Porter was calculated to detract from the value of the trademark, and clearly constituted 'blurring' and 'tarnishing'. The defence of 'parody', 'criticism' or 'commentary' under S 4(d) was not applicable, since Ms Porter was using a similar sign in the course of advertising her business, not in journalistic writings or other similar contexts. There was no absolute right to use one's own name in a trading context, if it could be shown that it was being used for purposes contrary to law.

Ms Porter submitted that the broader context needed to be considered. The design of her restaurant included a large cartoon image of herself laughing, so, taken with the use of her own name, there was no blurring or confusion, such as to damage the integrity of the trademark. Alternatively, even if it was recognised that there was a potential dilution, this was protected, as the intent was clearly to parody and criticise, and to focus public attention on the campaign to have the Swine Prohibition Law repealed. AgrarMega had been spending large sums of money lobbying for the repeal, and this meant that they were able to wield excessive power in the public arena. Ms Porter's rights to privacy had been damaged, as she would be denied use of her own name, and the protection of her right to free speech in the use of the name as a part of a wider campaign of protest against the meat industry was in the public interest, as part of the preservation of a free forum for public debate. Large companies should not be allowed to buy up and control bits of language and access to the public sphere.

(4a) Both sides accepted that Ms Porter's sign was a form of speech. The court heard arguments from Ms Porter that the campus speech code was designed to protect students from hostility and harassment on grounds of race, ethnicity, religion, gender, sexual orientation, disability status, etc. There was no such well-defined interest group as 'meat-eaters' who were in need of protection, as they formed the overwhelming majority. The university was under its charter required to promote educational goals, including discussion of matters of public interest, and had a positive obligation to protect minority opinions from being marginalised or excluded from the public sphere. While the sign had been strongly worded, it was directed at an activity, not a defined group of people with a socially recognised special interest in need of protection. Ms Porter had remained silent at the entrance and merely held the sign for students to see it. No reasonable person would seek to forbid or curtail freedom to dissent in the public sphere, and the fact that some students were offended merely indicated the strength of feeling attached to the topic. The value attached to free speech should not be judged by the response of those who were addressed by the remarks, since their emotional involvement meant that they could not make an objective or reasonable interpretation of the free speech interest at stake. Ms Porter was making available an alternative view as part of a free market of ideas which it was the duty of the university to protect and promote. While Ms Porter was offended by the sight of people eating meat, she did not seek to prevent students eating meat on campus.

The University of Hogsville argued that calling fellow students 'murderers', even if indirectly, was speech that 'denigrates or shows hostility or aversion' to a group. While that group had not been envisaged when the code was drafted, there was no logical reason to restrict its application, and 'meat-eaters' as a group fell within the wording of the code. Meat-eating, just as vegetarianism, could potentially form part of a religious or ideological code. Many students had complained that they had been made extremely uncomfortable and upset, and had avoided returning to the refectory. The sign was in large letters and in lurid red, and it was no substantial mitigation to argue that Ms Porter had remained silent. The code was designed specifically to protect the open access of all students to all facilities, and this was being compromised by Ms Porter in her creation of a hostile environment, calling many of her fellow students 'murderers'. There were many avenues on campus for her freedom of speech rights to be exercised. Whether the environment created was 'hostile' or not had to be judged primarily from the point of view of the addressees of the remarks, not obviously from the point of view of the speaker, nor from some hypothetical reasonable interpreter's point of view, since that 'reasonable interpreter' had no insight into whether or not the addressee would feel aggressed or intimidated.

B Rules, norms and the everyday

In modern cities signs are posted throughout the landscape stating rules of all kinds. However, the power of norms and express rules is highly contingent. Laws may be stated publicly but not be enforced, or be unenforceable. Signs in public places ('No smoking', 'No waiting', 'Keep off the grass'), with or without legal authority, may be regarded in some contexts as representing a merely theoretical threat of intervention if transgressed against. The state of a sign may be viewed as relevant to this – if it is peeling, partially legible or positioned ambiguously, it may be viewed as less 'potent' legally.

Some rules simply cannot be enforced on practical grounds, such as a rule observed in the Metro system of the capital city of an Asian country with an intermittent terrorist threat. The rule required of people entering the under-pass: 'Please put your belongings here [on a table] for inspection'. Any official or police officer attempting to follow this would have reduced the system to chaos, given the sheer volume of passengers and pedestrians entering the walk-way. Instead, the inspection was carried out about two feet away from the table at the top of the escalator, with a brief search or cursory glance into bags held out for inspection. Whether this procedure was a violation of the official rule might depend on a whole host of background facts, and the assumptions of various social actors, against which the rule was established.

One view might be that we can identify a specific linguistic quality or essence to this rule, a meaning to the words on the sign, and therefore we can assert confidently that the essential 'semantic' core was violated by the observed practice – the officials did not do what the sign suggested they should do.

This would mean that the rule was in fact being formally violated, but that distinct contextual practical factors came into play, so that the authority issuing the rule either did not monitor enforcement of the rule, regarded the practice as acceptable on practical grounds, or would tolerate it unless some event (inspection by a safety agency, a terrorist incident) led to pressure to 'tighten up'. If a particular official could be identified as being the one who 'let through' the bomb, then they could be singled out for blame for failing to enforce the rule. Alternatively perhaps the rule merely provided the official with the discretion to require that large suitcases or bulky packages had to be placed on the table, and this was clearly indicated in briefings given in relation to safety checks. Thus the authority issuing the rule might have intended that the officer exercise reasonable discretion as to whether to require all belongings be placed on the table. Such discretion might also to be used (whether intended or not by the authorities) to select particular 'suspicious' individuals for searches, against a background of assumptions about the category or categories of persons who might be involved in terrorist attacks. A Western tourist carrying a large bag might be exempted from placing it on the table, whereas someone falling into the suspect categories might have their similar or smaller bag searched more thoroughly. Having a simple rule but allowing discretion in practice does not of course exempt the identified official from potential blame.

Does the use of the word 'belongings' imply that pens, books and wallets had to be put on the table? To understand the word 'belongings' in this rule we could begin with a dictionary definition ('a person's movable possessions'; *New Oxford English Dictionary*), but in this context it would have to be understood as synonymous with 'bag'. A pen, a book or a wallet would not qualify, but a handbag or carrier-bag would. But is there a difference between the discretion used by the official to exclude pens, books and wallets, and the discretion used to decide that not every bag needed to be put on the table?

There is a complex social calculus at work here, where factors such as the smooth movement of passengers and pedestrians are balanced against the risk of a terrorist attack, in the context of the length of time since the last terrorist incident, the background briefing given to officials, the nature of the objects being taken into the Metro, the categories or perceived categories of people carrying those objects, the nature of background briefings and training, the expectations and behaviour of the passengers and pedestrians, general social and cultural beliefs and practices about how rules work, and implicit assumptions and explicit discussion about the nature and likely rigour of enforcement. At the centre of this is a written sign and an official, who under the authority of the sign searches bags, but generally does not require them to be placed on the table.

Questions for discussion

(1) Are we to regard that official as an 'interpreter' of the (language of) the sign, and, if so, to what extent is such an interpretation an individual act, dependent on personal qualities of the official and their individual view of the best way to balance the elements of the social calculus?

(2) Does it make sense to distinguish between (a) the (literal) meaning of the rule and (b) its interpretation, such that there is an evident and public gap between what the rule means and what it is made to do?

C Who owns language?

In law, ownership is generally not an indivisible absolute right, is also frequently bound up with obligations and duties, and may exist alongside parallel lesser rights. In *Robertson v Rochester Folding Box Co* (1902), Gray J. rejected the idea that property was concerned solely with objects or things (at 564):

> Property is not, necessarily, the thing itself, which is owned; it is the right of the owner in relation to it. The right to be protected in one's possession of a thing, or in one's privileges, belonging to him as an individual, or secured to him as a member of the commonwealth, is property, and as such entitled to the protection of the law.

This issue of ownership of language can arise under certain circumstances, for example where a language is understood as forming a cultural inheritance and collective property of a people. A document posted on the internet discussing state-sponsored Aboriginal language programmes in Australia laments the lack of legal protection for an intellectual property right in a language ([Owning Language] 2007):

> The paradox for communities is that while the actual material expressions of their cultural spirituality are protected by the law of copyright, there is no such protection of the language that provides the unique linguistic vehicle through which these icons of identity can be explored, discussed and inherited across generations.

The document argues for a form of collective cultural 'self-ownership', in that the identity that is being defended is owned absolutely, and this includes the languages which are fundamental to that identity.

The following is an extract from 'A Declaration of the Independence of Cyberspace', by the cyber-activist John Perry Barlow (barlow @eff.org) of the Electronic Frontier Foundation. This was proclaimed in Davos, on 8 February 1996, in response to the United States Telecom Reform Act of 1996. The full text is widely available on the internet.

Governments of the Industrial World, you weary giants of flesh and
steel, I come from Cyberspace, the new home of Mind. On behalf of the
future, I ask you of the past to leave us alone. You are not welcome
among us. You have no sovereignty where we gather. We have no elected
government, nor are we likely to have one, so I address you with no
greater authority than that with which liberty itself always speaks. I
declare the global social space we are building to be naturally independent of the tyrannies you seek to impose on us. You have no moral right
to rule us nor do you possess any methods of enforcement we have true
reason to fear. Governments derive their just powers from the consent of
the governed. [. . .] Cyberspace does not lie within your borders. Do not
think that you can build it, as though it were a public construction
project. You cannot. It is an act of nature and it grows itself through our
collective actions. [. . .] We are creating a world that all may enter without
privilege or prejudice accorded by race, economic power, military force,
or station of birth. We are creating a world where anyone, anywhere may
express his or her beliefs, no matter how singular, without fear of being
coerced into silence or conformity. Your legal concepts of property,
expression, identity, movement, and context do not apply to us. They are
all based on matter, and there is no matter here. Our identities have no
bodies, so, unlike you, we cannot obtain order by physical coercion. [. . .]
Your increasingly obsolete information industries would perpetuate
themselves by proposing laws, in America and elsewhere, that claim to
own speech itself throughout the world. These laws would declare ideas
to be another industrial product, no more noble than pig iron. In our
world, whatever the human mind may create can be reproduced and distributed infinitely at no cost. The global conveyance of thought no
longer requires your factories to accomplish.

Questions for discussion

(1) What concepts of ownership and authority are invoked in this piece?
(2) In what ways is cyberspace understood to be outside traditional state
control and why?
(3) What metaphorical understandings are attributed to traditional states and
how is metaphor used to critique their aims and policies?
(4) How is the right of agency of the author to speak on behalf of cyberspace
established?
(5) Stanley Fish argues that this idea of a realm of freedom without coercion
is a utopian fantasy. Do you agree?

The condition of speech being free is not only unrealizable, it is also
undesirable. It would be a condition in which speech was offered for no
reason whatsoever. Once speech is offered for a reason it is necessarily,

if only silently, negating all of the other reasons for which one might have spoken. Therefore the only condition in which free speech would be realizable is if the speech didn't mean anything. Free speech is speech that doesn't mean anything. (Lowe and Jonson 1998)

(6) In 2001, Maori protested about 'Bionicle' figures produced by Lego which used tropes, including language, from Maori culture in combination with Easter Island and Polynesian figures (Coombe 2003: 1189ff). One critic of a related website wrote (cited in Coombe and Hermann 2004: 564):

I am angered and disgusted to see so many Maori words used for nothing other than a kids' game, pretending to teach others how to pro- nounce our language, and looking to a Maori dictionary to make up new names to role-play. What right do you have to abuse our tongue? Who of you here are actually Maori?

Do you believe that intellectual property law should be used to prevent the cir- culation of images which members of those cultures argue do violence to cul- tural integrity?

D Popular meaning and statutory interpretation

In *Corkery v Carpenter* (1951), the issue at stake was an appeal against a con- viction for being drunk in charge of a carriage (Licencing Act 1872 S 12). Evans (1988: 75) characterises this as a case of verbal ambiguity, 'where some word [. . .] is capable of more than one meaning and it is not clear what meaning was intended'. The defendant (Corkery) had been pushing a bicycle while drunk and was also creating a disturbance. The definitional question that arose was whether a bicycle was a 'carriage' within the meaning of S 12. Legal argument made reference to other statutes and cases where the question or related questions had arisen (see discussion and summary in Evans 1988: 75–80). The defence argued a general principle of statutory interpretation 'that in statutes concerning matters relating to the general public words are presumed to be used in their popular meaning', as well as the words of a popular song 'Daisy Bell', which illustrated the distinction in popular usage between 'bicycle' and 'carriage':

It won't be a stylish marriage
I can't afford a carriage
But you'll look sweet upon the seat
Of a bicycle made for two.

The court, however, upheld the conviction and made the declaration that 'the doubts that have been expressed by text-book writers on the subject need no longer exist, as this court has now construed the word "carriage" in the Licencing Act 1872 as including a bicycle, whether it be a tradesman's bicycle or tricycle or the ordinary passenger bicycle – ordinarily called a push-bicycle – as was the case here'.

Questions for discussion

(1) When presented with the facts of a case such as this, it is usually fairly easy to form an intuitive (albeit partially informed) judgment about the correctness of the decision. What view have you formed?

(2) Do you find the words of the popular song to be persuasive as evidence about ordinary linguistic usage?

(3) The defendant was also charged with a separate count of malicious damage, contrary to S 12 of the Criminal Justice Administration Act 1914, as he had taken out his displeasure at the arrest on the fittings of his prison cell. If acquitted on the first charge, then the arrest and detention would have been unlawful, entitling the defendant to seek to break out of his cell. In this way the definitional question about 'bicycle' and 'carriage' also had implications for whether Corkery would be punished for damaging the cell or not. In giving judgment that the defendant had been lawfully arrested, Lord Goddard added that there was 'no excuse whatever for his breaking up the cell in the manner in which he did, and he was properly sentenced to three months' imprisonment' (at 107).

We could speculate that on a different pattern of facts, with a more appealing defendant who had not created a disturbance and caused damage, and could have been shown to have dismounted from his bicycle purely out of a concern for his own and others' safety, perhaps the court would have been more sympathetic. This speculation is not open to definitive determination by the outside observer, nor would it necessarily have occurred to the judge as a way of looking at the case in his pursuit of an interpretative strategy. If you thought that the defendant was wrongly convicted, does this additional information lead you to hesitate over your initial intuitive verdict? If you thought that he was correctly convicted, do you now feel more certain about that decision?

(4) Commenting on this and similar cases, Harris writes (Harris 1981: 192):

> The kind of descriptive diagnostic which operates in the case of the law is merely one very clear example of a principle which applies to communicational interactions generally. It is not a 'special case' except in that it probes and lays bare to an unusual degree the procedures and the rationale which underlie a determination of 'what is meant'. It comes to terms with the fact that there is no way in which language can provide explicitly and specifically for all conceivable eventualities.

Do you agree with this statement?

E Literal meaning and national security: *Adler v George* (1964)

The Official Secrets Act 1920, S 3, reads as follows: 'No person in the vicinity of any prohibited place shall obstruct [. . .] any member of His Majesty's forces engaged on guard, sentry, patrol, or other similar duty in relation to the prohibited place [. . .].' A protester was arrested *inside* a Royal Air Force Facility and charged under the Act. On appeal, the question for the court was whether 'in the vicinity' also included the meaning 'in' or 'inside'.

Structure of the problem

Category or linguistic frame (C) = 'in the vicinity'
Phenomenon, event or specific phrase (P) = 'in' or 'inside'

Does P fall within C?

Dictionary definitions of 'vicinity'

The region near or about a place; the neighbourhood or vicinage; the state or fact of being near a place; proximity, propinquity. (*MacQuarie*)

The area near or surrounding a particular place. (*New Oxford*)

If something is in the vicinity of a place, it is in the near-by area. (*COBUILD*)

Questions to consider

On the basis of these dictionary definitions, does 'in the vicinity' include 'in'? Consider:
(1) If I am in or inside the park, am I also in the vicinity of the park?

YES   NO   MAYBE

(2) If a cat is in the vicinity of a cardboard box, can that mean that the cat is also inside the box?

YES   NO   MAYBE

(3) Do you think that in general people would agree that (choose one answer):

(a) the core meaning of 'in the vicinity' definitely includes the meaning 'in';
(b) this is an obviously marginal case, that is, it is clear that (or most people would agree that) 'in' is marginal in relation to the core meaning of 'in the vicinity';
(c) this is a debatable case, that is, some people would think that 'in' falls within the core meaning of 'in the vicinity', others would think it was

marginal and others would argue that it falls outside the meaning of 'in the vicinity';

(d) 'in the vicinity' and 'in' have separate meanings and there is no overlap between them.

The argument made by the appellant (cited from p. 8)

The justices [in the original trial] were wrong, since the acts proved occurred on the station, and the offence charged related to something occurring in the vicinity of the station, and 'in the vicinity of' means 'near' or 'close to', and does not mean 'in' or 'on'. The term 'in the vicinity of' is not defined in the Official Secrets Act, 1920, and the natural or popular and accepted meaning of 'vicinity' which has to be applied is to be found in the general dictionaries, such as the Oxford English Dictionary and others.

The argument made by the prosecutor (cited from p. 9)

There is no direct authority, but it is submitted that, since the defendant could be on only one part of the station at a time, he was in the vicinity of all the other parts of the station at that time. The meaning of 'in the vicinity of', in the context of the Official Secrets Act, 1920, is wide enough to cover what the defendant was found to have done in this case; to hold otherwise would be to produce extraordinary results.

Background and intent of the law

If the court decides to look beyond the meanings of the words used and consider the wider circumstances and intent of the law, it would presumably consider:

(I) the aim of the act, namely the protection of the security of military bases, and national security

(II) the principle that citizens should not be made criminally liable without a clear legal justification, and that the benefit of the doubt should go to the accused person

(4) Which of these principles do you think should carry more weight?

(I)   (II)   (equal)

(5) What is your verdict? In reaching a verdict, you might want to consider whether we should give more weight to the wording/language of the act, the general intent of the act, or other principles such as that of 'lenity' – which states that in criminal matters the defendant should be given the benefit of the doubt in the case of any ambiguity.

(6) Check the original case record for the result.

F 'No vehicles across state lines': a famous vehicle case *McBoyle v United States* (1931)

McBoyle was convicted of transporting across a state line a stolen aeroplane, and the judgment was upheld by the Circuit Court of Appeals for the Tenth Circuit. The Supreme Court then considered an appeal in relation to whether the National Motor Vehicle Theft Act (1919) applied to aircraft. The statute stated (S 2). that

> (a) The term 'motor vehicle' shall include an automobile, automobile truck, automobile wagon, motor cycle, or any other self-propelled vehicle not designed for running on rails; [. . .] S. 3. That whoever shall transport or cause to be transported in interstate or foreign commerce a motor vehicle, knowing the same to have been stolen, shall be punished by a fine of not more than $5,000, or by imprisonment of not more than five years, or both.

Structure of the problem

Category or linguistic frame (C) = 'vehicle'
Phenomenon, event or specific phrase (P) = 'aeroplane'

Does P fall within C?

Questions to consider

(1) In ordinary usage, does C include P?

YES   NO   MAYBE

There then arises the specific question of whether the P falls under the C as defined or illustrated in the rule:

C .... vehicle (e.g. automobile, truck, wagon, motorcycle, any self-propelled vehicle not running on rails)
P .... aeroplane

(2) Is the P in this case a C as defined in the law?

YES   NO   MAYBE

A third set of considerations involves the intention of the law and the context of the particular case, as well as considerations of fairness and justice. These surrounding circumstances might be important if the case is marginal, that is, where there is some doubt about the answers to Questions 1 and 2.
(3) Are there any contextual or circumstantial reasons why we should or should not classify the P as a C?

YES   NO   MAYBE

Even if we decide 'maybe' for Questions 1–3, we have to make a decision:
(4) On the basis of the above, is the P ('aeroplane') a C ('vehicle')?

YES   NO

Give your reasons/explain your decision.

Summary of the judgment of the court

Justice Holmes conceded that the term 'vehicle' could and had been used to
include aircraft in some legislation: 'No doubt etymologically it is possible to
use the word to signify a conveyance working on land, water or air, and sometimes legislation extends the use in that direction [. . .] But in everyday speech
"vehicle" calls up the picture of a thing moving on land.' Legislative intent gave
no guidance: 'Airplanes were well known in 1919, when this statute was passed;
but it is admitted that they were not mentioned in the reports or in the debates
in Congress.' On balance, Justice Holmes held that the line should be drawn
clearly, on the grounds that 'it is reasonable that a fair warning should be given
to the world in language that the common world will understand, of what the
law intends to do if a certain line is passed'. Holmes argued that the rule as laid
down was 'in words that evoke in the common mind only the picture of vehicles
moving on land'. The court should not extend this to aircraft 'simply because it
may seem to us that a similar policy applies, or upon the speculation that, if the
legislature had thought of it, very likely broader words would have been used'.

(5) What are the main theoretical concepts appealed to in this ruling? Do
you agree with the reasoning?

G Grice and perjury

Perjury can be defined as follows:

> Offence committed by a person lawfully sworn as a witness or interpreter
> in a judicial proceeding who willfully makes a statement, material in that
> proceeding, which he knows to be false or does not believe to be true.
> (*Curzon Dictionary of Law*)

In everyday life, the line between deception and lying is not always crucial,
since we would frequently apply the same moral or social sanctions to deception as to literal lying. Depending on the context, an argument based on a
literal meaning might not work very well. Thus if you say to a child, 'Don't
hang around near the park at night' and the child goes into the park, it may
not be very persuasive for the child to say: 'I didn't hang around near the park,
I was hanging around in the park.' In a legal context, the issue is less

clear, since lying ('perjury') is a serious offence, but the line between (1) lying, (2) deceiving and (3) not volunteering information which is relevant to the question can be hard to draw.

The case of *Bronston v United States* (1973) raises some important issues. (See Tiersma 1999: 183–6; Solan 2004; Winter 2001: 297–309; Solan and Tiersma 2005: 215ff.) Bronston's film production company was in bankruptcy, and under cross-examination, Bronston was asked about his own personal assets (at 354):

Q. Do you have any bank accounts in Swiss banks, Mr Bronston?
A. No, Sir.
Q. Have you ever?
A. The company had an account there for about six months in Zurich.

It turned out that Bronston had had an account earlier in Zurich, but that he no longer had a bank account there. He was prosecuted for lying under oath when giving evidence, that is, for perjury, even though everything he said was literally true. Bronston was convicted, but his appeal was upheld by the US Supreme Court. It was held unanimously that Bronston had answered the questions truthfully and in so doing had fulfilled the requirements of a witness under oath. The court said that it was the responsibility of the lawyer to ask the follow-up question, or to clarify the answer given by the witness, and not that of the witness to volunteer information. The court explained the 'Gricean' point as follows (at 362–3):

Arguably, the questioner will assume there is some logical justification for the unresponsive answer, since competent witnesses do not usually answer in irrelevancies. Thus the questioner may conclude that the unresponsive answer is given only because it is intended to make a statement – a negative statement – relevant to the question asked. In this case, petitioner's questioner may have assumed that petitioner denied having a personal account in Switzerland; only this unspoken denial would provide a logical nexus between inquiry directed to petitioner's personal account and petitioner's adverting, in response, to the company account in Zurich.

Some critics of this decision have argued that the act of lying should be seen as a sub-category of deception. However, Solan (204: 189–93) points out that is possible to draft a law to include both direct lying and misleading statements and omissions, and this was not done in the US perjury statute. For example, the United States Securities and Exchange Commission rule (C.F.R. S240.10b5) makes it unlawful:

To make any untrue statement of a material fact or to omit to state a material fact necessary in order to make the statements made, in the light of the circumstances under which they were made, not misleading [. . .] in connection with the purchase or sale of any security.

The decision is, for Solan, defensible on the grounds of 'lenity' (the principle that in criminal law where a statute is uncertain the benefit of the doubt should be given to the defendant). Language games and the manipulation of presupposition are used by lawyers in cross-examination, so defendants are equally entitled to exploit the deniability that such resources create. Further, it is desirable that perjury be restricted to clear cases.

Deception can be defined as a deliberate attempt to leave the listener with a false or misleading impression. This problem also concerns a wider legal issue, which is that of 'omission', since in law omissions are not generally culpable, and there is no obligation to incriminate oneself. If lying involves giving none of the truth, which serves the speaker's purpose, that is, the misleading of the listener, then deception consists of giving as much of the truth as serves the speaker's purpose (i.e. of being 'economical with the truth'; see Durant 1996), that is, the misleading of the listener.

Consider the following exchange:

(a) Q. Fred, how many times did you enter the office on Wednesday?
     A. Five

Let us suppose that it turns out that Fred in fact went into the office twenty-five times on Wednesday, would we say that Fred was lying? On the one hand, five is included in twenty-five, that is to say, Fred was strictly telling the truth, since there were five separate occasions on which Fred entered the office. On the other, Fred's answer is clearly likely to deceive, since it appears to violate a cooperative norm of conversation (Grice's 'maxim of quantity'), namely that one gives the total rather than the part when asked about a quantity:

(b) Q. How long did you live in Singapore?
     A. One year.

If it turns out that the addressee lived there for ten years continuously, the questioner might well feel that the answer was a lie.

(c) Q. Do you have a dollar? I need one for the machine.
     A. Yes.

If we say that (a) and (b) are lies (deliberate false statements), but that (c) is not, since it is cooperative within Grice's terms (even if the addressee has ten dollars), we have introduced a contextual element to perjury. This fine line was recognised as problematic by the Supreme Court in Bronston, when it quoted in a footnote an 'illustration' given by the District Court (at 355, fn. 3):

[I]f it is material to ascertain how many times a person has entered a store on a given day and that person responds to such a question by saying five times when in fact he knows that he entered the store 50 times that day, that person may be guilty of perjury even though it is technically true that he entered the store five times.

The court commented that it was different in character from the exchange in Bronston, as there was nothing in the answer 'to alert the questioner that he may be sidetracked'. The comment continued (at 355–6):

Moreover, it is very doubtful that an answer which, in response to a specific quantitative inquiry, baldly understates a numerical fact can be described as even 'technically true'. Whether an answer is true must be determined with reference to the question it purports to answer, not in isolation. An unresponsive answer is unique in this respect because its unresponsiveness by definition prevents its truthfulness from being tested in the context of the question – unless there is to be speculation as to what the unresponsive answer 'implies'.

Solan comments (2004: 185): 'in deciding whether the statement is literally false, we will impose on the witness the obligation to understand the question reasonably within the context – hardly a literal act'. Solan's point is that an element of cooperation beyond truth-telling would be imposed by this criterion, since the witness is held liable to a standard of material relevance.

Winter (2001: 297–309), however, takes issue with the court's reasoning, and the court's lack of interest in Bronston's state of mind, which was restricted to whether he believed his statements to be true or not, and did not pay attention to his presumed intention to deceive:

The lower courts in *Bronston* read the statute in light of the social concept of a 'lie'. Similarly, they understood Bronston's testimony in relation to the pragmatics of ordinary conversation – in which people do not usually answer in irrelevances but generally respond with no more information than is necessary to be helpful. [Winter here refers to Grice's maxim of quantity in a footnote.] The Supreme Court, in contrast, read the statute against the assumptions of the crude rationalism that holds sway over much of the legal system [. . .]. A statement is perjury if and only if it is literally untrue. Similarly, the Court understood Bronston's testimony in reductive P-or not-P terms: The statement was either true or false, not according to how an ordinary person would understand the statement – presumably that would be 'subjective' – but according to whether it conformed to discernible, objective criteria.

Winter suggests that problems such as perjury should be settled with reference to ordinary language practice. Solan's argument by contrast rests on the alienation of courtroom discourse from ordinary language. Witnesses are just as entitled as cross-examining lawyers to take advantage of any possibilities of plausible deniability on offer.

Questions for discussion

(1) Do you agree that we should apply an everyday intuition about deception to decide the scope of perjury?

(2) What do you think Winter means by the 'crude rationalism' that he regards as dominating the law?

Further Reading

For contrasting survey-anthologies of legal theory and jurisprudence, see Bix (2006), *Jurisprudence: Theory and Context*; Coleman and Shapiro (2002), *The Oxford Handbook of Jurisprudence and Philosophy of Law*; Penner et al. (2002), *Introduction to Jurisprudence and Legal Theory*; and Patterson (2002), *Philosophy of Law and Legal Theory: An Anthology*. Other general works which take different positions on legal theory include Douzinas and Gearey (2005), *Critical Jurisprudence: The Political Philosophy of Justice*; and Morrison (1997), *Jurisprudence: From the Greeks to the Postmodernists*. Introductory or analytical survey works include Ingram (2006), *Law: Key Concepts in Philosophy*; Tebbit (2000), *Philosophy of Law*; McLeod (2007), *Legal Theory*. Cotterrell (2003), *The Politics of Jurisprudence*, and Ward (2004), *Introduction to Critical Legal Theory*, stress the 'critical' approach to jurisprudence. On law and language, in particular the indeterminacy debate, see Endicott (1996, 2002), and Schauer (1992).

For readings in particular domains of legal theory, see Delgado and Stefancic (2000a), *Critical Race Theory: The Cutting Edge*; Patterson (1994), *Postmodernism and Law*; Levinson and Mailloux (1988), *Interpreting Law and Literature: A Hermeneutic Reader*; Patterson (2004), *Wittgenstein and Law*; Morawetz (2000), *Law and Language*; and Marmor (1997), *Law and Interpretation: Essays in Legal Philosophy*. An excellent guide to the English legal system and common law method is found in Zander (2004), *The Law-Making Process*, and Twining and Miers (2004), *How to do Things with Rules: A Primer of Interpretation*. For an accessible discussion of statutory interpretation, see Evans (1998); a detailed reference work is Bennion (2002). On definition in law, see Harris and Hutton (2007). For a recent volume on legal interpretation, see Wagner et al. (2007).

Recent works in forensic linguistics include McMenamin (2002), Gibbons (2003) and Olsson (2004), all entitled *Forensic Linguistics*; (Coulthard and Johnson 2007), *An Introduction to Forensic Linguistics*; and Solan and Tiersma (2005), *Speaking of Crime: The Language of Criminal Justice*. The works of Roger Shuy are central to this field, including *The Language of Confession, Interrogation and Deception* (1998) and his recent *Creating Language Crimes*

(2005). Schane (2006), *Language and the Law*, offers a clear perspective on law from the point of view of linguistics. For studies of various aspects of the legal process, see Heffer (2005), *The Language of Jury Trial*; Cotterill (2003), *Language and Power in Court*, on the O. J. Simpson trial; the papers in Cotterill (2004), *Language in the Legal Process*; and Levi and Walker (1990), *Language in the Judicial Process*. For general discussion from different points of view, see Tiersma (1999), *Legal Language*, and Mellinkoff (1963), *The Language of the Law*. For articles on a range of relevant subjects, see the journal *Forensic Linguistics: The International Journal of Speech, Language and the Law*. The 'hate speech' issue is treated in Heumann and Church (2007), *Hate Speech on Campus*; Delgado and Stefancic (1997), *Must We Defend Nazis?*; and Gould (2005), *Speak No Evil*; and by Stanley Fish in his *There's No Such Thing as Free Speech . . . and it's a Good Thing Too* (1994). For readings from different disciplines engaged in the study of discourse, see Caldas-Coulthard and Coulthard (1996), *Texts and Practices*, and Jaworksi and Coupland (2006), *The Discourse Reader*. Greenawalt's *Speech, Crime and the Uses of Language* (1989) surveys issues of freedom of speech and restrictions on language use. On dialogical thinking and discourse, see Cristaudo (forthcoming), *The Star and the Cross*.

This book has drawn on many years of membership of a network of integrational linguists: see Toolan (1996), *Total Speech: An Integrational Linguistic Approach to Language*; Harris (1998), *Introduction to Integrational Linguistics*; Davis (2001), *Words: An Integrational Perspective*; Taylor (1997), *Theorizing Language*; and Harris and Wolf (1998), *Integrational Linguistics: A First Reader*.

References

Ainsworth, Janet (2005/6), 'Linguistics as a knowledge domain in the law', *Drake Law Review* 54: 651–9.

Alexander, Larry (1995), 'On statutory interpretation: fancy theories of statutory interpretation aren't', *Washington University Law Quarterly* 73(3): 1081–3.

Alexander, Larry and Emily Sherwin (2001), *The Rule of Rules: Morality, Rules, and the Dilemmas of Law*, Durham, NC: Duke University Press.

Althusser, Louis (1971), *Lenin and Philosophy and Other Essays*, trans. B. Brewster, New York: Monthly Review Press.

Anderson, Benedict (1983), *Imagined Communities: Reflections on the Origin and Spread of Nationalism*, London: Verso.

[AP] (2007), ' "That's so gay" girl not entitled to damages', Associated Press, 16 May, www.planetout.com/news/article.html?2007/05/16/1, accessed 17 February 2008.

Austin, J. L. (1956), 'A plea for excuses', *Proceedings of the Aristotelian Society* 57: 1–30.

Austin, J. L. (1962), *How to Do Things with Words*, Cambridge, MA: Harvard University Press.

Austin, J. L. (1970), *Philosophical Papers*, Oxford: Oxford University Press.

Austin, John (1832), *Province of Jurisprudence Determined: The First Part of a Series of Lectures on Jurisprudence, or, The Philosophy of Law*, London: John Murray.

Ayer, Alfred (1936), *Language, Truth and Logic*, London: Victor Gollancz.

Bacon, Francis (2000), *The New Organon*, eds Lisa Jardine and Michael Silverthorne, Cambridge: Cambridge University Press. First published 1620.

Bakhtin, Mikhail (1986), *Speech Genres and Other Late Essays*, trans. Vern W. McGee, eds Caryl Emerson and Michael Holquist, Austin: University of Texas Press.

Balkin, Jack (1987), 'Transcendental deconstruction, transcendent justice', *Michigan Law Review* 92: 1131–86.

Balkin, Jack (2003), 'Fox's trademark suit infringes on free speech', *Sun-Sentinel* (Florida), 19 August, p. 17A.

Balkin, Jack (2004), 'How rights change: freedom of speech in the digital era', *Sydney Law Review* 26(5): 5–16.

Barnes, Jeffrey (2006), 'The continuing debate about "plain language" legislation: a law reform conundrum', *Statute Law Review* 27: 83–132.

Barthes, Roland (1977), 'The death of the author', ed. and trans. Stephen Heath, *Image, Music, Text*, New York: Hill, pp. 142–8.

Baudrillard, Jean (1981), *For a Critique of the Political Economy of the Sign*, St Louis: Telos Press. First published 1973.

Beck, Anthony (1994), 'Is law an autopoietic system?', *Oxford Journal of Legal Studies* 14(3): 401–18.

Beck, Ulrich, Wolfgang Bonss and Christopher Lau (2003), 'The theory of reflexive modernization: problematic, hypotheses and research programme', *Theory Culture Society* 20(2): 1–33.

Bennion, Francis (1989), 'Brutus v Cozens and the meaning of ordinary words', www.francisbennion.com, accessed 13 November 2007.

Bennion, Francis (2002), *Statutory Interpretation: A Code*, 4th edn, London: Butterworths.

Bensen, Robert (1988), 'How judges fool themselves: the semiotics of the easy case', in Roberta Kevelson (ed.), *Law and Semiotics 2*, New York: Plenum, pp. 31–60.

Bentham, Jeremy (1821), *The Elements of the Art of Packing, as Applied to Special Juries, particularly in the Cases of Libel Law*, London: Effingham Wilson.

Bentham, Jeremy (1843), 'Essay on logic', in *Works of Jeremy Bentham 1838–1843*, vol. 8, ed. John Bowring, Edinburgh: Simpkin, Marshall, pp. 213–93.

Bentham, Jeremy (1970), *On Laws in General*, ed. H. L. A. Hart, London: Athlone Press. Based on a manuscript completed in 1782.

Bentham, Jeremy (1988), *A Fragment on Government*, ed. J. H. Burns and H. L. A. Hart, Cambridge: Cambridge University Press. First published 1776.

Bentham, Jeremy (2002), 'Nonsense upon stilts, or Pandora's box opened', in *Rights, Representation, and Reform: Nonsense Upon Stilts and Other Writings on the French Revolution*, eds Philip Schofield, Catherine Pease-Watkin and Cyprian Blamires, Oxford: Oxford University Press, pp. 317–88. First published 1795.

Bix, Brian (1993), *Law, Language and Legal Determinacy*, Oxford: Clarendon Press.

Bix, Brian (2002), 'Natural law: the modern tradition', in Jules Coleman and Scott Shapiro (eds), *The Oxford Handbook of Jurisprudence and Philosophy of Law*, Oxford: Oxford University Press, pp. 61–103.

Bix, Brian (2006), *Jurisprudence: Theory and Context*, 4th edn, London: Sweet and Maxwell.

Black, Henry (ed.) (1891), *Dictionary of Law Containing Definitions of the Terms and Phrases of American and English Jurisprudence, Ancient and Modern*, St Paul, MN: West.

Blackstone, William (1756), *An Analysis of the Laws of England*, Oxford: Clarendon Press.

Blackstone, William (1765–9), *Commentaries on the Laws of England*, 4 vols, Oxford: Clarendon Press.

Bloomfield, Leonard (1926), 'A set of postulates for the science of speech', *Language* 2(3): 153–64.

Borch, Christian (2005), 'Systemic power: Luhmann, Foucault and analytics of power', *Acta Sociologica* 48(2): 155–67.

Bork, Robert (1990), *The Tempting of America: The Political Seduction of the Law*, New York: Touchstone.

Bourdieu, Pierre (1991), *Language and Symbolic Power*, trans. Gino Raymond and Matthew Adamson, ed. John B. Thompson, Cambridge, MA: Harvard University Press.

Brion, Denis (1987), 'The shopping mall: signs of power', in Roberta Kevelson (ed.), *Law and Semiotics 1*, New York: Plenum, pp. 65–108.

Brion, Denis (1988), 'What is a hay baler? The semiotic answer from contract law', in Roberta Kevelson (ed.), *Law and Semiotics 2*, New York: Plenum, pp. 61–85.

Brisbin, Richard (1997), *Justice Antonin Scalia and the Conservative Revival*, Baltimore, MD: Johns Hopkins University Press.

Butler, Judith (1995), 'Burning acts, injurious speech', in A. Haverkamp (ed.), *Deconstruction is/in America: A New Sense of the Political*, New York: New York University Press, pp. 149–80.

Butler, Judith (1997), *Excitable Speech: A Politics of the Performative*, New York: Routledge.

Caldas-Coulthard, Carmen and Malcolm Coulthard (eds) (1996), *Texts and Practices: Readings in Critical Discourse Analysis*, London: Routledge.

Cameron, Deborah (1995), *Verbal Hygiene*, London: Routledge.

Campos, Paul (1995), 'This is not a sentence', *Washington University Law Quarterly* 73: 971–82.

Campos, Paul (1998), *Jurismania: The Madness of American Law*, New York: Oxford University Press.

Cardozo, Benjamin (1921), *The Nature of the Judicial Process*, New Haven, CT: Yale University Press.

Carrington, Paul (1995), 'Hail Langdell!', *Law and Social Inquiry* 20: 691–760.

Carty, Hazel (1996), 'Heads of damage in passing off', *European Intellectual Property Review* 18(9): 487–93.

Carty, Hazel (2004), 'Advertising, publicity rights and English law', *Intellectual Property Quarterly* 3: 209–58.

Castoriadis, Cornelius (1987), *The Imaginary Institution of Society*, trans. Kathleen Blaney Mclaughlin, Cambridge: Polity.

Chafee, Zechariah, Jr. (1947), 'Do judges make or discover law?', *Proceedings of the American Philosophical Society* 91(5): 405–20.

Chan, Johannes (1999), 'A search for identity: legal development since 1 July 1997', in Wang Gungwu and John Wong (eds), *Hong Kong in China: The Challenges of Transition*, Singapore: Times Academic Press, pp. 245–84.

Chen, Albert (2002), 'The constitution and the rule of law', in Lau Siu-kai (ed.), *The First Tung Chee-hwa Administration*, Hong Kong: Chinese University Press, pp. 69–88.

Chomsky, Noam (1965), *Aspects of the Theory of Syntax*, Cambridge, MA: MIT Press.

Chomsky, Noam (1986), *Knowledge of Language*, Westport, CT: Praeger.

Cicutti, Nic (1995), 'Seeking the right service', *Independent*, 26 March, http://findarticles.com/p/articles, accessed 28 January 2008.

Clark, Michael (2005), 'Deconstruction, feminism and law: Cornell and MacKinnon on female subjectivity and resistance', *Duke Journal of Gender Law and Policy* 12: 107–30.

Coetzee, J. M. (1996), *Giving Offence: Essays on Censorship*, Chicago: University of Chicago Press.

Cohen, Felix (1935), 'Transcendental nonsense and the functional approach', *Columbia Law Review* 35(6): 809–49.

Coleman, Jules and Scott Shapiro (eds), *The Oxford Handbook of Jurisprudence and Philosophy of Law*, Oxford: Oxford University Press.

Coleridge, Samuel Taylor (1816), *The Statesman's Manual*, London: Gale and Fenner.

[Conference Proceedings] (1995), 'Law and linguistics conference: proceedings', in 'What is Meaning in Legal Text? Northwestern University Law and Linguistics Conference', *Washington University Law Quarterly* 73(3): 800–970.

Conley, John and William O'Barr (1990), *Rules versus Relationships: The Ethnography of Legal Discourse*, Chicago: University of Chicago Press.

Conley, John and William O'Barr (1998), *Just Words: Law, Language and Power*, Chicago: University of Chicago Press.

Coombe, Rosemary (1998), *The Cultural Life of Intellectual Properties: Authorship, Appropriation, and the Law*, Durham, NC: Duke University Press.

Coombe, Rosemary (2003), 'Fear, hope and longing for the future of authorship and a revitalized public domain in global regimes of intellectual property', *DePaul Law Review* 52: 1171–91.

Coombe, Rosemary and Andrew Herman (2004), 'Rhetorical virtues: property, speech, and the commons on the world-wide web', *Anthropological Quarterly* 77(3): 559–74.

Cornell, Drucilla (1987), 'The problem of normative authority in legal interpretation', in Roberta Kevelson (ed.), *Law and Semiotics 1*, New York: Plenum, pp. 149–57.

Cornell, Drucilla (1991), *Beyond Accommodation: Ethical Feminism, Deconstruction, and the Law*, New York: Routledge.

Cornell, Drucilla (1992), *The Philosophy of the Limit*, New York: Routledge and Kegan Paul.

Cotterrell, Roger (2003), *The Politics of Jurisprudence: A Critical Introduction to Legal Theory*, 2nd edn, Oxford: Oxford University Press.

Cotterill, Janet (2003), *Language and Power in Court: A Linguistic Analysis of the O.J. Simpson Trial*, Basingstoke: Palgrave Macmillan.

Cotterill, Janet (ed.) (2004), *Language in the Legal Process*, Basingstoke: Palgrave Macmillan.

Coulthard, Malcolm and Alison Johnson (2007), *An Introduction to Forensic Linguistics: Language in Evidence*, London: Routledge.

[Craig-Martin, Michael] (1972), Interview, *Audio Arts* 1(2), 1973, www.tate.org.uk/britain/exhibitions/audioarts/cd1_2_transcript.htm, accessed 5 December 2007.

Crawford, Barclay and Nick Gentle (2007), 'The enemy within', *South China Morning Post*, Sunday 11 November, Agenda, p. 11.

Cristaudo, Wayne (forthcoming), *The Star and the Cross: Franz Rosenzweig and Eugen Rosenstock-Huessy's Post-Nietzschean Revivals of Judaism and Christianity*, Cambridge: Cambridge Scholar Press.

Culler, Jonathan (1982), *On Deconstruction: Theory and Criticism after Structuralism*, Ithaca, NY: Cornell University Press.

Culler, Jonathan (1986), *Saussure*, Fontana: London.

Culler, Jonathan (1988), *Framing the Sign: Criticism and its Institutions*, Oxford: Blackwell.

Cunningham, Clark, Judith Levi, Georgia Green and Jeffrey Kaplan (1994), 'Plain meaning and hard cases', *Yale Law Journal* 103: 1561–625.

Cutts, Martin (1996), 'Plain English in the law', *Statute Law Review* 17: 50–61.

Davis, Daniel (1996), 'Trade mark law: linguistic issues', *Language and Communication* 16(3): 255–62.

Davis, Hayley (1989), 'What makes bad language bad?', *Language and Communication* 9(1): 1–9.

Davis, Hayley (2001), *Words: An Integrational Perspective*, London: Curzon.

Dawkins, Richard (1976), *The Selfish Gene*, Oxford: Oxford University Press.

Deleuze, Gilles and Félix Guattari (1988), *Thousand Plateaus: Capitalism and Schizophrenia*, trans. Brian Massumi, London: Athlone.

Delgado, Richard and Jean Stefancic (1997), *Must We Defend Nazis? Hate Speech, Pornography and the New First Amendment*, New York: New York University Press.

Delgado, Richard and Jean Stefancic (2000a), *Critical Race Theory: The Cutting Edge*, 2nd edn, Philadelphia: Temple University.

Delgado, Richard and Jean Stefancic (2000b), 'Editors' Introduction', *Critical Race Theory: The Cutting Edge*, 2nd edn, Philadelphia: Temple University, pp. xv–xix.

Delgado, Richard and Jean Stefancic (2001), *Critical Race Theory: An Introduction*, New York: New York University Press.

Dennett, Daniel (1995), *Darwin's Dangerous Idea: Evolution and the Meanings of Life*, London: Penguin.

Derrida, Jacques (1974), *Glas*, trans. John P. Leavey and Richard Rand, Lincoln: University of Nebraska Press.

Derrida, Jacques (1976), *On Grammatology*, trans. G. C. Spivak, Baltimore, MD: Johns Hopkins University Press.

Derrida, Jacques (1990), 'Force of law: the mystical foundation of authority', *Cardozo Law Review* 11: 920–1045.

Dickens, Charles (1971), *Bleak House*, intro. J. Hillis Miller, London: Penguin. First published 1853.

Donaldson, Michael (1995), 'Some reservations about law and postmodernism', *American Journal of Jurisprudence* 40: 335–46.

Douglas, Mary (1987), *How Institutions Think*, London: Routledge and Kegan Paul.

Douzinas, Costas and Adam Gearey (2005), *Critical Jurisprudence: The Political Philosophy of Justice*, Oxford: Hart.

Durant, Alan (1996), 'Allusions and other "innuendo meanings" in libel actions: the value of semantic and pragmatic evidence', *Forensic Linguistics* 3(2): 195–210.

Duxbury, Neil (2007), 'Jhering's philosophy of authority', *Oxford Journal of Legal Studies* 27(1): 23–47.

Dworkin, Ronald (1975), 'Hard cases', *Harvard Law Review* 88(6): 1057–109.

Dworkin, Ronald (1986), *Law's Empire*, London: Fontana.

Dyzenhaus, David (1994), ' "Now the machine runs itself": Carl Schmitt on Hobbes and Kelsen', *Cardozo Law Review* 16(1): 1–19.

Eagleton, Terry (1998), 'Resources for a journey of hope', in Stephen Regan (ed.), *The Eagleton Reader*, Oxford: Blackwell, pp. 311–20.

Eco, Umberto (1984), *Semiotics and the Philosophy of Language*, Bloomington: Indiana University Press.

Edmonds, David and John Eidinow (2001), *Wittgenstein's Poker*, London: Faber and Faber.

Elliott, D. W. (1989), 'Brutus v Cozens – decline and fall', *Criminal Law Review* 10: 323–30.

Endicott, Timothy A. O. (1996), 'Linguistic indeterminacy', *Oxford Journal of Legal Studies* 16: 667–97.

Endicott, Timothy (2002), 'Law and language', in Edward N. Zalta (ed.), *The Stanford Encyclopedia of Philosophy*, Winter 2002 edn, http://plato.stanford.edu/archives/win2002/entries/law-language, accessed 17 July 2006.

Evans, Jim (1988), *Statutory Interpretation: Problems of Communication*, Auckland and Oxford: Oxford University Press.

Farber, Daniel (2000), 'Do theories of statutory interpretation matter? A case study', *Northwestern University Law Review* 94(4): 1409–44.

Finnis, John (2002), 'Natural law: the classical tradition', in Jules Coleman and Scott Shapiro (eds), *The Oxford Handbook of Jurisprudence and Philosophy of Law*, Oxford: Oxford University Press, pp. 1–60.

Fischl, Richard (1992), 'The question that killed Critical Legal Studies', *Law and Social Inquiry* 17(4): 779–820.

Fish, Stanley (1980), *Is there a Text in this Class? The Authority of Interpretative Communities*, Cambridge, MA: Harvard University Press.

Fish, Stanley (1984), 'Fish v. Fiss', *Stanford Law Review* 36(6): 1325–47.

Fish, Stanley (1989), *Doing What Comes Naturally: Change, Rhetoric, and the Practice of Theory in Literary and Legal Studies*, Durham, NC: Duke University Press.

Fish, Stanley (1994), *There's No Such Thing as Free Speech . . . and it's a Good Thing Too*, New York: Oxford University Press.

Fiss, Owen (1982), 'Objectivity and interpretation', *Stanford Law Review* 34(4): 793–63.

Fogle, Randy (1993), 'Is calling someone gay defamatory? The meaning of reputation, community mores, gay rights, and free speech', *Law and Sexuality* 3: 165–99.

Foucault, Michel (1977), 'What is an author?', trans. Donald F. Bouchard and Sherry Simon, in *Language, Counter-Memory, Practice*, Ithaca, NY: Cornell University Press, pp. 124–7.

Frank, Jerome (1970), *Law and the Modern Mind*, Gloucester, MA: Peter Smith. First published 1930.

Franken, Al (2003), *Lies (And the Lying Liars Who Tell Them): A Fair and Balanced Look at the Right*, New York: Penguin.

Franken, Al (2008), Personal website: transcript of *Fox News Network, LLC, v. Penguin Group (USA), Inc., and Alan S. Franken* 2003, http://alfrankenweb.com/foxcourt.html, accessed 2 February 2008.

Frankfurter, Felix (1947), 'Some reflections on the reading of statutes', *Columbia Law Review* 47: 527–46.

Frug, Mary (1991), 'Law and postmodernism: the politics of a marriage', *University of Colorado Law Review* 62: 483–8.

Fuchs, Matthew (2005/6), 'Free exercise of speech in shopping malls: bases that support an independent interpretation of Article 40 of the Maryland Declaration of Rights', *Albany Law Review* 69: 449–88.

Fuller, Lon (1958), 'Positivism and fidelity to law: a reply to Professor Hart', *Harvard Law Review* 71: 630–72.

Fuller, Lon (1969), *The Morality of Law*, 2nd edn, New Haven, CT: Yale University Press.

Gaonkar, Dilip Parameshwar (2002), 'Towards new imaginaries: an introduction', *Public Culture* 14: 1–19.

Garfinkel, Harold (1956), 'Conditions of successful degradation ceremonies', *American Journal of Sociology* 61: 420–4.

Garfinkel, Harold (1967), *Studies in Ethnomethodology*, Englewood Cliffs, NJ: Prentice Hall.

Garfinkel, Harold (1968), 'Oral contributions', in R. J. Hall and K. S. Crittenden (eds), *Proceedings in the Purdue Symposium on Ethnomethodology*, Institute Monograph Series No. 1, Purdue, CA: Purdue University.

Garner, Bryan (2003), 'Legal lexicography: a view from the front lines', *English Today* 9: 33–42.

Gibbons, John (ed.) (1994), *Language and the Law*, London: Longman.

Gibbons, John (2003), *Forensic Linguistics: An Introduction to Language in the Justice System*, Oxford: Blackwell.

Goble, G. W. (1933), 'Law as science', *Scientific Monthly* 37(3): 229–40.

Goddard, Cliff (1996), 'Can linguists help judges know what they mean? Linguistic semantics in the court-room', *Forensic Linguistics: The International Journal of Speech, Language and the Law* 3(2): 250–72.

Golanski, Alani (2002), 'Linguistics in law', *Albany Law Review* 66: 61–121.

Goldstein, Robert Justin (2000), *Flag Burning and Free Speech: The Case of* Texas v Johnson, Lawrence: University Press of Kansas.

Goode, Roy (2004), *Commercial Law*, 3rd edn, London: Penguin.

Goodrich, Peter (1987a), *Legal Discourse: Studies in Linguistics, Rhetoric and Legal Analysis*, London: Macmillan.

Goodrich, Peter (1987b), 'Psychoanalysis in legal education: notes on the violence of the sign', in Roberta Kevelson (ed.), *Law and Semiotics 1*, New York: Plenum, pp. 193–213.

Goodrich, Peter (1990), *Languages of Law: From Logics of Memory to Nomadic Masks*, London: Weidenfeld and Nicolson.

Goodrich, Peter (2005), 'Slow reading', in Peter Goodrich and Mariana Valverde (eds), *Nietzsche and Legal Theory*, New York: Routledge, pp. 185–200.

Gould, Jon (2005), *Speak No Evil: The Triumph of Hate Speech Regulation*, Chicago: University of Chicago Press.

Graff, Gerald (1982), ' "Keep off the grass"; "drop dead" and other indeterminacies: a response to Sanford Levinson', *Texas Law Review* 60: 405–13.

Graham, Phil (2006), *Hypercapitalism: New Media, Language, and Social Perceptions of Value*, New York: Peter Lang.

Gray, Kevin and Susan Gray (2005), *Elements of Land Law*, 4th edn, Oxford; Oxford University Press.

Greenawalt, Kent (1989), *Speech, Crime and the Uses of Language*, New York: Oxford University Press.

Greenawalt, Kent (2002), 'Constitutional and statutory interpretation', in Jules Coleman and Scott Shapiro (eds), *The Oxford Handbook of Jurisprudence and Philosophy of Law*, Oxford: Oxford University Press, pp. 268–310.

Gregg, Benjamin (1999), 'Using legal rules in an indeterminate world: overcoming the limitations of jurisprudence', *Political Theory* 27(3): 357–78.

Grice, H. P. (1975), 'Logic and conversation', in P. Cole and J. L. Morgan (eds), *Syntax and Semantics, Vol. 3, Speech Acts*, New York: Academic Press, pp. 41–58.

Griffith, J. A. G. (1997), *The Politics of the Judiciary*, 5th edn, London: Fontana.

Griffiths, Andrew (2003), 'Modernising trade mark law and promoting economic efficiency: an evaluation of the Baby Dry judgement and its aftermath', *Intellectual Property Quarterly* 1: 1–37.

Habermas, Jürgen (1987), *The Theory of Communicative Action: Reason and the Rationalization of Society*, vol. 2, trans. Thomas McCarthy, Boston: Beacon Press.

Habermas, Jürgen (1996), *Between Facts and Norms: Contributions to a Discourse Theory of Law and Democracy*, trans. William Rehg, Cambridge, MA: MIT Press.

Habermas, Jürgen (1998), 'Reply to symposium participants, Benjamin N. Cardozo School of Law', in Michael Rosenfeld and Andrew Arato (eds), *On Law and Democracy: Critical Exchanges*, Berkeley: University of California Press, pp. 379–452.

Hale, Matthew (1736), *The History of the Pleas of the Crown*, 2 vols, London: E. and R. Nutt and R. Gosling.

Hare, Ivan (2006), 'Crosses, crescents and sacred cows: criminalising incitement to religious hatred', *Public Law* Autumn: 521–38.

Harkness, Jason (1998), 'A linguistic inspection of the law of defamation', *Auckland University Law Review* 8: 653–84.

Harpham, Geoffrey Galt (2002), *Language Alone: The Critical Fetish of Modernity*, London and New York: Routledge.

Harpwood, Vivienne (2005), *Modern Tort Law*, 5th edn, London: Routledge-Cavendish.

Harris, Marvin (1987), *Cultural Anthropology*, 2nd edn, New York: Harper and Row.

Harris, Roy (1981), *The Language Myth*, London: Duckworth.

Harris, Roy (1987), *The Language Machine*, London: Duckworth.

Harris, Roy (1990), 'Lars Porsena revisited', in Christopher Ricks and Leonard Michaels (eds), *The State of the Language*, London: Faber and Faber, pp. 411–21.

Harris, Roy (1998), *Introduction to Integrational Linguistics*, Oxford: Pergamon.

Harris, Roy and Christopher Hutton (2007), *Definition in Theory and Practice: Language, Lexicography and the Law*, London: Continuum.

Harris, Roy and Talbot Taylor (1989), *Landmarks in Linguistic Thought: The Western Tradition from Socrates to Saussure*, London: Routledge.

Harris, Roy and George Wolf (eds) (1998), *Integrational Linguistics: A First Reader*, Oxford: Pergamon.

Hart, H. L. A. (1954), 'Definition and theory in jurisprudence', *Law Quarterly Review* 70: 37–60.

Hart, H. L. A. (1982), *Essays on Bentham: Studies in Jurisprudence and Political Theory*, Oxford: Clarendon Press.

Hart, H. L. A. (1983), 'Positivism and the separation of law and morals', in *Essays in Jurisprudence and Philosophy*, Oxford: Clarendon Press, pp. 49–87. First published 1958.

Hart, H. L. A. (1994), *The Concept of Law*, 2nd edn, postscript eds P. Bulloch and J. Raz, Oxford: Clarendon Press. First published 1961.

Haugen, Einar (1987), *Blessings of Babel: Bilingualism and Language Planning*, Berlin: Walter de Gruyter.

Hayakawa, S. I. (1974), *Language in Thought and Action*, 3rd edn, London: George Allen and Unwin.

Hayek, Friedrich A. von (1946), *The Road to Serfdom*, London: Routledge.

Hayek, Friedrich A. von (1982), *Law, Legislation and Liberty*, 3 vols in one, London: Routledge and Kegan Paul.

Heffer, Chris (2005), *The Language of Jury Trial: A Corpus-Aided Analysis of Legal–Lay Discourse*, Basingstoke: Palgrave Macmillan.

Heidegger, Martin (1998), *Pathways*, ed. William McNeill, Cambridge: Cambridge University Press. First published 1927.

Heritage, John (1984), *Garfinkel and Ethnomethodology*, Cambridge: Polity.

Heumann, Milton and Thomas Church (1997), *Hate Speech on Campus: Cases, Case Studies and Commentary*, Boston: Northeastern University Press.

Higgins, Worth (1997), ' "Proper names exclusive of biography and geography": maintaining a lexicographic tradition', *American Speech* 72(4): 381–94.

Hill, Archibald A. (1954), 'Prescriptivism and linguistics in English teaching', *College English* 15(7): 395–9.

[HK Government] (2008), Annex 3, Personalized Vehicle Registration Marks (PVRMs) Scheme, Transport Department, HK Government, www.td.gov.hk/home/index.htm, accessed 3 January 2008.

Hobbes, Thomas (1998), *Leviathan*, Oxford: Oxford University Press. First published 1651.

Hofrichter, Jesse (2006/7), 'Tool of the trademark: brand criticism and free speech problems with the Trademark Dilution Revision Act Of 2006', *Cardozo Law Review* 28: 1923–60.

Hogan, Patrick Colm (1996), *On Interpretation: Meaning and Inference in Law, Psychoanalysis, and Literature*, Athens: University of Georgia Press.

Holborow, Marnie (2006), 'Putting the social back into language: Marx, Vološinov and Vygotsky reexamined', *Studies in Language and Capitalism* 1: 1–28.

Holland, Ray (1999), 'Reflexivity', *Human Relations* 52(4): 463–84.

Holmes, Oliver (1896/7), 'The path of the law', *Harvard Law Review* 10: 457–78.

Holmes, Oliver (1898/9), 'Law in science and science in law', *Harvard Law Review* 12: 443–63.

Holmes, Oliver (1967), *The Common Law*, ed. Mark de Wolfe Howe, Cambridge, MA: Harvard University Press. First published 1881.

Hume, Baron David (1797), *Commentaries on the Law of Scotland, Respecting the Description and Punishment of Crimes*, 2 vols, Edinburgh: Bell and Bradfute.

Hunt Alan and Gary Wickham (1994), *Foucault and Law: Towards a Sociology of Law as Governance*, London: Pluto.

Hutchinson, Allan (2000), *It's All in the Game: A Non-Foundationalist Account of Law and Adjudication*, Durham, NC: Duke University Press.

Hutchinson, Allan (2004), 'Judges and politics: an essay from Canada', *Legal Studies* 24: 275–93.

Hutton, Christopher (1995), 'Law lessons for linguists? Accountability and acts of professional communication', *Language and Communication* 16(3): 205–14.

Hutton, Christopher (2005), *Race and the Third Reich: Linguistics, Racial Anthropology and Genetics in the Dialectic of Volk*, Cambridge: Polity.

Ingber, Stanley (1984), 'The marketplace of ideas: a legitimizing myth', *Duke Law Journal* 1(1): 1–91.

Ingram, David (2006), *Law: Key Concepts in Philosophy*, London: Continuum.

[Iventure] (2007), ' "Keep entrepreneur free": entrepreneurs continue battle with Entrepreneur Magazine (EMI)', www.entrepreneur.net/index.html, accessed 13 December 2007.

Jackson, Bernard (1988), *Law, Fact and Narrative Coherence*, Liverpool: Deborah Charles.

Jackson, Bernard (1997), *Semiotics and Legal Theory*, Liverpool: Deborah Charles. First published 1985.

Jason-Lloyd, Leonard (2005), *An Introduction to Policing and Police Powers*, London: Routledge-Cavendish.

Jaworksi, Adam and Nikolas Coupland (eds) (2006), *The Discourse Reader*, London and New York: Routledge.

Jhering, Rudolf von (1985), 'In the heaven for legal concepts: a fantasy', *Temple Law Quarterly* 58: 799–842. First published 1884.

Jones, Peter (2001), 'Cognitive linguistics and the Marxist approach', in René Dirven, Bruce Hawkins and Esra Sandikcioglu (eds), *Language and Ideology: Theoretical Cognitive Approaches*, Amsterdam: John Benjamins, pp. 227–51.

Kaplan, Jeffrey, Georgia Green, Clark Cunningham and Judith Levi (1995), 'Bringing linguistics into judicial decision-making: semantic analysis submitted to the US Supreme Court', *Forensic Linguistics* 1: 81–98.

Kearns, Paul (2007), 'The ineluctable decline of obscene libel: exculpation and abolition', *Criminal Law Review* September: 667–76.

Kellner, Douglas (2003), 'Jean Baudrillard', in George Ritzer (ed.), *The Blackwell Companion to Major Contemporary Social Theorists*, Oxford: Blackwell, pp. 310–31.

Kelman, Mark (1987), *A Guide to Critical Legal Studies*, Cambridge, MA: Harvard University Press.

Kennedy, Duncan (1983), *Legal Education and the Reproduction of Hierarchy: A Polemic against the System*, Cambridge, MA: Afar.

Kennedy, Randall (1989), 'Racial critiques of legal academia', *Harvard Law Review* 102(8): 1745–819.

Kennedy, Randall (2003), *Nigger: The Strange Career of a Troublesome Word*, New York: Vintage Books.

Kerouac, Jack (1959), *Dharma Bums*, New York: New American Library.

Kevelson, Roberta (1988), *The Law as a System of Signs*, New York: Plenum.

Kim, Pauline T. (2007), 'Lower court discretion', *New York University Law Review* 82: 383–442.

King, Michael (2006), 'What's the use of Luhmann's theory?', in Michael King and Chris Thornhill (eds), *Luhmann on Law and Politics: Critical Appraisals and Applications*, Hart: Oxford, pp. 37–52.

Kirby, Vicki (2006), *Judith Butler: Live Theory*, London: Continuum.

Klein, Naomi (1999), *No Logo*, New York: Picador.

Knight, Dean (2006), ' "I'm not gay – not that there's anything wrong with that!": are unwanted imputations of gayness defamatory?', *Victorian University of Wellington Law Review* 37: 249–79.

Korzybski, Alfred (1948), *Science and Sanity: An Introduction to Non-Aristotelian Systems and General Semantics*, 3rd edn, Lakeville, CT: International Non-Aristotelian Library, distributed by Institute of General Semantics.

Kowinski, William (1985), *The Malling of America: An Inside Look at the Great Consumer Paradise*, New York: William Morrow.

Kozinski, Alex (1993), 'Trademarks unplugged', *New York University Law Review* 68: 960–78.

Kuhn, Thomas (1962), *The Structure of Scientific Revolutions*, Chicago: University of Chicago Press.

Lee, Colleen and Helen Wu (2007), 'G.O.D. boss sorry for "14K" T-shirts', *South China Morning Post*, Saturday 3 November, p. C3.

Leiter, Brian (2003), 'American legal realism', in W. Edmundson and M. Golding (eds), *The Blackwell Guide to the Philosophy of Law and Legal Theory*, Oxford: Blackwell, pp. 50–66.

Lenoble, Jacques (1998), 'Law and undecidability: toward a new vision of the proceduralization of law', in Michael Rosenfeld and Andrew Arato (eds), *On Law and Democracy: Critical Exchanges*, Berkeley: University of California Press, pp. 37–81.

Levi, Judith and Anne Walker (1990), *Language in the Judicial Process*, New York: Plenum.

Levinson, Standford and Steven Mailloux (1988), *Interpreting Law and Literature: A Hermeneutic Reader*, Evanston, IL: Northwestern University Press.

Lévi-Strauss, Claude (1966), *The Savage Mind*, London: Weidenfeld and Nicolson. First published 1962.

Llewellyn, Karl (1950), 'Remarks on the theory of appellate decision and the rules and canons of how statutes are to be interpreted', *Vanderbilt Law Review* 3: 396–406.

Lobban, Michael (1991), *The Common Law and English Jurisprudence*, Oxford: Clarendon Press.

Locke, John (2001), *An Essay Concerning Human Understanding*, Ontario: Batoche Books. First published 1690.

Love, Nigel (1998), 'The fixed-code theory', in Roy Harris and George Wolf (eds), *Integrational Linguistics: A First Reader*, Oxford: Pergamon, pp. 49–67.

Lowe, Peter and Annemarie Jonson (1998), ' "There is no such thing as free speech": an interview with Stanley Fish', *Australian Humanities Review*, February, www.lib.latrobe.edu.au/AHR/archive/Issue-February-1998/fish.html, accessed 28 January 2008.

Luhmann, Niklas (1986) 'The autopoiesis of social systems', in F. Geyer and J. Van d. Zeuwen (eds), *Sociocybernetic Paradoxes: Observation, Control and Evolution of Self-Steering Systems*, London: Sage, pp. 172–92.

Luhmann, Niklas (1988), 'Closure and openness: on reality in the world of law', in Gunther Teubner (ed.), *Autopoietic Law: A New Approach to Law and Society*, Berlin: Walter de Gruyter, pp. 335–48.

Luhmann, Niklas (1989), *Ecological Communication*, trans. John Bednarz, Chicago: University of Chicago Press.

Luhmann, Niklas (2004), *Law as Social System*, trans. Klaus A. Ziegert, eds Fatima Kastner, Richard Nobles, David Schiff and Rosamund Ziegert, intro. Richard Nobles and David Schiff, Oxford: Oxford University Press.

MacKinnon, Catharine (1989), *Towards a Feminist Theory of the State*, Cambridge, MA: Harvard University Press.

MacKinnon, Catharine (1993), *Only Words*, Cambridge, MA: Harvard University Press.

Manchester, Colin, David Salter and Peter Moodie (2000), *Exploring the Law: The Dynamics of Precedent and Statutory Interpretation*, London: Sweet and Maxwell.

Marmor, Andrei (ed.) (1997), *Law and Interpretation: Essays in Legal Philosophy*, Oxford: Clarendon Press.

Marmor, Andrei (2005), *Interpretation and Legal Theory*, 2nd edn, Oxford and Oregon: Hart.

Marx, Karl (1889), *Capital*, ed. Friedrich Engels, trans. Samuel Moore and Edward Aveling, London: Swan Sonnenshein.

Matsuda, Mari (1989), 'Racist speech: considering the victim's story', *Michigan Law Review* 187: 2320–81.

McLeod, Ian (2007), *Legal Theory*, 4th edn, Basingstoke: Palgrave Macmillan.

McMenamin, Gerald (2002), *Forensic Linguistics: Advances in Forensic Stylistics*, Boca Raton, FL: CRC Press.

Mellinkoff, David (1963), *The Language of the Law*, Boston: Little, Brown.

Mensch, Elizabeth (1981), 'Freedom of contact as ideology (Review of P. S. Atiyah, *The Rise and Fall of Freedom of Contract*, 1979)', *Stanford Law Review* 33: 753–72.

Mercuro, Nicholas and Steven G. Medema (2006), *Economics and the Law: From Posner to Postmodernism and Beyond*, Princeton, NJ: Princeton University Press.

Messinger, Adam (2007), 'The capitalization of google as a verb', www. adammessinger.com, accessed 13 December 2007.

Milovanovic, Dragan (1983), 'Weber and Marx on law: demystifying ideology and law – toward an emancipatory political practice', *Contemporary Crises* 7: 353–70.

Mill, John Stuart (1999), *On Liberty*, Ontario: Broadview Literary Texts. First published 1869.

Miller, J. Hillis (1971), 'Introduction', in Charles Dickens, *Bleak House*, London: Penguin, pp. 11–34.

Milroy, James and Lesley Milroy (1991), *Authority in Language: Investigating Language Prescription and Standardization*, 2nd edn, London: Routledge.

Mitchell, Paul (2005), *The Making of the Modern Law of Defamation*, Oxford: Hart.

Moore, Michael (1985), 'A natural law theory of interpretation', *Southern California Law Review* 58: 277–398.

Morawetz, Thomas (ed.) (2000), *Law and Language*, Aldershot: Ashgate/Dartmouth.

Morgan, Bronwen and Karen Yeung (2007), *An Introduction to Law and Regulation: Texts and Materials*, Cambridge: Cambridge University Press.

Morrison, Mary Jane (1989), 'Excursions into the nature of legal language', *Cleveland State Law Review* 37(2): 271–336.

Morrison, Wayne (1997), *Jurisprudence: From the Greeks to the Postmodernists*, London: Cavendish.

Munro, Colin (2007), 'A jester's licence? Comedy and defamation law', *Scots Law Times* 20: 135–7.

Nietzsche, Friedrich (2000), 'On truth and lie in an extra-moral sense', in Clive Cazeaux (ed.), *Continental Aesthetics Reader*, New York: Routledge, pp. 53–62. First published 1873.

Nobles, Richard and David Schiff (2006), *A Sociology of Jurisprudence*, Oxford: Hart.

[NOW] (2008), Website of the National Organization of Women Foundation, www.nowfoundation.org/index.html, accessed 4 February 2008.

O'Connell, Lisa (1999), 'Marriage acts: stages in the transformation of modern nuptial culture', *Differences: A Journal of Feminist Cultural Studies* 11(1): 68–111.

Ogden, Charles (1951), *Bentham's Theory of Fictions*, New York: Harcourt, Brace.

Olsson, John (2004), *Forensic Linguistics: An Introduction to Language, Crime and the Law*, London: Continuum.

Orwell, George (1972), 'Politics and the English language', in David Lodge (ed.), *20th Century Literary Criticism*, London: Longman, pp. 360–9. First published 1947.

[Owning Language] (2007), 'Owning language: copyright, ethics and the development of Aboriginal language programs', www.aare.edu.au/01pap/low01352.htm, accessed 17 December 2007.

Patterson, Dennis (ed.) (1994), *Postmodernism and Law*, Aldershot: Dartmouth.

Patterson, Dennis (ed.) (2002), *Philosophy of Law and Legal Theory: An Anthology*, Malden, MA: Blackwell.

Patterson, David (ed.) (2004), *Wittgenstein and Law*, Aldershot: Ashgate.

Penner, James, David Schiff and Richard Nobles (eds) (2002), *Introduction to Jurisprudence and Legal Theory*, London: Elsevier.

Peters, John Durham (1993), 'Distrust of representation: Habermas on the public sphere', *Media, Culture, Society* 15: 541–71.

Philips, Alfred (2002), *Lawyers' Language: How and Why Legal Language is Different*, London: Routledge.

Philips, Susan U. (1998), *Ideology in the Language of Judges: How Judges Practice Law, Politics, and Courtroom Control*, New York and Oxford: Oxford University Press.

Phillips, Jeremy (2004), 'No marks for Hitler: a radical reappraisal of trade mark use and political sensitivity', *European Intellectual Property Review* 26(8): 327–30.

[PLAN] (2008), Website of the Pro-Life Action League, www.prolifeaction.org/nvs, accessed 4 February 2008.

Pocock, J. G. A. (1971), *Politics, Language and Time: Essays on Political Thought and History*, London: Methuen.

Pollner, Melvin and Emerson, Robert (2001), 'Ethnomethodology and ethnography', in P. Atkinson, A. Coffey, S. Delamont, J. Lofland and L. Lofland (eds), *Handbook of Ethnography*, London: Sage, pp. 118–35.

Posner, Richard (1983), *The Economics of Justice*, Cambridge, MA: Harvard University Press.

Posner, Richard (1988), *Law and Literature: A Misunderstood Relation*, Cambridge, MA: Harvard University Press.

Posner, Richard (2001), *Frontiers of Legal Theory*, Cambridge, MA: Harvard University Press.

Pound, Roscoe (1908), 'Mechanical jurisprudence', *Columbia Law Review* 8: 605–23.

Probert, Walter (1959), 'Law and persuasion: the language-behavior of lawyers', *University of Pennsylvania Law Review* 108(1): 35–58.

Raval, Suresh (1980), 'Intention and contemporary literary theory', *Journal of Aesthetics and Art Criticism* 38(3): 261–77.

Rawls, John (1955), 'Two concepts of rules', *Philosophical Review* 64: 3–32.

Renteln, Alison (2004), *The Cultural Defense*, New York and Oxford: Oxford University Press.

Richards, I. A. (1968), *Coleridge on Imagination*, London: Routledge and Kegan Paul.

Richardson, Megan (2004), 'Trade marks and language', *Sydney Law Review* 26: 193–220.

Robertson, Geoffrey (1999), *The Justice Game*, London: Vintage.

Rogers, W. V. H. (2006), *Winfield and Jolowicz on Tort*, London: Sweet and Maxwell.

Rorty, Richard (1979), *Philosophy and the Mirror of Nature*, Princeton, NJ: Princeton University Press.

Rorty, Richard (1982), *Consequences of Pragmatism*, Brighton: Harvester.

Rumfelt, Eileen (2006), 'Political speech: priceless – *MasterCard v. Nader* and the intersection of intellectual property and free speech', *Emory Law Journal* 55(2): 389–421.

Russell, Bertrand (1959), 'Introduction', in Ernest Gellner, *Words and Things: An Examination of, and an Attack on, Linguistic Philosophy*, London: Gollancz, pp. 13–15.

Sacks, Harvey (1992a), 'Topic; utterance placement; "activity occupied" phenomena; formulations; euphemisms', in *Lectures on Conversation*, vol. 1, Oxford: Blackwell, pp. 535–46.

Sacks, Harvey (1992b), 'The inference-making machine', in *Lectures on Conversation*, vol. 1, Oxford: Blackwell, pp. 113–25.

Sacks, Harvey, Emmanuel Schegloff and Gail Jefferson (1974), 'A simplest systematics for the organization of turn-taking for conversation', *Language* 50(4): 696–735.

Saunders, David (1997), *Anti-Lawyers: Religion and the Critics of Law and State*, London: Routledge.

Saussure, Ferdinand de (1983), *Course in General Linguistics*, trans. Roy Harris, London: Duckworth. First published 1916.

Scalia, Antonin (1997), *A Matter of Interpretation: Federal Courts and the Law*, Princeton, NJ: Princeton University Press.

Schaefer, Walter (1958), 'The language of law: a symposium (foreword)', *Western Reserve Law Review* 9: 117–18.

Schane, Sanford (2006), *Language and the Law*, London: Continuum.

Schauer, Frederick (1985), 'Easy cases', *Southern California Law Review* 58: 399–440.

Schauer, Frerderick (1988), 'Formalism', *Yale Law Journal* 97(4): 509–48.

Schauer, Frederick (ed.) (1992), *Law and Language*, New York: New York University Press.

Schegloff, Emmanuel (1992), 'Repair after last turn: the last structurally provided defense of intersubjectivity in conversation', *American Journal of Sociology* 97: 1295–345.

Sealy, Len and Richard Hooley (2005), *Commercial Law: Texts, Cases and Materials*, Oxford: Oxford University Press.

Searle, John (1964), 'How to derive "ought" from "is"', *Philosophical Review* 73(1): 43–58.

Shapiro, Martin (1981), 'On the regrettable decline of law French: or Shapiro jettet le brickbat', *Yale Law Journal* 90: 1198–204.

Shuy, Roger (1998), *The Language of Confession, Interrogation and Deception*, Thousand Oaks, CA: Sage.

Shuy, Roger (2002), *Linguistic Battles in Trademark Disputes*, Basingstoke: Palgrave Macmillan.

Shuy, Roger (2005), *Creating Language Crimes: How Law Enforcement Uses (and Misuses) Language*, Oxford: Oxford University Press.

Simmel, Georg (1990), *The Philosophy of Money*, trans. Tom Bottomore, David Frisby and Kaethe Mengelberg, ed. David Frisby, 2nd edn, London: Routledge. First published 1907.

Solan, Lawrence (1993), *The Language of Judges*, Chicago: University of Chicago Press.

Solan, Lawrence (2004), 'The Clinton scandal: some legal lessons from linguistics', in Janet Cotterill (ed.), *Language in the Legal Process*, Basingstoke: Palgrave Macmillan, pp. 180–95.

Solan, Lawrence and Peter Tiersma (2005), *Speaking of Crime: The Language of Criminal Justice*, Chicago: University of Chicago Press.

Solum, L. B. (1996), 'Indeterminacy', in Dennis Patterson (ed.), *A Companion to Philosophy of Law and Legal Theory*, Malden, MA: Blackwell, pp. 488–502.

Stein, Gertrude (1922), *Geography and Plays*, Boston: Four Seas.

Stein, Jess (1958), 'Outside pressures', *College Composition and Communication* 9(2): 94–7.

Stone, Martin (1995), 'Focusing the law: what legal interpretation is not', in Andrei Marmor (ed.), *Law and Interpretation: Essays in Legal Philosophy*, Oxford: Clarendon Press, pp. 31–96.

Stone, Martin (2002), 'Formalism', in Jules Coleman and Scott Shapiro (eds), *The Oxford Handbook of Jurisprudence and Philosophy of Law*, Oxford: Oxford University Press, pp. 166–205.

Sullivan, Robert (1994), 'Enlightenment, autonomy, the law, and Jeremy Bentham's Pannomium', *Legal Studies Forum* 18: 163–76.

Swift, Jonathan (1712), *Proposal for Correcting, Improving and Ascertaining the English Tongue*, 2nd edn, London: Printed for Benjamin Tooke.

Swift, Jonathan (1960), *Gulliver's Travels and other Writings*, ed. Louis A. Landa, Boston: Houghton Mifflin. First published 1726.

Talbot, Mary, Karen Atkinson and David Atkinson (eds) (2003), *Language and Power in the Modern World*, Edinburgh: Edinburgh University Press.

Taylor, Talbot (1997), *Theorizing Language*, Oxford: Pergamon.

Tebbit, Mark (2000), *Philosophy of Law: An Introduction*, London: Routledge.

[TELA] (2007), 'Film censorship guidelines for censors', www.tela.gov.hk/english/doc/forms/filmcensorship.pdf, accessed 3 January 2008.

Teubner, Gunther (1989), 'How the law thinks: toward a constructivist epistemology of law', *Law and Society Review* 23: 727–57.

Thumma, Samuel and Jeffery Kirchmeier (1999), 'The lexicon has become a fortress: the United States Supreme Court's use of dictionaries', *Buffalo Law Review* 47: 227–301.

Tiersma, Peter (1987), 'The language of defamation', *Texas Law Review* 66: 303–50.

Tiersma, Peter (1999), *Legal Language*, Chicago: University of Chicago Press.

Tobin, Jeffrey (2007), *The Nine: Inside the Secret World of the Supreme Court*, New York: Doubleday.

Toolan, Michael (1996), *Total Speech: An Integrational Linguistic Approach to Language*, Durham, NC: Duke University Press.

Toolan, Michael (2002), 'The language myth and the law', in Roy Harris (ed.), *The Language Myth in Western Culture*, London: Curzon, pp. 159–82.

Torremans, Paul (2005), *Intellectual Property Law*, 4th edn, Oxford: Oxford University Press.

Tushnet, Mark (1991), 'Critical Legal Studies: a political history', *Yale Law Journal* 5: 1515–44.

Twining, William and David Miers (2004), *How to Do Things with Rules: A Primer of Interpretation*, 4th edn, London: Butterworths.

Unger, Roberto (1983), *The Critical Legal Studies Movement*, Cambridge, MA: Harvard University Press.

Wagner, Anne, Werner Wouter and Deborah Cao (eds) (2007), *Interpretation, Law and the Construction of Meaning*, Dordrecht: Springer.

Waismann, Friedrich (1965), *The Principles of Linguistic Philosophy*, ed. R. Harré, London: Macmillan.

Waldron, Jeremy (2000), ' "Transcendental nonsense" and system in law', *Columbia Law Review* 100(1): 16–53.

Ward, Ian (2004), *Introduction to Critical Legal Theory*, London: Cavendish.

Wendel, Bradley W. (2005), 'Professionalism as interpretation', *Northwestern University Law Review* 99: 1167–233.

Werbach, Kevin (1994), 'Looking it up: dictionaries and statutory interpretation', *Harvard Law Review* 107: 1437–53.

Weschler, Lawrence (1999), *Boggs: A Comedy of Values*, Chicago: University of Chicago Press.

West, Robin (1988), 'Jurisprudence and gender', *University of Chicago Law Review* 55: 1–72.

Westerhaus, Jennifer (2003), 'Review of Roger Shuy, *Linguistic Battles in Trademark Disputes*, 2002', *International Journal of Speech, Language and the Law* 10(2): 292–6.

White, James Boyd (1987), 'Thinking about our language', *Yale Law Journal* 96: 1960–83.

White, James Boyd (1990), *Justice as Translation: An Essay in Cultural and Legal Criticism*, Chicago: University of Chicago Press.

Wicke, Jennifer (1991), 'Postmodern identities and the politics of the postmodern (legal) subject', *boundary 2* 19(2): 10–33.

Widdowson, Henry (2003), *Defining Issues in English Language Teaching*, Oxford: Oxford University Press.

Wilkins, John (1688), *Essay towards a Real Character and a Philosophical Language*, London: S. Gellibrand.

Williams, Glanville L. (1945–6), 'Language and the law', *Law Quarterly Review* 61, 71–86, 179–95, 293–303, 384–406; 62: 387–406.

Williams, Patricia (1987), 'Alchemical notes: reconstructing ideals from deconstructed rights', *Harvard Civil Rights – Civil Liberties Law Review* 22: 410–33.

Wilson, Roy and Brian Galpin (1962), *Maxwell on the Interpretation of Statutes*, London: Sweet and Maxwell.

Wimsatt, William K. and Monroe C. Beardsley (1946), 'The intentional fallacy', *Sewanee Review* 54: 468–88.

Winter, Steven (2001), *A Clearing in the Forest: Law, Life, and Mind*, Chicago: University of Chicago Press.

Wipperfürth, Alex (2005), *Brand Hijack: Marketing without Marketing*, New York: Penguin.

Wittgenstein, Ludwig (1978), *Philosophical Investigations*, trans. G. E. M. Anscombe, Oxford: Blackwell. First published 1953.

Wolin, Richard (2004), *The Seduction of Unreason*, Princeton, NJ: Princeton University Press.

Woodlee, Yolanda (1999), 'D.C. Mayor acted "hastily", will rehire aide', *Washington Post* online issue, 24 February, www.washingtonpost.com, accessed 23 January 2008.

Zander, Michael (2004), *The Law-Making Process*, 6th edn, Cambridge: Cambridge University Press.

Legal Cases Cited

Abrams v United States 250 U.S. 616 (1919)

Adler v George [1964] 2 QB 7

Antoniades v Villiers [1990] 1 AC 417

B and S v Leathley [1979] Crim. L.R. 314

Bayer Co. v United Drug Co. 272 F. 505 (S.D.N.Y. 1921)

Bravado Merchandising Services Ltd v Mainstream Publishing (Edinburgh) 1996 S.L.T. 597

British Sugar v James Robertson [1996] R.P.C. 281

British Telecommunications Plc & Ors v One In A Million Ltd & Ors [1998] EWCA Civ 1272 (CA)

Bronston v United States 409 US 352 (1973)

Brown v Gould [1972] Ch 53

Brutus v Cozens [1973] AC 854

Butterley Co. v New Hucknall Colliery Co. [1910] A. C. 381

Camden (Marquis) v Inland Revenue Commissioners [1914] 1 KB 641

Cassidy v Daily Mirror Newspapers Ltd [1929] 2 KB 331

Charleston v News Group Newspapers [1995] 2 AC 65

Church of the Holy Trinity v United States 143 U.S. 457 (1892)

Clore v Theatrical Properties Ltd and Westby & Co [1936] 3 All ER 483 (CA)

Community for Creative Non-Violence v Watt 703 F.2d 586 (1983)

Corkery v Carpenter [1951] 1 KB 102

Dyson v Qualtex [2006] EWCA 166

Eastman Photographic Materials Co. v Comptroller-General of Patents, Designs, and Trade-Marks [1898] A. C. 571.

Fey v King 190 NW 519 (1922)

First National Bank v Bellotti 435 U.S. 765 (1978)

Ford Motor v 2600 (2001) 177 F. Supp. 2d 661, 2001 U.S. Dist. Lexis 21302 (E.D. Michigan, 2001)

Fox News Network, LLC, v Penguin Group (USA), Inc., and Alan S. Franken, US District Court, Southern District of New York 03 Civ. 6162 (RLC)(DC) (2003)

Garner v Burr [1951] 1 KB 31

Grey v Pearson (1857) 6 HL Cas 61

Heyden's Case (1584) 3 Co Rep 7a

Hilder v Dexter [1902] A.C. 474

Hill v East and the West India Dock Co (1884) 9 App Cas 448

HKSAR v Ng Kung Siu & Another [1999] 3 HKLRD 907

Hulton & Co v Jones [1910] A.C. 20

Inland Revenue Commissioners v Williamson (1928) 14 TC 335 (CS)

Investors Compensation Scheme Ltd v West Bromwich Building Society (1998) 1 W. L.
    R. 896

John Angus Smith v United States 508 U.S. 223 (1993)

Kimberley-Clark v Fort Sterling Limited [1997] FSR 877

Langbridge's Case Year Book of 19 Edward III, 375 (1345)

Lee v Ventura County Superior Court 9 Cal.App.4th 510 (1992)

Liverpool City Council v Irwin [1976] 1 Q.B 319 (C.A.)

Liversidge v Anderson [1942] AC 206 (HL)

Lochner v State of New York 198 U.S. 45 (1905)

Mandla v Dowell Lee [1983] 2 A.C. (HL)

Marbury v Madison 5 U.S. (1 Cranch) 137 (1803)

Mattison v Hart (1854) 14 CB 357

McBoyle v United States 283 U.S. 25 (1931)

Miranda v Arizona 384 U.S. 436 (1966)

Morse v Frederick 127 U.S. 2618 (2007)

National Organization for Women v Scheidler 510 U. S. 249 (1994)

*Office for Harmonisation in the Internal Market (OHIM) v WM Wrigley JR Company
    (Doublemint)* [2004] R.P.C. 18 (ECJ)

Olmstead v United States 277 U.S. 438 (1928)

Palsgraf v Long Island Railroad Co. 162 N.E. 99 (N.Y.) (1928)

Pepper v Hart [1993] AC 593 (HL)

Perfection: Joseph Crosfield and Sons' Application (1909) 26 RPC 837

Procter & Gamble Company v Office for Harmonisation (OHIM) in the Internal Market
    [2002] Case C-383/99 P (ECJ)

Pruneyard Shopping Center v Robins 447 U.S. 74 (1980)

R.A.V v St. Paul 505 U.S. 377 (1992)

R v Caldwell [1982] AC 382

R v Derby Justices, ex p DPP (1999), reported in *The Times*, 17 August, 1999

R v Judge of the City of London Court [1982] 1 QB 273

R v R [1992] 1 A.C. 599

R v Secretary of State for Transport, ex p. Factortame Ltd [1991] AC 603 (ECJ and HL)

R (Wilkinson) v IRC [2006] 1 All E.R 529

Re Barlow's Will Trusts [1979] 1 WLR 278

*Re Mr Prime Minister John Piss the Family Court and Legal Aid Applicant and Minister
    for Foreign Affairs and Trade* [2000] AATA 1028

Re Rowland [1963] Ch 1 (CA)

Reckitt & Colman v Borden [1990] R.P.C. 341 (HL)

Reddaway v Banham [1896] A.C. 199 (HL)

Riggs v Palmer 115 N.Y. 506 (1889)

River Wear Commissioners v Atkinson (1877) 2 App. Cas. 743

Robertson v Jackson (1845) 2 C. B. 412

Robertson v Rochester Folding Box Co 171 N.Y. 538 (1902)

Roe v Wade 410 U.S. 113 (1973)

S. v H.M. Advocate 1989 S.L.T. 469

Scheidler v National Organization for Women 537 U.S. 393 (2003)

Scheidler v National Organization for Women 547 U.S. 9 (2006)
Schroeder Music Publishing Co Ltd v Macaulay [1974] 1 WLR 1308
Shore v Wilson (1842) 9 Cl. & F. 355
Sim v Stretch [1936] 2 All ER 1237
Slim v Daily Telegraph Ltd [1968] 2 QB 157
Société des Produits Nestlé SA v Mars UK Ltd [2005] E.T.M.R. 96 (ECJ)
Southern Pacific Company v Jensen 244 US 205 (1917)
Spartan Steel & Alloys Ltd v Martin & Co (1973) 1 Q.B. 27
Stevens v Gourley (1859) 7. C. B. (N.S.) 99
Street v Mountford [1985] AC 809
Texas v Johnson 491 U.S. 397 (1989)
Thomas Montgomery v Thompson and Others (1891) A.C. 217
United States v Phelps 877 F.2d 28 (1989)
United States v John Angus Smith 957 F.2d 835 (1992)
Virginia v Black et al. 538 U.S. 343 (2003)

Index

abortion, 96, 99–100
Abrams v United States (1919), 120
absolutism, 63
abstraction(s), 15–16, 28, 39
  definitional test for, 51, 53
  distrust of, 54, 55
  in lexicography, 86, 93–4
absurdity, 71–2, 73, 96–7
academy, 119
accountability, 27–8, 42–3
  of authors and speakers to law, 117
  democratic, 81
  of law to public debate, 141
  natural and classical, 43
  in a 'situated practice', 159
  and transparency, 143–4
  and wordplay, 104–5
activism, 31
  and critique of language and text, 17, 18
  and trademarks, 131
Acts of Parliament, framed in intelligible language,
  88; *see also* statutory interpretation
Adamic language, 1, 3, 37, 39, 179
adjudication
  an 'inference-making machine' in, 44
  contextual case-specific, 79
  ex post quality of common law, 52
  fidelity to text of the law, 29, 64, 68, 150
  as indeterminate, 17
  institutional structure and political justification,
    152
  and interstitial law-making, 29, 95, 150, 179
  inviting politics into, 95
  and legal interpretation, 152
  mystification of, 141–2, 145
  and narratives of litigants, 144–5
  'presumptive formalism', 13
  scientific approach, 12
  see also judges
Adler v George (1964), 195–6
Advertising, 117, 126, 135, 188
'affirmative action', 31
agency
  assumption by critic, 146
  attributed to language itself, 115

authorial establishment of right of, 192
  and control over meaning, 183–4
  economic as rational maximisation, 21
Alien Contract Labor Act (US 1885), 96
alienation, 5, 14, 20, 137, 164, 202
'alternative means test', 114
Althusser, Louis, 115
ambiguity, 97–8, 193–4
anthropological linguistics, 144
anthropology, 141, 142, 143, 148
  reflexive or postmodern turn, 143
anti-foundationalism, 18, 25, 39, 61
anti-semitism, 20
Anticybersquatting Consumer Protection Act (US)
  (1999), 33
Antoniades v Villiers (1990), 156
apologising, Austin on, 58
arbitrariness, of linguistic form and meaning, 35–6,
  40, 67
arbitration
  in cases of uncertainty, 156–7
  informal mechnanisms, 23
'archetypation', 52
arguments, 'slippery-slope', 94, 111
Armstrong, Sir Robert, 172
art, reflexivity in, 162, 165
art criticism, interpretation in, 160
artist
  analogy with judge, 146
  counterfeit, 105–7
Atkin, Lord, 67
attention, 'real-time' form of, 170
audit, 70
'audit culture', 162
Augustine, Saint, of Hippo, 2
Austin, J. L., 166, 167
  speech act theory, 55–6, 57–8, 108
Austin, John, 10
  command theory of law, 53
authoritarianism, in language, 125–9
authority
  asymmetry in context, 24
  demystification of law's, 143
  of dictionaries, 100–1
  divine, 1–2, 5, 62–3